IP SANs

IP SANs

A Guide to iSCSI, iFCP,
and FCIP Protocols
for Storage Area Networks

Tom Clark

✦✦Addison-Wesley

Boston • San Francisco • New York • Toronto • Montreal
London • Munich • Paris • Madrid • Capetown
Sydney • Tokyo • Singapore • Mexico City

Many of the designations used by manufacturers and sellers to distinguish their products are claimed as trademarks. Where those designations appear in this book, and Addison-Wesley, Inc. was aware of a trademark claim, the designations have been printed with initial capital letters or in all capitals.

The author and publisher have taken care in the preparation of this book, but make no expressed or implied warranty of any kind and assume no responsibility for errors or omissions. No liability is assumed for incidental or consequential damages in connection with or arising out of the use of the information or programs contained herein.

The publisher offers discounts on this book when ordered in quantity for special sales. For more information, please contact:

Pearson Education Corporate Sales Division
201 W. 103rd Street
Indianapolis, IN 46290
(800) 428-5331
corpsales@pearsontechgroup.com

Visit AW on the Web: www.aw.com/cseng/

Library of Congress Cataloging-in-Publication Data

Clark, Tom, 1947 Aug. 12–
    IP SANs : a guide to iSCSI, iFCP, and FCIP protocols for storage area networks / Tom Clark.
        p.   cm.
    Includes bibliographical references and index.
    ISBN 0-201-75277-8
    1. Storage area networks (Computer networks) 2. Computer network protocols. I. Title.
TK5105.86 .C53 2001
004.6'8—dc21

                                                                    2001045777

ISBN 0-201-75277-8
Text printed on recycled paper
1 2 3 4 5 6 7 8 9 10—MA—0504030201
First printing, November 2001

This book is
dedicated to
my daughters,
Shannon and Willa

✳

Contents

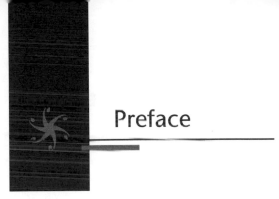

Preface

THE FOLLOWING WORK provides an overview of a new technology for creating storage area networks (SANs) with conventional Transmission Control Protocol/Internet Protocol (TCP/IP) and Gigabit Ethernet networking. IP-based storage networking continues the work initially started by Fibre Channel of providing flexible, high-performance block data access for storage applications. SANs have already proved their practical value in facilitating applications such as server clustering, storage consolidation, and tape backup. With continued market momentum, storage networking is expected to capture more than half the new storage deployments within the next few years.

The unique contribution of storage over IP solutions is the ability to integrate storage networking into mainstream data communications. For customers, the economies of scale provided by common infrastructure and common management make a compelling argument for the adoption of IP SANs, whereas Fibre Channel, despite the effort of certain authors, is still viewed as problematic and must be maintained as a separate network. As often happens in high technology fields, one group of vendors breaks the very hard ground of technical issues, only to see others behind them sowing and reaping the newly tilled and now-fertile soil.

Although IP storage can leverage many of the advances made by Fibre Channel, it has its own issues to address. The Internet Engineering Task Force (IETF) is currently working on multiple protocols for transporting block data over IP networks. The IETF activity consists of ongoing discussions on the requirements of storage data over IP and a series of Internet drafts that embody the work in progress. A detailed analysis of the standards specifications for these protocols is well beyond the scope of this short book, and well beyond the endurance of its author. The IP storage technical documentation, however, is readily available on the IETF Web site listed in the bibliography. The curious reader will also find there the latest versions of standards drafts and Requests for Comments (RFCs) for auxiliary protocols such as security and quality of service, which would be quickly outdated if included here.

The scope of the following text also includes an overview of Fibre Channel technology. This is provided as a basis to appreciate the challenges of IP storage and to acquaint readers from the internetworking world with SAN concepts first aired by Fibre Channel. As with IP storage specifications, this book cannot detail Fibre Channel standards. For granular detail, the reader may reference Robert Kembel's *Fibre Channel Consultant* series, which includes a recent book on fabric switches, or the reader may examine the appropriate Fibre Channel standards directly. A more comprehensive overview of Fibre Channel topologies and products is also included in my previous work, *Designing Storage Area Networks*.

This book is intended for information technology (IT) managers, administrators, consultants, and technical staff responsible for networking and storage management. Storage and networking have traditionally resided in two distinct worlds. Typically, people from an internetworking background are not familiar with storage issues, whereas storage administrators may need to know little about IP internetworking. Storage networking is a melding of these technologies into an integrated solution. IP storage networking offers some relief to networking personnel because the interconnects, bandwidth provisioning, and transport management for IP SANs are drawn from mainstream IP networking. For storage administrators, understanding IP storage is also facilitated by the more accessible expertise within IT staff who are already familiar with the IP component of IP SANs. To satisfy readers from both worlds, this text does not assume prior knowledge of either IP networking or storage concepts. The respective readers may skim at will through material they already understand and may dwell on the passages that contain new content. Although it is difficult to write a single book for such a potentially diverse readership, it is hoped that regardless of specific technical background, the reader will in the end close the cover with an understanding of the benefits that IP storage can provide.

The particular prejudices at work throughout the text will become obvious. Fibre Channel was a pioneering technology. It was the first to develop and implement successfully in viable products a number of new capabilities that have benefited IT in general. A stable and relatively error-free switched gigabit transport, a fully functional serial protocol for block data transmission, and innovative treatment of networked servers and storage have been leveraged by IP storage vendors to accelerate the development of IP SANs.

Despite the technical attributes of Fibre Channel, however, historical momentum and massive resources are on the side of IP and Gigabit Ethernet technology. Although Fibre Channel storage solutions will continue to ship in significant volumes for some time to come, the tide of storage networking will eventually turn at customer direction toward the network infrastructure that already dominates mainstream data communications. The challenge for all storage network vendors and customers alike will be to make this transition as painless as possible.

Organization

The following text provides an overview of multiple technologies that must eventually coexist within enterprise networks. Networks must necessarily maintain a medley of products as new technologies are introduced and as the most recent legacy-branded products are transitioned to less critical areas. For storage, a network may require support for direct-attached Small Computer Systems Interface (SCSI) disks and tape, Fibre Channel switches and storage, and the newly introduced IP storage devices. The text therefore devotes some space to examining the attributes of each storage technology with the aim of clarifying alternatives for technology convergence.

Chapter 1 provides a historical perspective on storage issues and what problems must be resolved to achieve viable, shared storage solutions. Because the Technical Council of the Storage Networking Industry Association (SNIA) has provided a general framework for understanding shared storage, Chapter 2 reviews the SNIA Shared Storage Model to position IP SANs within storage networking as a whole.

For successful deployment, storage over IP has dependencies on both legacy and current technologies. Chapter 3 examines storage networking transports and components, including SCSI and Fibre Channel, as well as the Gigabit Ethernet infrastructure on which IP storage itself resides. The foundation protocol for all storage networking solutions is provided by the SCSI Architectural Model, or SAM-2. The main features of the SCSI architecture are reviewed in Chapter 4.

Chapters 5, 6, and 7 cover IP, the User Datagram Protocol, and TCP respectively. These chapters are intended primarily for readers unfamiliar with IP concepts, although references are also made to features that affect IP SANs.

Chapter 8 examines the three IP storage protocols currently under development in the IETF. The Fibre Channel over IP (FCIP) protocol represents a Fibre Channel extension strategy and relies on IP only to connect remote

Fibre Channel SANs. The Internet Fibre Channel Protocol (iFCP) maps IP addresses to Fibre Channel end nodes and enables the replacement of Fibre Channel fabrics with IP storage networking. The Internet SCSI (iSCSI) protocol enables replacement of Fibre Channel end devices with native IP storage devices, and thus represents a radical shift from current Fibre Channel deployments. These three protocols provide a spectrum of solutions, from simple Fibre Channel extension to migration to displacement.

The IP storage transport protocols are by no means the sole focus of the IETF standards initiatives. Management of IP SANs is also a critical issue. Chapter 9 reviews the Internet Storage Name Server (iSNS) protocol that has been supported by the IP storage community as a means of rationalizing discovery and management of IP storage devices and interconnects.

Two key components that have been lacking in Fibre Channel SANs are security of storage data as it traverses the network and quality of service to ensure proper delivery. Chapter 10 reviews mainstream IP security features that can be used for IP storage networks, whereas Chapter 11 examines class-of-service and quality-of-service standards and standards initiatives. These chapters validate in principle the marketing claims of IP storage vendors that IP SANs may leverage the advanced functionality already deployed for enterprise IP networks.

Although IP storage networking is generally viewed as the successor to Fibre Channel, InfiniBand has also been promoted as a homogeneous solution for everything data related. Chapter 12 provides an overview of the InfiniBand architecture and how it may integrate into IP storage solutions.

Technology development would have little purpose if it did not solve real customer problems. Chapter 13, therefore, offers application studies to demonstrate how IP storage solutions may be applied, including server cluster, storage consolidation, LAN-free and server-free tape backup, and metropolitan and wide area applications for SANs. In many respects, a diagram of an IP SAN solution for a specific application may not differ significantly from a comparable Fibre Channel SAN solution. Boxes reside in the middle, lines are drawn, boxes sit at the end. The substantive difference, however, is how easy those boxes are to acquire, deploy, manage, and maintain. In the end, the customer does not and should not have to worry about the underlying plumbing. The customer simply expects to turn on the spigot and for data to appear. If that is convenienced by IP SANs, then the mission of IP storage vendors is accomplished.

Lastly, Chapter 14 discusses new technologies in general and the inflated expectations that invariably accompany them, and then reviews the fundamental prerequisites that must be met for successful adoption of IP storage networking. IP storage has the potential to alter traditional concepts of data access at a much more fundamental level than previously viewed via Fibre Channel SANs. If IP storage is successful, storage-specific issues may gradually disappear as networked storage access becomes more ubiquitous.

Acknowledgments

Attempting to provide a concise overview of an emerging technology would not be possible without the support and insights of many people, in particular my coworkers whose day jobs frankly do not provide much time for reviewing and critiquing manuscripts. I would like to thank Karen Gettman, my editor, and Emily Frey of Addison-Wesley for managing this project and facilitating the reviews and compilation of the manuscript. Without their constant support and efficiency in handling publication issues, seeing this work through to completion would not have been possible.

I would also like to thank my peers who reviewed the text, offering suggestions and corrections for sections that were admittedly churned out under an extreme deadline. My thanks to Mark Carlson, Charles Monia, Gary Orenstein, Milan Merhar, and Paul Massiglia for helping to maintain technical and sometimes political correctness of the text, and for improving its readability.

As in my previous work on SANs, my frontline editor is my wife, Lou. For that work, she endured arbitrated loop primitive signals and primitive sequences as well as the internal mechanism of the 8b/10b encoder, things in which an avid gardener would normally find little interest, especially in the spring. In reviewing this manuscript, she diligently waded through the first draft chapters, meticulously circling my punctuation and grammatical errors, and highlighting sentence structures that were obviously written at the end of a 12-hour stint. After my four months of weekends in front of the PC, she began referring to herself as a "single wife." Now that this text is complete, however, life can return to normal. On any given Sunday I may now find myself at the business end of a wheelbarrow, working through the second eight yards of compost that sits in our driveway. The lilies and grasses will be great this summer.

Technology development is a collective effort driven by both cooperation and competition. As an umbrella technology, storage networking has attracted some of the brightest minds in the industry and it has been my good fortune to work with and be inspired by talented and highly creative technologists from both the storage and networking fields. The storage networking community is like a very large and extended (and sometimes dysfunctional) family. Despite the occasional vendor bickering, most are committed to the common goal of advancing the industry. This has been demonstrated repeatedly by the time and energy vendors have invested in the SNIA Interoperability Committee and the large interoperability demonstrations we have held at Storage Networking World conferences. I would therefore like to acknowledge all the active players in the storage networking industry whose cooperative energy and efforts have been an ongoing inspiration. In particular, I would like to thank Sheila Childs, Co-Chair of the SNIA Interoperability Committee; Dona Stever, Chair of the SNIA Technology Center Committee; and Gary Phillips, SNIA executive board member for their dedication and example. Special recognition should also be given to Bob Perera and Stan Worth. Although their respective companies are competitors in the marketplace, Bob and Stan have jointly led SNIA interoperability efforts to advance practical solutions for storage networking and have set an excellent example of vendor cooperation for others.

Finally, I would like to acknowledge Aamer Latif and the forward-looking professional team at Nishan Systems for their work in pioneering IP storage solutions that facilitate technology convergence and provide a much smoother migration path to future SANs. In the early days of SAN adoption, I was often asked by customers why storage networking could not be implemented on their existing Ethernet LANs. The obvious answer was that no one had solved the problem of block storage data over IP, and therefore Fibre Channel was the only viable solution. Unbeknown to any of us, however, the problem was in fact being addressed in deep stealth mode by Nishan, long before other vendors took up the challenge. The concurrent efforts by Nishan in development of the iSCSI, iFCP, and iSNS protocols, and convergence of Fibre Channel and IP storage have made my job as an advocate of storage networking much easier.

Tom Clark
Seattle, Washington, U.S.A.
tclark@nishansystems.com
designingsans@verizon.net

Introduction

IP SANs are applying conventional technologies to solve new problems that have evolved around data storage. Although the current crisis in data storage and availability has been slow in maturing, it now presents an immense obstacle for expanding information networks. Customers are running out of storage space and are feeling the press of time.

1.1 Space and Time

Enterprise networks are facing an explosion of data demands from their users. Applications have become more sophisticated, content more rich and diverse, consumers of data more numerous, and expectations for data access driven higher. The catalyst for this explosive growth in information and information access has been forged by a fundamental change in how data is used and by a profound change in the underlying infrastructure that delivers it.

For most of a generation, large computer systems centralized the data services in the enterprise and tightly controlled information content, format, and access. User requests for changes in data formatting (for example, adding a new field in a customer information display) might be queued for months as rows of monastic COBOL programmers patiently scribed code. Remote access to data relied on expensive, point-to-point leased lines and proprietary communications equipment that inherently limited access. In the end, these monolithic computer systems and networks failed to accommodate user demands for more flexible access to more diverse information and have been superseded by more powerful, more affordable, and more dispersed computer systems and networks. UNIX and Windows platforms have displaced mainframes, and networks built on open standards have displaced proprietary ones.

Today, the typical enterprise data center is a maze of 19" racks housing discrete UNIX and Windows servers and their attached storage. A rack or group of racks may be dedicated to a specific department of the enterprise, such as finance, engineering, or human resources. Whereas previously these departments would have shared computing time on a large mainframe, they now control their own computing resources. And although previously they would have had to stand in line with program change requests in hand, they can now install their own specialized applications and generate their own data content. Data generation is further facilitated by new enabling technologies based on visual programming utilities and Hypertext Markup Language that place powerful content creation tools into the hands of any literate person. Multiply this scenario by the thousands of enterprise networks that have undergone this transformation, and it is easy to appreciate the surge in the volume of new data anticipated during the next few years.

Concurrent with this metamorphosis of computing environments, the nature and use of data itself has changed. Information previously presented as dry text has become rich in content, graphical, animated, and dynamic. Nested links to more granular information allow the user to navigate to the desired level of detail or to click through to associated topics. Static columns of numbers in a spreadsheet may be accompanied by colored charts and graphs; a text document may embed a spreadsheet, graphics, or logo; a human resources record may include an employee photograph as well as scanned documents; and a user may casually append a multimegabyte PowerPoint presentation to an e-mail message.

With the ability of more people to generate more data that has more content, enterprise networks are challenged with providing the space to store data and reducing the time to deliver it. For enterprise networks, space and time are indeed a continuum, because ever-increasing storage requirements stress the ability of networks to provide prompt delivery, and more ubiquitous and efficient networks stress the ability of storage systems to absorb newly generated data. Previously viewed as two separate entities within the enterprise, storage and networking are melding into a single concern.

Today's enterprise networks have, after a long struggle between contending technologies, almost universally converged on the Transmission Control Protocol/Internet Protocol (TCP/IP) as the transport protocol of choice, and Ethernet as the underlying infrastructure. Analogous to the Betamax versus VHS wars in the video-recording industry, TCP/IP and Ethernet were not necessarily the best technologies to triumph over their contenders. They do have, however, the proven advantages of open systems compliance, resiliency to disruption, flexibility in deployment, ubiquity, and affordability as networks scale. Over time, the TCP/IP protocol has been enriched with auxiliary management, security, and encryption capabilities, whereas Ethernet has matured from a shared, low-speed topology to a high-performance, multigigabit switched transport.

Until recently, networks terminated at the user, at the far end of the system, and the server or computing resource terminated at the point of data access. Network managers have been responsible for allocating bandwidth and monitoring the transport of data from source to destination, but have not been responsible for what happens to the data once it arrives. Likewise, systems and storage administrators have been focused on the placement and security of data under their charge, but have been largely oblivious to the external network infrastructure. As networking and storage technologies merge, these previously separate areas of responsibility are also merging.

During the past 20 years, the more dynamic development of enterprise networking has been in stark contrast to the more conservative pace of storage systems. For decades, the dominant paradigm in storage has been defined by channel architectures at the high end and the Small Computer Systems Interface (SCSI) at the medium to low end of enterprise systems. SCSI is both a protocol and a cabling standard. The SCSI protocol is optimized for the movement of large blocks of data between storage systems and hosts, typically servers. Parallel SCSI cabling provides a parallel data path for the efficient transport of bytes of data over limited distances. Although parallel SCSI performance has gradually increased from 20 megabytes per second (MBps) to higher speeds, it has maintained a rigid master/slave relationship between servers and attached storage resources. Because the server in this case is the owner of and sole gateway to its attached storage, access to the data residing on that storage is vulnerable to server failure.

Perhaps the most significant advance in storage technology was initiated by the creation of serial SCSI, or SCSI-3. Although previous developments provided greater efficiency in data movement, lower profile disk drives, and greater disk capacity, none of these accomplishments altered the server/storage paradigm. SCSI-3 enabled the SCSI protocol to be transported on more flexible networking infrastructures, and thus cut the thick umbilical cord of parallel cabling that previously bound storage to individual servers. With storage now a peer on a common network with multiple servers, its data is accessible even if individual servers fail.

Networking for storage resources on its own, however, would not be viable if it lacked the performance of the technology it hoped to replace. For serialized SCSI to replace parallel SCSI, a quantum leap in network performance was needed. This breakthrough was achieved by gigabit networking—first in the form of Fibre Channel, followed by Gigabit Ethernet. At gigabit speeds, it is possible to conquer time, delivering data as quickly as server resources can digest it. And with large storage pools now networked to multiple servers, space can be mastered as well.

Storage networking has undergone a fairly rapid adoption cycle from early market products to acceptance as a mainstream enterprise solution. Because of the central role that data plays for institutions and commercial enterprises, issues of data placement, security, and transport are universal. Today, all major suppliers of host systems and storage resources provide solutions based on storage networking as their flagship offerings. Although these solutions are being adopted initially by the top-tier enterprise customers, they are steadily penetrating the mainstream market. This rate of adoption will be accelerated by the emergence of new storage network solutions such as storage data over IP.

The first-generation storage networks for block data transport were enabled by Fibre Channel technology. Fibre Channel is a gigabit transport that provides high-performance, long-distance fiber-optic cabling (as much as 10 km), flexible peer networking, and upper layer protocol support for SCSI-3. Although Fibre Channel supports a variety of upper layer protocols, including IP, engineering development has focused on storage applications. A variety of products, including Fibre Channel host bus adapters (HBAs) for servers, Fibre Channel–attached storage arrays, Fibre Channel–attached tape libraries, and Fibre Channel switches and hubs, have enabled the first enterprise-class storage network solutions.

The challenge Fibre Channel has faced is common to any new technology that must engineer a total solution from the ground up. Creating standards for physical and logical layer interfaces, developing and testing entirely new architectures, undergoing long periods of interoperability testing and validating standards compliance, establishing agreement among the developers of hardware and software products for practical implementations, and demonstrating to the market that the solutions offered are viable, scalable, and enduring have been difficult tasks. Add to this considerable set of challenges the fact that storage networking itself introduces entirely new concepts and issues unrelated to the underlying plumbing. Management of storage networks, for example, is complex simply because networking and storage management tools must be combined. The management complexity often associated with current Fibre Channel storage area networks (SANs) will remain, even if Fibre Channel disappears.

While Fibre Channel developers have been struggling with these issues, new IP-based storage network initiatives have emerged. IP and Ethernet could not offer a viable alternative to Fibre Channel as long as Ethernet's performance was limited to Fast, 100-megabit per second (Mbps) Ethernet. Storage traffic for enterprise applications requires at least ten times that bandwidth. Ethernet vendors, however, have benefited directly from the development of Fibre Channel technology. The physical layer and data encoding mechanisms of Fibre Channel were borrowed (or stolen, depending on whom you ask) to accelerate the development of Gigabit Ethernet. With the appropriate bandwidth now in hand, Gigabit Ethernet is now positioned to compete with Fibre Channel for the storage networking market. The development of 10 Gigabit Ethernet will provide something of an advantage until Fibre Channel reaches parity.

What is wrong with Fibre Channel? Probably nothing that additional years of engineering could not fix. The interoperability and maturity of Fibre Channel end systems, however, has not been matched by Fibre Channel fabrics, largely because of competitive interests among the fabric vendors themselves. Without interoperability between director-class and departmental switches, it is not possible to build an enterprise-class storage network. In addition, security mechanisms such as encryption and authentication, transport management platforms, and traffic prioritization methods, which are already available for IP and Gigabit Ethernet networks, are still under construction in Fibre Channel protocol standards. With the tens of thousands of engineers at work on IP solutions arrayed against less than a thousand Fibre Channel engineers, it will be difficult for Fibre Channel vendors to deliver full and robust solutions quickly to an increasingly competitive market.

Given the availability and stability of Fibre Channel end systems, it is likely that Fibre Channel–based storage and IP-based storage networking products will be successful for some time to come. No one technology displaces all others, at least not overnight. IP-based storage solutions will become more pervasive over time, though, if for no other reason than the historical momentum that IP and Ethernet have gained throughout mainstream data communications. Customers will always gravitate to solutions that are more familiar, more affordable, and more compatible with their existing infrastructures.

1.2 Text Overview

The following work has been written for a fairly diverse audience and thus has several goals. Readers from networking fields who are interested in storage networking will hopefully find useful material for understanding the unique attributes of storage, particularly for TCP/IP and Gigabit Ethernet storage network configurations. Readers from system administration and storage-related fields may be unfamiliar with networking concepts, and through the text may gain a clearer understanding of the implications of combining storage and networking technologies. Managers and consultants will hopefully benefit from the discussion of real-world implementations that leverage the benefits of both Fibre Channel and Gigabit Ethernet solutions.

Although the focus of this work is on IP-based storage networks, storage networking as an architecture sits above any specific product implementation. To put storage networking into perspective and to define more clearly the role of IP-based solutions, Chapter 2 provides an overview of the Storage Networking Industry Association (SNIA) shared storage architecture. This model defines abstract layers of application, record/file system, block, and services subsystems in which various components of storage network hardware and applications may be placed. This overview should make it easier to distinguish between issues that are transport specific and those that are independent of the underlying infrastructure. It should also clarify the distinction between block-level storage over IP and file-level solutions such as network-attached storage (NAS). Additional information on the SNIA is provided in Appendix B.

To understand the issues associated with storage data over IP, it is useful to understand the common requirements of storage devices and how networking technologies can adapt to them. Chapter 3, Storage Networking Building Blocks, examines attributes of storage, traditional SCSI cabling, Fibre Channel technology, Gigabit Ethernet, NAS, and the broad challenges that storage over IP must overcome. Readers already familiar with one or another aspect of these technologies may fast-forward through the appropriate passages.

Chapter 4 provides an overview of the SCSI protocol. Operating systems typically access storage resources via a SCSI interface. The SCSI Architectural Model (SAM) details this implementation and defines SCSI commands that are used to transport data blocks from source to destination. Serial SCSI, or SCSI-3, enables SCSI commands and data to traverse a serial network topology such as Gigabit Ethernet, and thus is the fundamental enabler for block-oriented storage networks.

Chapters 5, 6, and 7 cover the IP, the User Datagram Protocol (UDP), and the TCP respectively. These chapters are intended primarily for readers unfamiliar with networks based on IP routing, although attention is also given to the consequences of transporting blocks of storage data over UDP/IP and TCP/IP infrastructures. Issues such as routing, flow control, session management, and packet transmission algorithms are discussed, as well as approaches to TCP/IP processing overhead on host systems.

The primary discussion of IP-based storage networking occurs in Chapter 8. The three main IP protocols currently under development in the IP Storage (IPS) Work Group of the Internet Engineering Task Force (IETF) are Fibre Channel over IP (FCIP), Internet Fibre Channel Protocol (iFCP), and Internet SCSI (iSCSI). Each of these protocols provides different capabilities for IP storage networks, and each confronts unique issues in enabling stable, high-speed performance. Because the standards activity of the IPS Work Group is an ongoing effort, the focus of this discussion is the enduring issues of each protocol, not the particular problems addressed by a specific standards draft. For successful implementation in real-world products, IP storage protocols are also dependent on technology advances made outside the IETF's purview. These dependencies, such as TCP off-load engines (TOEs), are discussed elsewhere in the text. Additionally, some IP storage initiatives are derivations of the IPS Work Group's efforts. Fibre Channel Protocol over UDP/IP, for example, utilizes the same basic mechanism as iFCP, but substitutes datagram service for TCP.

Plugging storage components into a common network may provide connectivity, but does not ensure that hosts will discover and be able to establish sessions with their storage resources. Chapter 9 explains the discovery and name service originally developed for Fibre Channel SANs, and their extension to IP-based storage networks via the Internet Storage Name Service (iSNS). The iSNS protocol leverages the Domain Name Service (DNS) function created for LAN and Internet device recognition, and extends it to include Fibre Channel's device discovery scheme.

Chapter 10 explores security issues common to all storage networking architectures and describes the role of Fibre Channel zoning, virtual LANs (vLANs) and encryption/authentication for securing storage data. One of the benefits of IP-based storage networks is its ability to use well-established virtual network and encryption methods to safeguard block data.

Chapter 11 reviews class-of-service and quality-of-service (QoS) protocols that have been developed for mainstream IP networking. Because storage data is invariably mission critical, IP storage is a natural beneficiary of these QoS services. Traffic priroritization, differentiated services (DiffServ), Resource Reservation Protocol (RSVP), and Multiprotocol label switching (MPLS) may offer customers additional tools for leveraging IP for SANs.

No discussion of new technologies for storage networking would be complete without some reference to InfiniBand. Chapter 12 provides a brief overview of InfiniBand technology and the Virtual Interface (VI) protocol. Although InfiniBand is optimized for a more efficient server-to-server communication and promises to displace traditional bus architectures, servers will still need access to stored data. For successful deployment, InfiniBand-based servers will necessarily require bridge and gateway products to an installed base of Fibre Channel and IP-based storage devices.

Having been sufficiently immersed in storage networking and IP-related technical issues, it should be useful to see how IP-based storage networks are appearing in the real world. Chapter 13 provides a series of application studies, including server clustering, backup, storage consolidation, disaster recovery, and metro and wide area storage networks based on IP. Many of these solutions may be constructed with a combination of Fibre Channel and IP/Gigabit Ethernet products, and in the future an admixture of InfiniBand as well.

Chapter 14 offers a summary of the prerequisites for IP storage technology and projects its developmental road map through further advances. The emergence of 10 Gigabit Ethernet, for example, offers the breakthrough bandwidth required for safely mixing a wide variety of IP-based traffic, including storage data. Storage arrays with 10 Gigabit Ethernet interfaces enable storage consolidation on an unprecedented scale. Future evolution of Fibre Channel, IP storage, and Infiniband hold significant promise for enterprise networks, which can select from a variety of high-performance products to meet specific needs. As IP-based storage becomes more ubiquitous and merged into mainstream networking, storage-specific issues will hopefully fade from view.

1.3 Chapter Summary

- The exponential growth of data is exceeding the capabilities of traditional storage and traditional networking paradigms.

- Data generation and use has been facilitated by fundamental changes in computing environments and by the transformation of data into rich content.

- Data access now requires more flexible connectivity for storage and higher speed transports for delivery.

- Storage and networking are converging into more homogenous infrastructures via storage networking technologies.

- First-generation Fibre Channel SANs are now confronted by solutions based on more familiar IP and Gigabit Ethernet.

- Storage networking technologies may coexist for some time, but IP-based SANs have the advantage of historical momentum, manageability, and ubiquity.

2 — Shared Storage

SHARING OF STORAGE RESOURCES is enabled by networking technology. The following discussion examines the benefits of shared storage, and how sharing can be accomplished through different network implementations.

2.1 Captive Storage

The value of sharing storage resources is clear when we consider the consequences of binding storage to individual servers. A typical direct-attached storage configuration consists of a server with a SCSI adapter card (or integrated SCSI interface) and several disks or disk arrays connected by a daisy chain of parallel cabling. The end points of this cabling string must be properly terminated to avoid signaling errors along the chain.

Although there are inherent limitations in SCSI cabling such as distance and number of devices supported, these are cosmetic issues compared with the exclusive binding of the disk resources to the server. Depending on cable type and the SCSI interface, strings are normally limited to approximately 25 m overall. Typically, fewer than 15 devices can appear on the string, although larger capacity disk arrays help reduce this number in practical installations. Proper termination is a requirement, but most often this is just an annoyance to the administrator. As shown in Figure 2–1, each server maintains its own storage resources via the SCSI chain.

As a further inconvenience, the entire SCSI chain may have to be quiesced to perform maintenance or to add/remove a disk resource. Data access is thus lost for the duration—a situation that end users have still not come to appreciate despite 20 years of conditioning. Additionally, because the SCSI chain is a common bus among all attached disks, the slowest SCSI interface dictates the performance of the string. This has made it difficult to migrate SCSI-based systems from current to next-generation products.

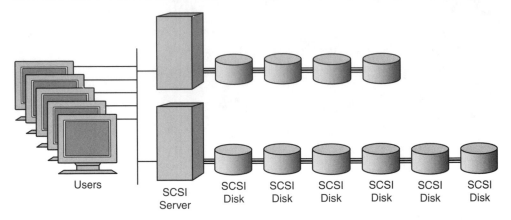

Figure 2–1 A typical SCSI daisy chain.

Despite these shortcomings, SCSI-attached storage is an entrenched technology and is widely deployed in enterprise networks. It is familiar, easy to acquire, relatively low cost, and, until the advent of high-availability operations and the explosion of data storage requirements, has served its purpose.

If capacity, administration, and high-availability access were not issues, parallel SCSI would endure. Unfortunately for enterprise networks, high availability, cost of administration, and increasing capacity requirements have all become very critical issues. Enterprises cannot continue adding and administering additional servers simply because servers are the exclusive keepers of storage. Enterprises also cannot afford the loss in business revenue that accompanies server failures. Consequently, despite the familiarity and lower cost of SCSI-attached storage, network managers are being forced by their own internal budgets and by the requirements of business operations to consider alternative solutions that can enable storage to be shared.

The transition from captive to shared storage has several implications. The traditional parallel SCSI bus gives way to serial network cabling. Because serial network architectures typically support long distances (when fiber-optic cabling is used), distance limitations are largely overcome. Depending on the topology, the number of devices supported on a single network may be practically unlimited. Because an individual storage array is no longer dependent on the activity of a shared bus, storage resources can also be installed and removed from the network without disruption to ongoing traffic. And, most important, a storage resource is no longer a subordinate to a master server. Servers and storage devices are peers. If an individual server fails, other servers on the peer network can access the data stored in the array.

Although there are other application benefits that are discussed later, the elevation of storage from a captive resource to an independent and central entity within the storage network most accurately reflects the position that data has assumed for enterprise networks. This transition has facilitated new ways of thinking about storage and has engendered creative solutions for storage access.

2.2 The SNIA Shared Storage Model

To clarify the roles of new storage networking technologies and applications, the SNIA has been developing a shared storage architectural model. The Shared Storage Model is a work-in-progress of the SNIA Technical Council, which in turn is composed of technologists from a variety of SNIA member companies.

An architectural model provides value by abstracting a complex technology into its most basic components. It has particular value for storage networking, because as a technology it embodies entirely new concepts, structures, applications, and infrastructures. NAS and SAN, for example, have struggled in the marketplace as contending storage networking solutions. Marketing-driven distinctions, however, become transparent when an architectural model is applied. As shown in the following examples, NAS and SAN occupy the same space vis-à-vis upper layer applications.

As shown in Figure 2–2, the SNIA model abstracts the application layer (for example, server and workstation software applications) from the underlying storage domain that serves as the repository for data that user applications manipulate. The storage domain itself includes several layers, including a file/record subsystem for organizing data, and a block subsystem that includes block aggregation layers for organizing data in bulk. The block subsystem includes the physical devices (disk and tape) on which data is stored. Auxiliary service subsystems provide a variety of functions, including device discovery, management, security, availability, and storage planning.

At this most abstract level, all specific storage networking implementations including NAS, Fibre Channel, and Gigabit Ethernet fall under the general heading of *storage domain*. This highlights the commonality of file-oriented and block-oriented infrastructures in relation to the upper layer applications. A rank-and-file end user, for example, simply wants fast, reliable access to information. The underlying plumbing that enables this should be transparent. Plumbing, however, is very important, particularly to the plumbers themselves. Their role is to determine the requirements for data

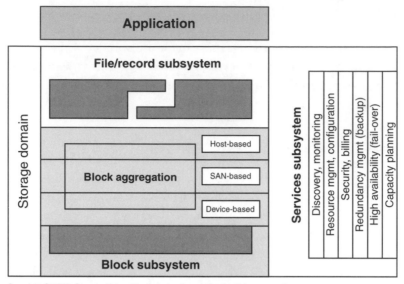

Figure 2–2 The SNIA Shared Storage Model.

access that different applications demand and to optimize the plumbing infrastructure for them.

For discussions on IP-based storage, the distinction between file and block access methods is of practical importance. A file, after all, ultimately resides somewhere on disk, and has been written there with standard cylinder, head, and sector block addressing. A call for a file by its file system name or handle thus triggers a lower level block access process. As the server of the file assembles it for transport, the file is in turn "packetized" for transmission across a LAN. The distinction between file and block in terms of storage networking, then, turns on whether the recipient of the data receives a file that has been processed from blocks, or receives the blocks directly. Block-oriented access, because it sits closer to the arrays and lower levels of the operating system, ensures high performance. File-oriented access enables other higher level functionality, such as cross-platform access between heterogeneous operating systems.

The organization of data blocks (block aggregation) may occur at the host, storage network, or device level. A disk array, for example, may receive data blocks from the host via a storage network, but provides the intelligence for distributing blocks (striping and/or mirroring) across its disks. Alternately, this function could be served by software RAID (redundant array of independent disks) on the host striping data to a collection of disks, by a storage appliance sitting between the host and storage resources, or by an intelligent controller on the HBA.

In Figure 2–3, the framework of the general architectural model is used to demonstrate the function of block-oriented SANs within the storage domain. In this example, the SAN sits between servers or workstations and the target disk subsystems. The SAN may use Fibre Channel or Gigabit Ethernet to provide connectivity between hosts and storage, and in either case offers the benefit of high bandwidth, support for longer distances (vis-à-vis parallel SCSI cabling), peer-to-peer networking, and the ability to implement advanced features such as storage consolidation, resource sharing, and high availability.

A differentiating feature of both Fibre Channel and Gigabit Ethernet SANs is the ability to transport blocks of data using the serial SCSI protocol. Because the operating systems that support applications view storage resources as SCSI devices, a SAN infrastructure can directly replace traditional parallel SCSI-attached storage with no change to the operating system. The same reads and writes of SCSI blocks that were previously performed to disks attached to a parallel SCSI bus can now be executed over a more flexible network topology. In the configuration shown in Figure 2–3, additional disk resources or additional servers can be added without disruption to

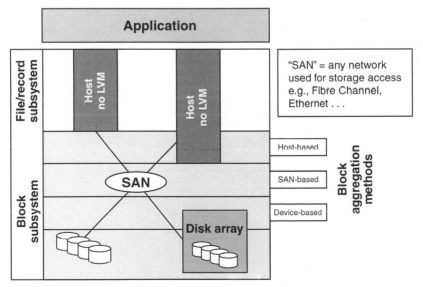

Copyright © 2000, Storage Networking Industry Association (work in progress)

Figure 2–3 SNIA Shared Storage Model—SAN.

ongoing transactions. Additionally, because all hosts have potential visibility to shared storage resources, failover and other high-availability methods are also enabled.

The SAN example depicts hosts that interface to the application layer. The applications themselves may be running on remote client workstations connected by a LAN to SAN-attached file servers, or on application servers (for example, database servers) directly attached to the SAN. An e-mail client, for example, may send e-mail as a file to an exchange server. The data manager of the server (for example, NT Files System, NTFS) in turn uses block methods to write the data to disk. Requests for reads and writes of records by a data-mining application are likewise converted into block methods by the server's data manager. In either case, the SAN-attached host sends and receives block data across the SAN to storage subsystems. This is a primary distinction between SAN and NAS.

As shown in Figure 2–4, a NAS system reaches from the file/record subsystem down to the block subsystem and the physical storage devices. Whereas SANs serve up blocks of data from disk, NAS devices serve up assembled files. In this respect, NAS resembles the traditional file server architecture, minus the overhead of file server administration and the complexity of a full-featured operating system.

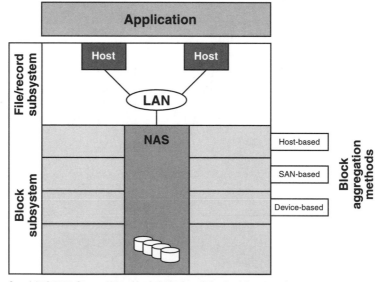

Figure 2–4 The SNIA Shared Storage Model—NAS.

NAS systems are optimized for heterogeneous file access. Although SCSI block methods may be used to exchange data between the NAS intelligence and its attached disk arrays, this is generally hidden within the NAS enclosure. The visible access to applications is through the Network File System (NFS) or Common Internet File System (CIFS) protocols over IP. Because NFS and CIFS can be run on a variety of operating systems, users only need to install the appropriate NFS or CIFS clients to enable access. Enterprise networks can deploy NAS devices to serve Windows, Solaris, UNIX, and Linux workstations, provided the appropriate protocol drivers are installed.

As shown in Figure 2–4, the application's access to NAS storage is over the LAN. LAN bandwidth is a potential bottleneck for Fast Ethernet networks, but the availability of switched Gigabit Ethernet LAN technology makes this less of an issue. In terms of protocol overhead, SANs have the advantage of a low-impact serial SCSI transport that requires minimal central processing unit (CPU) resources for protocol processing. Because NAS must rely on NFS or CIFS over TCP/IP, it must accommodate meta-data processing in addition to protocol overhead and CPU interrupts. NAS is rarely deployed when throughput performance is the main priority.

One of the major contributions of NAS technology is the concept of a storage appliance. A customer could, after all, install a traditional file server with SCSI-attached storage and load NFS or CIFS to facilitate heterogeneous storage access. File servers, however, require administration, both for the operating system and for the attached storage devices. In the end, the administrative costs of a homegrown NAS solution far outweigh the initial acquisition costs. NAS vendors have addressed this problem by making their devices as streamlined as possible, both in terms of efficiency in file serving and simplicity in configuration and management, and pretuning and configuring the operating system parameters.

In some vendor offerings, SAN and NAS technologies may be combined. As shown in Figure 2–5, a NAS processor (head) may use a SAN back end to enable more efficient access to storage arrays over Fibre Channel or Gigabit Ethernet (IP storage). Whether SAN technology is used for NAS storage is vendor dependent, but an internal SAN infrastructure for a NAS device offers the benefits generally associated with SANs: high bandwidth, flexible networking, and the ability to grow storage capacity on the fly.

New developments in both SAN and NAS technologies may further blur the lines between them and may reveal more clearly their marketing origins.

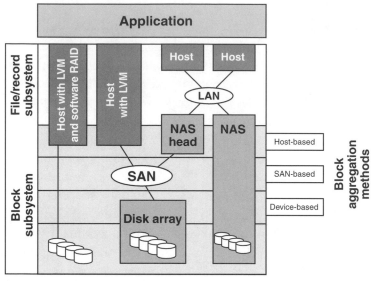

Figure 2–5 The SNIA Shared Storage Model—NAS/SAN.

IP storage, for example, makes it possible to transport file-oriented NAS requests and block-oriented IP/SCSI requests across common, homogeneous Gigabit Ethernet networks. Object-oriented storage initiatives (for example, Object-Based Storage Device) are redefining file and block access at a more fundamental level, and are driving meta-data processing intelligence further into storage systems themselves.

In the meantime, customers are selecting SAN and NAS solutions based on their own application requirements. SANs are normally chosen for high-performance applications that require gigabit speeds and the throughput that block data access provides. Server clustering, storage consolidation, backup, and disaster recovery, for example, may be implemented with Gigabit Ethernet-based SANs that, like NAS, leverage the benefits of IP. NAS solutions are generally chosen for heterogeneous file access and for appliance installations when simplified management is desired. Storage consolidation may also be addressed by NAS, however, and some vendors combine NAS and SAN backup solutions into a single offering. Because enterprise networks usually have a wide variety of application requirements, it is common to see both NAS and SAN deployed across the enterprise.

2.3 Storage Networking Layers

A network is a complex of physical components and logical functions that must work together harmoniously to ensure data integrity and efficient delivery. The common reference for network architectures is the Open System Interconnection (OSI) model that defines a seven-layer structure for the most common network functions. As shown in Table 2–1, the OSI model partitions network processes into sequential functions that user data must traverse as it moves from the upper layer application to transport across the physical network. As the user data is passed down by an application for transmission across the network, it is wrapped in successive envelopes of information, roughly corresponding to the layers represented below.

A file transfer, for example, would acquire an information envelope (header) on the file's format from the presentation layer, layer 6. The session layer, layer 5, would add additional information that may be useful for maintaining the file transfer session between sender and recipient. As the data is packetized, the transport layer appends additional information to track acknowledgment of receipt. Layer 3 appends network addressing required for routing across the network, whereas layer 2 specifies the type of media from which the data originated. Finally, the user data with all the necessary

---

TABLE 2–1   OSI REFERENCE MODEL

Layer	Title	Description
7	Application	Application layer: e-mail, file transfer, and so on, interface
6	Presentation	Application data formatting: application specific
5	Session	End-to-end session control: netbios, application specific
4	Transport	Transmission control: TCP, UDP
3	Network	Routing protocol: IP
2	Data link	Access method: ethernet, token ring, and so on
1	Physical	Physical transport: twisted pair, fiber optics, coaxial, and so on

nested headers is encapsulated for transport on the physical media, layer 1. At the receiving end, each header envelope is verified and removed by the receiving host until the data that composed the original file is reassembled and passed to the upper layer application for processing.

This is an idealized representation of network layering. In practical implementation, some of these functions are combined into a single layer or are omitted altogether. Layer 2 switching, for example, does not mandate a routing protocol; an upper layer application may absorb presentation or session functions. The value of the OSI Reference Model is not that it serves as a blueprint for how network architectures should be designed, but it serves as a useful reference for comparing how different network architectures are actually implemented.

Table 2–2 compares the layered structures of IP networking, Gigabit Ethernet, and Fibre Channel in relation to the OSI Reference Model. IP networking assumes an underlying network topology, and thus only defines the network addressing and transport layers. Gigabit Ethernet, on the other hand, assumes that it will be carrying some upper layer data that may or may not contain network routing protocols, and thus only defines the mechanisms required for properly accessing its supporting media at gigabit speeds. The Fibre Channel stack terminates at its upper layer protocol interface, which typically is SCSI-3. Because some functions are combined at different split points of the OSI Reference Model, there is not always a one-to-one equivalence between the different architectures.

There are several fundamental principles of data handling common to all networking technologies. These basic networking principles include

- Serial transport

- Access method

- Addressing

- Packetizing of data

- Routing of packets

- Upper layer protocol support

Because these networking fundamentals also form the foundation of storage networks, it is important to understand how each contributes to the network infrastructure and how each affects the operation of network interfaces in a storage environment.

TABLE 2–2   OSI, IP, GIGABIT ETHERNET, AND FIBRE CHANNEL STACKS

Layer	Title	IP Routed Networks	Switched Gigabit Ethernet	Fibre Channel
7	Application	NFS, CIFS, FTP,	May support	SCSI-3,
6	Presentation	SNMP, TFTP,	TCP/IP,	VI,
5	Session	TELNET,	UDP/IP, or other	IP
		FCP, SCSI-3	network	
			protocols	
4	Transport	TCP, UDP		FC-4
3	Network	IP		Protocol interface
				FC-3 Encryption, authentication
2	Data link	LAN, MAN, WAN, options for LLC/media access control (MAC)	MAC client sublayer	FC-2 Framing, flow control, class of service
			MAC control	
				FC-1 Encoding, Link controls
			MAC	
1	Physical	Physical	Physical	
				FC-0 Physical

2.3.1 Serial Transport

Networking is a serial transport. The digital ones and zeros that compose all data are transmitted sequentially, 1 bit at a time, from source to destination. Serial transmission enables data to be shipped over longer distances with fewer resources at a faster data rate. Serial transmission over fiber-optic cabling, for example, can extend tens of kilometers; over satellite, hundreds of kilometers. Alternately, a parallel transport such as SCSI cabling must use multiple lines to send groups of bits concurrently. Because of electrical and clocking considerations, parallel transmission is severely limited in distance, usually to less than 25 m. Serializing data for transport at gigabit speeds poses additional challenges, as discussed later.

2.3.2 Access Method

A networked device requires an access method to gain control of the transport media. The access method is particularly important for shared media, such as standard or Fast Ethernet and Fibre Channel arbitrated loop. Standard Ethernet uses carrier sense and collision detection, although switched Gigabit Ethernet circumvents collision detection by establishing dedicated unshared links. Regardless of the underlying transport, a form of media access control (MAC) is necessary for ensuring data integrity.

2.3.3 Addressing

Each device on a network must have a unique identity. This identity is established by a unique address, and, depending on the upper layer protocols that a device supports, a single networked computer may have a unique address corresponding to each protocol layer.

An Ethernet interface card in a server, for example, has a unique MAC address that is assigned by the manufacturer. The 6-byte MAC address is used when data is exchanged between computers on the same LAN segment. If a user wishes to communicate with another device on a different segment, a network protocol such as IP is required. Each device communicating via a network protocol must have, in addition to a unique MAC address, a unique network address. IP provides an addressing scheme for billions of unique network addresses, although address allocation must be administered to avoid duplications and to guarantee proper routing of data. Fibre Channel uses a 3-byte network address, as well as an 8-byte World Wide Name (WWN) to ensure uniqueness for every device.

2.3.4 Packetizing of Data

User data is sent across the network in discrete packets or frames. A large graphic file, for example, must be divided into multiple small packets for transport across the network. Each packet contains a portion of the original file, as well as sequencing and source/destination addressing in a packet header. At the receiving end, the network-specific addressing and sequence information is removed, and the data is reassembled to recreate the original file. Segmentation of larger blocks of data into packets or frames occurs in both Fibre Channel and IP networks. Fibre Channel end devices, however, expect to receive frames in the order in which they were sent (in-order delivery) for successful reassembly to occur. In-order delivery for IP networks is provided by the TCP layer.

2.3.5 Routing of Packets

Networks may be composed of multiple physical segments joined by routers or switches. Physical segmentation of a network is often required to avoid overloading the transport with too many users and thus degrading performance. Users on a single shared LAN segment can communicate directly with each other. If a user wishes to communicate with someone on a different LAN segment, a router or switch must forward the data. Managing the bandwidth available on a single segment and allocating sufficient router or switch ports for access to the rest of the network are fundamental challenges of network design.

In addition to getting packets across multiple segments, routing enables redundant links to be created between those segments. A meshed network is a topology that provides multiple data paths between its participants. If a single link fails, the meshed network can route data around the failure and still get data to its final destination.

One of the distinct advantages of using IP for storage networking is its ability to route storage traffic automatically across dispersed network segments for metropolitan, wide area, and disaster recovery applications.

2.3.6 Upper Layer Protocol Support

Network topologies and protocols provide the communications infrastructure for upper level applications. The network protocol layer is only responsible for moving data from one point to another. What is actually done with the data once it arrives is the responsibility of upper level protocols. IP, for example, routes packets through the network to the intended destination. Sitting above IP, the TCP or UDP formats the data for handoff to the application and ensures that the appropriate upper layer application receives that data. For IP-based storage networks, the payload is SCSI-3 commands, data, and status, either in the form of Fibre Channel Protocol (FCP) or as native serial SCSI.

2.4 Chapter Summary

Captive Storage

- Legacy SCSI-attached storage makes data captive behind an individual server.

- SCSI attachment imposes limitations on distance and device connectivity, as well as downtime for servicing or adds/moves/changes.

- Shared or networked storage establishes storage as a peer-to-server resource.

- Networked storage overcomes limitations of distance and population and facilitates nondisruptive changes or additions.

Shared Storage

- The SNIA shared storage model presents an abstraction of application and storage domains.

- Within the storage domain, NAS and SANs built on Fibre Channel or Gigabit Ethernet service data requests to the application level.

- Data access may be through records (for example, a database) or file systems, or combinations of both.

- NAS is file oriented and facilitates cross-platform access.

- SANs based on Fibre Channel or Gigabit Ethernet are block oriented and optimize performance.

- Enterprise networks typically use both NAS and SAN solutions.

Storage Networking Layers

- The OSI Reference Model depicts seven layers of network functionality: physical, data link, network, transport, session, presentation, and application.

- Specific network architectures may implement only some of these layers or combine them into single layers.

- TCP/IP and UDP/IP may carry upper layer protocols, including serial SCSI.

- Moving data serially allows higher speeds and longer distances between servers and storage.

- Access to physical transport involves low-level protocols to ensure data integrity.

- Network addressing is required to identify each participant uniquely and to route data properly across the infrastructure.

- Large blocks of data must be segmented into packets or frames for orderly shipment through the network.

- Routing of data packets between different network segments is performed by routers and switches.

- IP routing facilitates complex storage networks that span metropolitan and regional boundaries.

- Networking enables the movement of data whose source and destination are ultimately upper level application interfaces.

- For IP-based SANs, the serial SCSI protocol rides over a Gigabit Ethernet infrastructure to move blocks of data to and from disk.

3

Storage Networking Building Blocks

A STORAGE NETWORK may be composed of a wide variety of hardware and software products. Software products invariably involve management of some kind: management of logical volumes, management of disk resources, management of tape subsystems and backup, and management of the network transport status. Hardware products include the storage end systems and their interfaces to the network as well as the switches and bridge products that provide connectivity. Storage network interfaces typically include legacy SCSI, Fibre Channel, and Gigabit Ethernet. Just as first-generation Fibre Channel SANs accommodated legacy SCSI disk and tape devices, IP-based storage networks must incorporate both Fibre Channel and legacy SCSI devices. The challenge for vendors is to make this complexity disappear, and find inventive ways to integrate new and old technologies with minimal user involvement.

The following sections discuss the major building blocks of storage networks and highlight the technical aspects that differentiate them.

3.1 Storage Networking Terminology

Storage networking end systems include storage devices and the interfaces that bring them into the network. RAID arrays, just a bunch of disks (JBODs), tape subsystems, optical storage systems, and host adapter cards installed in servers are all end systems. The interconnect products that shape these end systems into a coherent network are discussed in the following sections on Fibre Channel, Gigabit Ethernet, and NAS. New SAN products such as virtualization devices and SAN appliances that front-end storage may, depending on implementation, also be considered end systems from the standpoint of storage targets, or interconnects from the standpoint of hosts.

3.1.1 RAID

RAID is both a generic term for intelligent storage arrays and a set of methods for the placement of data on multiple disks. Depending on the methods used, RAID can both enhance storage performance and enable data integrity. Because logic is required to distribute and retrieve data safely from multiple disk resources, the RAID function is performed by an intelligent controller. The controller may be implemented in either hardware or software, although optimal performance is through hardware, in the form of application-specific integrated circuits (ASICs) or dedicated microprocessors. A RAID array embeds the controller function in the array enclosure, with the controller standing between the external interface to the host and the internal configuration of disks. RAID arrays may include eight to ten internal disks for departmental applications or many more for data center requirements.

The performance problem that RAID solves stems from the ability of host systems to deliver data much faster than storage systems can absorb it. When a server is connected to a single disk drive, reads or writes of multiple data blocks are limited by the buffering capability, seek time, and rotation speed of the disk. While the disk is busy processing one or more blocks of data, the host must wait for acknowledgment before sending or receiving more. Throughput can be significantly increased by distributing the stream of data block traffic across several disks in an array, a technique called *striping*. In a write operation, for example, the host can avoid swamping the buffering capacity of any individual drive by subdividing the data blocks into several concurrent transfers sent to multiple targets. This simplified RAID is called *level 0*. If the total latency of an individual disk restricted its bandwidth to 10 to 15 MBps, then eight disks in an array could saturate a gigabit link that provided approximately 100 MBps of effective throughput.

Although boosting performance, RAID 0 does not provide data integrity. If a single disk in the RAID set fails, data cannot be reconstructed from the survivors. Other RAID techniques address this problem by either writing parity data on each drive in the array or by dedicating a single drive for parity information. RAID 3, for example, writes byte-level parity to a dedicated drive, and RAID 4 writes block-level parity to a dedicated drive. In either case, the dedicated parity drive contains the information required to reconstruct data if a disk failure occurs. RAID 3 and RAID 4 are less commonly used as stand-alone solutions because the parity drive itself poses a performance bottleneck problem. RAID 5 is the preferred method for striped data because it distributes block-level parity information across each drive in the array. If an individual disk fails, its data can be reconstructed from the parity information contained on the other drives, and parity operations are spread out among the disks.

The RAID striping algorithms range from simple to complex and thus imply much higher logic at the RAID 5 level. More logic implies more expense. RAID 5 controllers must not only provide the intelligence to distribute data and parity information across multiple drives, but must also be able to reconstruct data automatically in case of a disk failure. Typically, additional drives are provisioned in standby mode (spare), available for duty if a primary disk fails. The additional manipulation of data provided by RAID 5 also implies latency, and vendors of these products compete on the basis of performance and optimized controller logic.

Storage applications may also require full data redundancy. If, for example, the RAID controller failed or a break occurred along the cable plant, none of the RAID striping methods would ensure data availability. RAID level 1 achieves full data integrity by trading the performance advantage of striping for the integrity of data replication. This is accomplished by mirroring. In disk mirroring, every write operation to a primary disk is repeated on a secondary or mirrored disk. If the primary disk fails, a host can switch over to the backup disk. Mirroring on its own is subject to two performance hits: once for the latency of disk buffering, seek time, and spindle speed, and once for the additional logic required to write to two targets simultaneously. The input/output (I/O) does not complete until both writes are successful. Mirroring is also an expensive data integrity solution because the investment in storage capacity is doubled with every new installation. Mirroring, however, is the only solution that offers a near-absolute guarantee that data will be readily available in the event of disk failure. In addition, because data is written to two separate disk targets, the targets themselves may be separated by distance. Mirroring thus provides a ready solution for disaster recovery applications, provided sufficient latency and bandwidth are available between primary and remote sites. Storage replication over distance also makes mirroring a prime application for IP-based storage solutions.

RAID implementations may be combined to provide both striping throughput and data redundancy via mirroring. RAID 0 + 1, for example, simply replicates a RAID 0 disk set to create two separate copies of data on two separate, high-performance arrays. Just as mirroring doubled the cost of the capacity of a single drive, RAID 0 + 1 doubles the cost of a RAID striping array. As shown in Figure 3–1, data blocks are striped over disks in each array, providing an exact copy of data that can be written or read at high

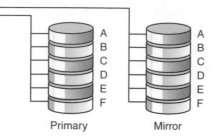

Figure 3–1 RAID 0 + 1 striping plus mirroring. Blocks A, B, C, D, E, and F of a single data file.

speed. Some implementations may combine RAID 5 with RAID 1 for an even higher level of data integrity and availability.

Because RAID implementations treat the drives in an array as a single resource, homogeneity of access is imposed on each individual drive. The performance of the disk set is thus determined by the lowest common denominator. The disk with the slowest access time will dictate the performance of all other drives. RAID-based storage arrays are thus typically populated with the same drive type per set, including unused hot spares that can be brought on-line if a drive fails. As newer, lower cost, and higher capacity drives are constantly introduced into the market, however, a customer may replace a failed disk with a much higher performing unit. The performance and capacity advantage of the newer unit will not be realized because the operational parameters of the original drive will throttle the new disk.

The main components of a RAID subsystem include the interface (parallel SCSI, Fibre Channel, or Gigabit Ethernet), the RAID controller logic, the backplane that accommodates the disks, the disks themselves, and the enclosure, including power supplies and fans. At the high end of the RAID food chain, RAID arrays may provide redundant power supplies and fans, diagnostic and "phone home" features for servicing, and high-performance logic to optimize RAID operations. At the low end, RAID may be implemented via software on a host system with data striped to unrelated disks (JBOD). Software RAID places additional burdens on the server or host because CPU cycles must be devoted to striping across multiple targets. The RAID function may also be provided by an HBA or interface card, which off-loads the host CPU and manages striping or mirroring functions to disk targets. This is advantageous from the standpoint of the host, but, as with software RAID, places additional transactions on the storage network for the parity operations. Despite higher cost, a RAID subsystem offers optimal performance for both RAID functions and storage network traffic compared with software or adapter card implementations.

A RAID enclosure hides the access method between the RAID controller and the disks it manages. The external interface between the host systems and the array may be parallel SCSI, Fibre Channel, or Gigabit Ethernet. The internal interface between the RAID controller and disks may be parallel SCSI or Fibre Channel, and at the very low end of the spectrum, even Integrated Drive Electronics (IDE). This separation between the internal workings of the array and the external interface provides flexibility in designing low-, medium-, and high-end RAID systems that target different markets. It also facilitates the introduction of new external interfaces such as IP over Gigabit Ethernet, which although not trivial from an engineering standpoint at least do not require redesign of the entire subsystem including the back-end disks.

In Figure 3–2, the basic architecture of RAID subsystems is shown with the variations of external interfaces and internal disk configurations. If Fibre Channel disks are used, the internal Fibre Channel disk interface may be based on a shared loop or switched fabric (discussed later).

RAID systems are a powerful component of storage networks. They offer the performance and data integrity features required for mission-critical applications, and the flexibility (given sufficient budget) for resilient data replication and disaster recovery strategies. They also provide, depending on vendor implementation, the ability to scale to terabytes of data in a single, highly available storage resource. In a storage network based on Fibre Channel or Gigabit Ethernet, the resources of a RAID array may be shared by multiple servers, thus facilitating data availability and reduction of storage management costs through storage consolidation.

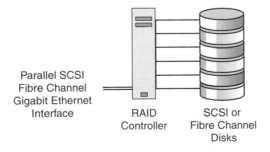

Parallel SCSI
Fibre Channel
Gigabit Ethernet
Interface   RAID   SCSI or
Controller   Fibre Channel
Disks

Figure 3–2 Basic architecture of a RAID subsystem.

3.1.2 JBODs

A JBOD is an enclosure with multiple disk drives installed in a common backplane. Unlike a RAID array, a JBOD has no front-end logic to manage the distribution of data over the disks. Instead, the disks are addressed individually, either as separate storage resources or as part of a host-based software or an adapter card RAID set. JBODs may be used for direct-attached storage based on parallel SCSI cabling, or on a storage network with, typically, a Fibre Channel interface.

The advantage of a JBOD is its lower cost vis-à-vis a RAID array, and the consolidation of multiple disks into a single enclosure that share power supplies and fans. JBODs are often marketed for installation in 19-inch racks and thus provide an economical and space-saving means to deploy storage. As disk drives with ever-higher capacity are brought to market, it is possible to build JBOD configurations with hundreds of gigabytes of storage.

Because a JBOD has no intelligence and no independent interface to a storage network, the interface type of the individual drives determines the type of connectivity to the SAN. An IP-based storage network using Gigabit Ethernet as a transport would therefore require Gigabit Ethernet/IP interfaces on the individual JBOD disks, or a bridge device to translate between Gigabit Ethernet and IP to Fibre Channel or parallel SCSI. Over time, disk drive manufacturers will determine the type of interface required by the market.

As shown in Figure 3–3, a JBOD built with SCSI disks is an enclosed SCSI daisy chain and offers a parallel SCSI connection to the host. A JBOD built with Fibre Channel disks may provide one or two Fibre Channel interfaces to the host and internally is composed of shared loop segments. In either configuration, a central issue is the vulnerability of the JBOD to individual disk failure. Without the appropriate bypass capability, the failure of a single drive could disable the entire JBOD.

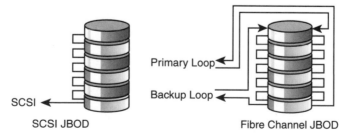

Figure 3–3 JBOD disk configurations.

Management of a JBOD enclosure is normally limited to simple power and fan status. In-band management may be provided by the SCSI Enclosure Services protocol, which can be used in both parallel SCSI and Fibre Channel environments. Some vendor offerings also allow the JBOD to be divided into separate groups of disks via a hardware switch or jumpers. As shown in Figure 3–4, a single Fibre Channel JBOD may appear as two separate resources to the host.

How the individual disk drives within a JBOD are used for data storage is determined by the host server or workstation, or by RAID intelligence on an HBA. Windows Disk Administrator, for example, can be used to create individual volumes from individual JBOD disks, or can assign groups of JBOD disks as a volume composed of a striped software RAID set. Software RAID will increase performance in reads and writes to the JBOD, but will also give exclusive ownership of the striped set to a single server. Without volume-sharing middleware, multiple servers cannot simultaneously manage the organization of striped data on a JBOD without data corruption. The symptom of unsanctioned sharing is the triggering of endless check disk sequences as a host struggles with unexpected reorganization of data on the disks. Generally, software RAID on JBODs offers higher performance and redundancy for dedicated server-to-storage relationships, but does not lend itself to server clustering or serverless tape backup across the SAN.

One means of leveraging JBODs for shared storage is the use of storage virtualization appliances that sit between the host systems and the JBOD targets. The virtualization appliance manages the placement of data to multiple JBODs or RAID arrays, while presenting the illusion of a single storage resource to each host. This makes it possible to dispense with software RAID on the host because this function is now assumed by the appliance. Essentially, storage virtualization fulfills the same function of an intelligent RAID controller, except that the virtualization appliance and storage arrays now sit

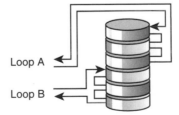

Figure 3–4 Dividing a Fibre Channel JBOD backplane into separate loops.

in separate enclosures across the storage network. As with Dorothy in *The Wizard of Oz,* however, one really should pay attention to the little man behind the curtain. Although presenting a simplified view of storage resources to the host systems, storage virtualization appliances must necessarily assume the complexity of managing data placement and be able to recover automatically from failures or disruptions. This is not a trivial task.

3.1.3 Tape Subsystems

Data storage on media of different kinds divides into a hierarchy of cost per megabyte, performance, and capacity. Generally, higher cost per megabyte brings greater performance and, ironically, lower capacity. At the high end, solid-state storage offers the performance of memory access, but with limited capacity. Spinning media such as disk drives in RAID configurations can support gigabit access speeds, with the capacity of more than a terabyte of data. Tape subsystems may only support a fifth of that speed, but large libraries can store multiple terabytes of data. At the low-performance end of the scale, optical media libraries offer nearly unlimited storage capacity. The two most commonly used solutions—disk and tape—are deployed for a sequential storage strategy, with normal data transactions based on disk, followed by periodic backup of that data to tape. Hierarchical storage management applications may be used to rationalize this process and to determine the frequency of and appropriate migration of data from disk to tape, and sometimes from tape to optical storage.

Securing a backup copy of data as a safeguard against disk or system failure is a universal problem. No institution or enterprise is likely to survive a loss of mission-critical information. In addition, a company may be obliged to keep reliable copies of its data according to government or commercial regulations. Financial institutions, for example, must keep long-term records of their transactions, which may require both tape and optical storage archiving.

If spinning disk media could provide affordable, scalable, and highly reliable long-term storage, mirroring would suffice. Although this solution is strongly supported by disk manufacturers, mirroring for ever-increasing amounts of data has proved too costly to implement. Tape, by contrast, has proved to be economical, scalable, and highly reliable, and despite the advances made by disk technology, tape is likely to endure as the primary tool for the archival preservation of data.

In its pure SCSI incarnation, tape provides a secure copy of data, but its performance is constrained by the typical topology in which it is deployed. For optimal performance in traditional environments, a SCSI tape device can be attached to a server/storage SCSI daisy chain. In this configuration, the tape device (like the storage arrays) becomes captive to an individual server. Each server would thus require its own tape unit for backup, multiplying the cost of tape systems and management throughout the network. Alternately, a dedicated tape backup server and SCSI-attached tape library can provide centralized backup over the LAN. This facilitates resource sharing, but places large block data transfer on the same LAN that is used for user traffic. The bandwidth of the LAN itself may create additional problems. The backup window, or period of time in which a nondisruptive backup could occur, may not be sufficient for the amount of data that requires duplication to tape.

The conflict between backup requirements and the constraints imposed by LAN-based backup is resolved by storage networking. By placing tape subsystems on a storage network, they become shared resources for multiple servers and can now move backup traffic independently of the LAN. This simultaneously reduces costs, simplifies administration, and provides greater bandwidth for backup streams. LAN-free backup on a storage network has also enabled new backup solutions. Even on a SAN, the backup traffic moves from disk storage to server and from server to tape. The server is in the backup path because it is responsible for reads from disk and for writes to tape. However, because servers, storage, and tape subsystems are now peers on the storage network, data paths can be enabled directly between disk storage and tape resources. Server-free backup is predicated on intelligent backup agents on the SAN that can perform the server's read/write functions for tape. A third-party copy (extended copy) agent may be embedded in the tape library, in the SAN switch, or in a SAN-to-SCSI bridge used to connect a SCSI tape library. Because the third-party copy agent assumes the task of reading from disk and writing to tape, server CPU cycles are freed for user transactions. LAN-free and server-free backup solutions for IP-based SANs are discussed further in Chapter 13.

The internal design of a tape subsystem is vendor specific, but typically includes an external interface for accessing the subsystem, controller logic for formatting data for tape placement, one or more tape drives that perform the write and read functions, robotics for manipulating tape cartridges and feeding the drives, and slots to hold the cartridges while not in use. Vendors may promote a variety of tape technologies, including advanced intelligent tape, linear tape-open, and digital linear tape, which are differentiated by performance and capacity.

The external interface to a tape library may be legacy SCSI, Fibre Channel, or Gigabit Ethernet. Although each tape drive within a library may only support 10 to 15 MBps of throughput, multiple drives can leverage the bandwidth provided by a gigabit interface. Theoretically this would allow multiple servers (or third-party copy agents) to back up simultaneously to a single library over the SAN, although the library controller must support this feature. Another potential performance enhancement is provided by the application of RAID striping algorithms to tape, or tape RAID. As with disk RAID, tape RAID implies additional complexity and logic, and therefore additional expense.

The initiative for IP-based SCSI solutions for tape was launched by SpectraLogic Corporation in the spring of 2001. Tape, like storage arrays, relies on block SCSI data for moving large volumes of data efficiently. SCSI over IP on Gigabit Ethernet infrastructures provides tape vendors with much greater flexibility in deploying their solutions. The Gigabit Ethernet network may be a dedicated SAN or a virtual segment (VLAN) of an enterprise network. Backups may thus occur wherever sufficient bandwidth has been allocated, and familiar IP and Ethernet management tools can be leveraged to monitor backup traffic. Because third-party copy is infrastructure neutral, serverless backup can also be used for IP-based tape subsystems.

3.1.4 SCSI Over IP-to-Parallel SCSI Bridges

Like first-generation Fibre Channel SANs, IP-based SANs must accommodate legacy devices, including SCSI disk arrays and SCSI tape subsystems. SCSI tape libraries, in particular, represent a substantial investment, and few information technology (IT) administrators have the luxury of discarding a valuable resource simply because interface technology has improved. The common denominator between the IP SAN and the legacy tape device is the SCSI protocol. The legacy tape device, however, supports parallel SCSI, or the SCSI-2 protocol. The IP SAN supports serial SCSI, or the SCSI-3 protocol. The function of a bridge is to translate between the two SCSI variants, and to make the SCSI-2 tape or storage subsystem appear to be a bona fide IP-addressable device.

An IP storage-to-SCSI bridge may provide multiple parallel SCSI ports to accommodate legacy units, and one or more Gigabit Ethernet ports to front the SAN. Just as a Fibre Channel-to-SCSI bridge must assign a Fibre Channel address to each legacy SCSI device, an IP storage-to-SCSI bridge must proxy IP addresses. The specific type of serial SCSI-3 supported by the Gigabit Ethernet ports on the bridge is vendor dependent, but may be iSCSI or iFCP.

SAN bridges provide a valuable function, both for preserving the customer's investment in expensive subsystems and for making those subsystems participants in a shared storage network. Although bridges are normally used to bring tape subsystems into a SAN, legacy SCSI disk arrays can also be supported. In some vendor implementations, even SCSI hosts (for example, servers with SCSI adapter cards) can be accommodated. This enables an IP storage network to be constructed with SCSI end systems only, using IP and Gigabit Ethernet as the SAN infrastructure. Customers with large SCSI installations could thus enjoy the benefits of shared storage networking without investing in new host adapters, storage, or tape.

3.1.5 Host Adapters

Host adapter cards provide the interface between the server or workstation internal bus and the external storage network. Interface cards are available for different bus architectures and may offer different physical connections for network interface. The adapter card vendor also supplies a device driver that allows the card to be recognized by the operating system. The device driver software may also perform protocol translation or other functions if these are not already executed by onboard logic.

Whether Fibre Channel or Gigabit Ethernet, the HBA or network interface card (NIC) must provide reliable gigabit communication at the physical and data link levels. As discussed later, Gigabit Ethernet has taken the physical layer and data encoding standards from Fibre Channel. Above the data encoding level, however, Gigabit Ethernet must appear as standard Ethernet to provide seamless integration to operating systems and applications.

For storage networking, two additional components may appear on the host Gigabit Ethernet interface card. To support storage data transfer efficiently, a storage NIC must incorporate an upper protocol layer for serial SCSI-3. This may be an iSCSI interface or an FCP interface. The purpose of this protocol interface is to deliver SCSI data to the operating system with high performance and low processor overhead. Fibre Channel FCP has solved this SCSI delivery issue, whereas the iSCSI initiative is reengineering an entirely new solution.

The second component that may be embedded on a storage NIC is additional logic to off-load TCP/IP processing from the host CPU. At gigabit speeds, TCP overhead may completely consume the resources of a host system. This would be unacceptable for servers in a storage network, which must simultaneously service both disk and user transactions. TCP off-load engines (for those lacking enough acronyms, TOEs) may be provided by software routines or, more efficiently, in ASICs or dedicated processors onboard the NIC.

Figure 3–5 depicts the basic functions of a Fibre Channel HBA, whereas Figure 3–6 shows the basic components of a storage NIC.

Both adapters provide transmit and receive connections to the storage network, which may be via fiber-optic or copper cabling. Both adapter types provide a clock and data recovery (CDR) logic to retrieve gigabit signaling from the inbound bit stream. Both provide serializing/deserializing logic to convert serial bits into parallel data characters for inbound streams, and convert parallel into serial for outbound streams. The mechanism for data encoding is provided by an 8b/10b encoding scheme originally developed by IBM and discussed in further detail later. For transmission on gigabit links, the data encoding method also uses special formatting of data and commands known as *ordered sets*.

Above the ordered set logic, a storage NIC will include a LAN controller chip, auxiliary logic and memory, an optional TOE, and hardware-based or software drivers for the serial SCSI-3 protocol. All of this functionality is made physically accessible to the host platform through the PCI, S-bus, or other bus interface and is logically accessible through the host device driver supplied by the manufacturer.

One of the often-cited benefits of IP-based storage networking is the ability to leverage familiar hardware and management software to deploy and maintain a SAN. In the example given here of a storage network adapter, there are clearly common components to ordinary Ethernet NICs. It is unlikely, however, that off-the-shelf Gigabit Ethernet NICs will be suited to storage applications. Without embedded logic to speed serial SCSI processing

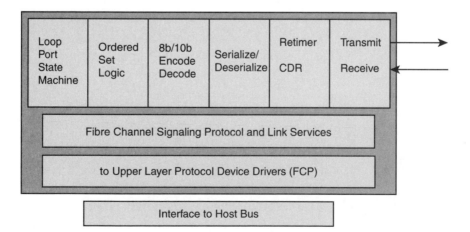

Figure 3–5 A Fibre Channel HBA.

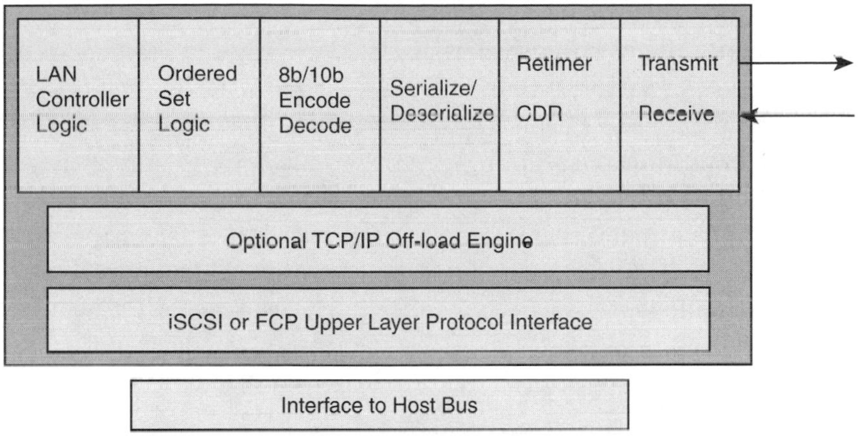

Figure 3–6 A storage over IP NIC.

and to off-load TCP overhead, a standard Gigabit Ethernet NIC will not provide the performance required for storage applications. From a management and support standpoint, however, the distinction between a specialized storage NIC and a standard NIC are minimal when compared with Fibre Channel HBAs.

3.2 Legacy SCSI Cabling

SCSI cabling is a parallel wiring plant analogous to common personal computer parallel printer cabling. In the SCSI cable, each bit of a data byte is given its own wire. A SCSI cable may have 8 (narrow SCSI) or 16 (wide SCSI) data lines, plus control lines to manage device selection and data transmission. The effective transmission rate is governed by the number of data lines provided and the clock rate at which bytes of data are sent concurrently. Although new parallel SCSI designs such as high-voltage differential and low-voltage differential (LVD) have enabled higher throughput, the overall distance limitation of SCSI cabling is 25 m, and device support is limited to 15 devices on a SCSI chain.

In a parallel SCSI configuration, the sending party places the 8 or 16 bits of data on the cable plant and toggles a control line to indicate transmission. Small differences in propagation delay may occur as the data bits are sent, so it is essential that the receiving device be able to capture all bits accurately within a certain window of time. This window is known as *skew*. The greater the differences in propagation delay along the length of the cable, the wider the window must be for all data bits to be captured. Parallel transmission thus favors shorter cable lengths to minimize skew and to avoid data corruption. To achieve an effective bandwidth greater than serial gigabit transports, the SCSI cable must be less than 12 m long.

Distance limitations and limited device population have relegated SCSI technology to the middle and low end of the storage market, where resource sharing and high availability are not required. Additionally, adds, moves, or changes in a SCSI configuration may necessitate downtime and disruption to users. This is less likely to be the case in gigabit storage networking.

3.3 Network-Attached Storage

Like the acronym SAN, NAS is largely a marketing term that has, through repeated use, gained a technical definition. The primary distinction between NAS and SAN rests on the difference between data files and data blocks. NAS transports files; SANs transport blocks. NAS uses file-oriented delivery protocols such as NFS and CIFS, whereas SANs use block-oriented delivery protocols such as SCSI-3. Because data blocks are the raw material from which files are formed, NAS also has a block component. These blocks are addressed on a per-file basis, using meta-data (directory information) to determine which file to use. The block access methods of a NAS device, however, are typically hidden in the NAS enclosure. To the outside world, the NAS device is a server of files and directories.

NAS accomplishes the central goal of storage networking: the sharing of storage resources through the separation of servers and storage over a common network. Like SAN-based storage, NAS overcomes the limitations of parallel SCSI and enables a more flexible deployment of shared storage. In redundant configurations, NAS can also provide highly available, nondisruptive storage access.

As shown in Figure 3–7, a NAS architecture includes disk arrays for data placement, a NAS processor, and an external interface to the user network. This architecture has a number of implications. Although the block data transport of a SAN normally occurs over a dedicated storage network (or VLANs within a Gigabit Ethernet network), the file transport of a NAS device assumes direct connectivity to the user network. NAS performance is thus partially determined by the bandwidth available on the messaging network. In addition, although the NAS processor is optimized for file transport, it is essentially a thin server sitting on a LAN "front-ending" storage

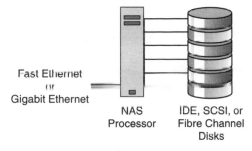

Fast Ethernet
or
Gigabit Ethernet

NAS
Processor

IDE, SCSI, or
Fibre Channel
Disks

Figure 3–7 NAS architecture.

arrays. To avoid the definition of NAS as "network-attached server" or simply "file server," vendors of NAS products have attempted to make the thin server component so thin that it is invisible from the user's perspective. The term *NAS* is therefore always linked in marketing literature to the concept of "appliance"—a device that is simply plugged into the network and requires little administration. Finally, the connection between NAS intelligence and its disks is immaterial from a user's perspective. Although SAN storage is predicated on high-performance gigabit interfaces for storage (either directly or via bridge products), a NAS device may rely on parallel SCSI, IDE, or Fibre Channel for storage connectivity.

The challenge of NAS vendors is to make their products more appliance-like and to reduce the overhead of NFS/CIFS protocols over TCP/IP. Although TCP/IP imposes its own latency on file transactions, NFS and CIFS also engender latency as file transfer sessions are established and torn down, and as files are found through directory lookup. Chip-based TOEs offer some relief, although the main initiative from some NAS vendors for dealing with latency is support of the Direct Access File System (DAFS) over the VI protocol. DAFS relies on remote direct memory access (RDMA) techniques to move data directly to systems memory. If a NAS controller can place file data directly into the memory of the client efficiently, transport latency is offset by the higher performance of file data placement.

The convergence of NAS and SAN is accelerated by the development of IP storage networks. With 10Gb backbones and gigabit interfaces to end devices, both file and block data can share a common network infrastructure. This promotes the deployment of shared storage solutions on the basis of user application requirements, without the artificial limits imposed by incompatible network topologies.

3.4 Fibre Channel

As the first network architecture to implement storage networking applications successfully, Fibre Channel has faced substantial challenges in product development, standardization, interoperability, and market acceptance. It has also achieved technological breakthroughs in the areas of gigabit transport and upper layer protocol support for SCSI-3, which ironically have made it vulnerable to competing storage network technologies. As the pioneer of storage networking, Fibre Channel has had to create its own vocabulary, and this, in turn, has made it difficult for customers to understand, deploy, and support. The basic lexicon of Fibre Channel is reviewed here.

3.4.1 Fibre Channel Layers

Fibre Channel standards are developed in the National Committee of Industrial Technology Standards (NCITS) T11 standards body, which has defined a multilayer architecture for the transport of block data over a network infrastructure. As shown in Table 3–1, Fibre Channel layers are numbered from FC-0 to FC-4.

The upper layer, FC-4, establishes the interface between the Fibre Channel transport and upper level applications and operating system. For storage applications, FC-4 is responsible for mapping the SCSI-3 protocol for transactions between host initiators and storage targets. The FC-3 layer is still in standards development, and includes facilities for data encryption and

TABLE 3–1 FIBRE CHANNEL LAYERED ARCHITECTURE

Fibre Channel Layer	Layer Title	Comments
FC-4	Upper layer protocol interface	SCSI-3, IP, VI, and so on
FC-3	Common services	Under development
FC-2	Data delivery	Framing, flow control, service class
FC-1	Ordered sets/byte encoding	8b/10b encoding, link controls
FC-0	Physical interface	Optical/electrical, cable plant

compression. The FC-2 layer defines how blocks of data handed down by the upper level application are segmented into sequences of frames for handoff to the transport layers. This layer also includes class-of-service implementations and flow control mechanisms to facilitate transaction integrity. The lower two layers, FC-1 and FC-0, focus on the actual transport of data across the network. FC-1 provides facilities for encoding and decoding data for shipment at gigabit speeds, and defines the command structure for accessing the media. FC-0 establishes standards for different media types, allowable lengths, and signaling.

Collectively, the Fibre Channel layers fall within the first four layers of the OSI model: physical, data link, network, and transport. Fibre Channel assumes a single unpartitioned network and homogeneous address space for the network fabric. Although theoretically this address space can be quite large (15.5 million addresses in a switched fabric), a single network space has implications for large Fibre Channel SANs. Without network segmentation, the entire fabric is potentially vulnerable to disruption in the event of failures.

3.4.2 FC-0: Fibre Channel Physical Layer

As the first successful serial gigabit transport, Fibre Channel has defined the basic principles and methods required for data integrity over high-speed serial links. At the physical layer, these include standards for gigabit signaling, supported cable types, allowable cable distances, and physical interfaces. Because Gigabit Ethernet has borrowed heavily from the Fibre Channel physical layer standards, it is useful to understand what they provide.

Unlike SCSI parallel cabling, a serial network cabling scheme does not have a separate control line to signal the rate of data transmission so that the recipient can accurately capture data. In a serial implementation, this clock signaling must be embedded in the bit stream itself. Fibre Channel uses an FC-1-defined byte-encoding scheme and CDR circuitry to recover the clock signal from the serial bit stream. The physical layer standards dictate that data integrity for gigabit transmission must be no less than 10^{-12} bit error rate, or a maximum of 1 bit error every 16 minutes over 1Gb media. To meet or exceed this rigorous standard, the physical interfaces and cabling must minimize the amount of jitter or timing deviation that may occur along the physical transport.

Deviations from the original clock signaling, or jitter, may be the result of natural propagation delays through fiber-optic or copper cabling as well as unnatural transients from poorly designed interfaces, laser optics, circuit boards, or power supplies. Jitter may be measured and represented in graphical form by an *eye diagram* on a test scope, as illustrated in Figure 3–8. The crossover points or intersections forming the eye represent signaling transitions to high or low voltages. Ideally, all transitions should occur at precisely the same interval. If this were the case, the eye would be perfectly formed and the CDR circuitry could recover all data bits with no bit errors whatsoever. In reality, some deviation will always be present. If the jitter is too extreme, the CDR will miss one or several bits, resulting in the corruption of data. This will in turn trigger recovery routines at the higher layers.

If jitter reduction is essential for Fibre Channel's 1.0625-Gbps clock rate, it is even more essential for Gigabit Ethernet's faster 1.25 Gbps. The faster the clock, the greater the statistical occurrence of bit errors over the same time span. A faulty transceiver, substandard fiber-optic cabling or connectors, exceeding cable distance guidelines, improperly shielded copper components, or simply bad product design can introduce system instability at the physical layer.

For cable plant, Fibre Channel accommodates both copper and fiber-optic cabling. Copper cabling is typically twin axial as opposed to shielded twisted pair, and is deployed for intracabinet and intercabinet usage. Intracabinet copper cabling may be used within an enclosed 19-inch rack for connecting storage devices or HBAs to Fibre Channel hubs or switches. The maximum length of intracabinet copper is 13 m. Intercabinet copper cabling may be used externally to 19-inch racks, to a maximum of 30 m. Both varieties are problematic because any copper cable plant is succeptable to electromagnetic interference (EMI) and may create ground loop problems between devices.

For both Fibre Channel and Gigabit Ethernet, fiber-optic cabling is the preferred cable plant because of its immunity to EMI. Fiber-optic cable types

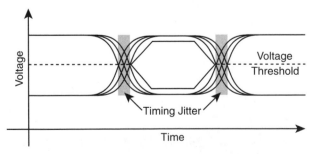

Figure 3–8 An eye diagram showing timing deviations in a gigabit stream.

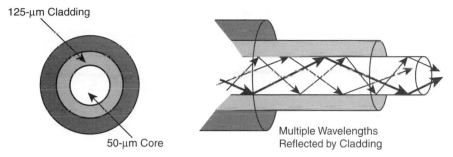

Figure 3–9 Multimode fiber-optic cable.

are distinguished by "mode," or by the frequencies of light waves that the optical cable supports.

Multimode cabling is used with shortwave laser light and has either a 50-μm or 62.5-μm core with 125-μm cladding. The reflective cladding around the core restricts light to the core. As shown in Figure 3–9, a shortwave laser beam is composed of hundreds of light modes that reflect off the core at different angles. This dispersion effect reduces the total distance at which the original signal can be reclaimed. In Fibre Channel configurations, multimode fiber supports 175 m with 62.5-μm/125-μm cable, and supports 500 m with 50-μm/125-μm cable.

Single-mode fiber is constructed with a 9-μm core and 125-μm cladding. Single mode is used to carry long-wave laser light, which has little of the dispersion effect of multimode lasers because the diameter of the core is matched to the wavelength of the light. With a much smaller diameter core and a single-mode light source, single-mode fiber supports much longer distances, currently as much as 10 km at gigabit speeds.

At either end of the cable plant, transceivers or adapters are used to bring the gigabit bit stream onto the circuit boards of HBAs or controller cards. Gigabit interface converters, or GBICs, connect the cabling to the device interface. Small-form factor GBICs are steadily replacing the older SC connectors, because they enable higher port density for switches. Optical transceivers may be permanently mounted onto the HBA, storage, or switch port, or may be removable to facilitate changes in media type or to service a failed unit.

3.4.3 FC-1: Fibre Channel Link Controls and Data Encoding

Suppose that the cable plant, transceivers, and interfaces all provided a stable physical layer transport for gigabit transmission. Turning bits of serial data into intelligible bytes is still an issue. If raw data bytes were dropped serially onto a gigabit transport, it would be impossible to tell where one byte ended and another began. Sending a stream of hex 'FF' bytes, for example, would create a sustained direct current (DC) voltage on the link, making it impossible to recover the embedded clock signaling needed to establish byte boundaries.

Fibre Channel standards have addressed this problem by using a byte encoding algorithm first developed by IBM. The 8b/10b encoding method converts each 8-bit data byte into two possible 10-bit characters. To avoid sustained DC states, each of the two 10-bit characters will have no more than six total ones or zeros. Of all the possible 10-bit characters that can be generated by standard 8-bit data bytes, about half will have an equal number of ones and zeros. The 8b/10b encoding scheme thus ensures a healthy mix of ones and zeros that allows recovery of the embedded clock signaling and thus recovery of data.

Because the 8b/10b encoder generates two different 10-bit characters for each byte, which one should be used for data transmission? This selection is made based on the *running disparity* of the character stream (Figure 3–10). If a 10-bit character has more ones than zeros, it has *positive disparity*. If it has more zeros than ones, it has *negative disparity*. An equal number of ones and zeros results in *neutral disparity*. The concept of running disparity is key to maintaining a more consistent distribution of ones and zeros in the bit

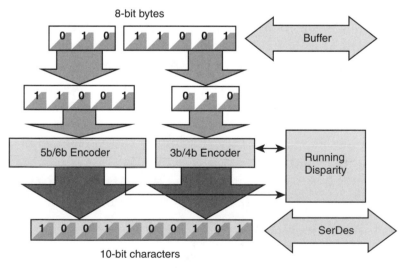

Figure 3–10 8b/10b encoding logic.

stream. A 10-bit data character with positive disparity should be followed by a character with neutral disparity (which leaves the running disparity positive), or by a character with negative disparity (which would leave the running disparity negative). This alternation between positive and negative disparity patterns ensures that no sequential combination of 10-bit characters will result in persistent ones or zeros bit states.

For all the 10-bit characters that can be generated by standard data bytes, none have more than four ones or zeros in sequence. Running disparity maintains this minimal occurrence for data characters. Some nonstandard 10-bit combinations, however, result in five ones or zeros in sequence. These characters are reserved as special characters and are inserted into the character stream as a means to establish boundaries between 10-bit characters. In Fibre Channel standards, the presence of a special "K28.5" character is monitored by the CDR circuitry. As soon as five ones or zeros in sequence are detected, the CDR can begin buffering sets of 10 bit streams that can then be converted accurately to valid 8-bit data bytes.

Fibre Channel standards for the FC-1 layer leverage the 8b/10b encoding method to create a command syntax known as *ordered sets*. The 8b/10b encoding scheme and running disparity ensure that the embedded gigabit signaling can be recovered and that data bytes can be successfully retrieved. Ordered sets are composed of four 10-bit characters, or 40 bits that constitute a transmission word. The ordered set leads with the special K28.5 character to indicate that the transmission word is a link-layer command or a signal of a change in state. The three data characters following the K28.5 character define the function of the ordered set; for example, start of frame (SOF), end of frame (EOF), initialization, and class of service.

Gigabit Ethernet has borrowed the ordered set command and signaling structure from Fibre Channel, but as we see later, uses fewer commands. Fibre Channel ordered sets are divided into frame delimiters, primitive signals, and primitive sequences. Frame delimiters mark the frame boundaries and may include frame sequencing information for multiframe transmissions. Primitive signals include the IDLE ordered set, which is used to maintain CDR when no user data is present on the link. Primitive sequences are ordered sets that must occur at least three times on the link before any action is taken (for example, a loop initialization or LIP primitive). Fibre Channel standards define more than 20 ordered sets for frame delimiting, more than 10 for primitive signals, and more than 15 for primitive sequences. Because only a single instance of a primitive signal is required to initiate an action, the CDR mechanism for gigabit transmission must be very precise.

3.4.4 FC-2: Fibre Channel Framing, Flow Control, and Class of Service

The data bytes that were encoded by FC-1 for reliable transmission on the physical media were handed down by FC-2 as a series of frames. The FC-2 layer receives blocks from the upper layer protocol (for example, FCP) and subdivides those into sequences of frames that can be reassembled on the other end. Frames are grouped into *sequences* of related frames. A database record, for example, may be written to disk as a single sequence of frames. The sequence is the smallest unit of error recovery in Fibre Channel. If a transmission word within a frame is corrupted and cannot be recovered, the entire sequence of frames must be retransmitted. At gigabit speeds, it is more efficient simply to retransmit an entire sequence of frames than to buffer and provide recovery constantly at the frame level. In the hierarchy of frame delivery at FC-2, multiple sequences of frames can occur within a single *exchange*. The exchange binding between two communicating devices maximizes utilization of the link between them and avoids constant setup and teardown of logical connections.

Fibre Channel framing allows for a variable-length frame with a payload of 0 to 2,112 bytes. Because the Fibre Channel maximal frame size does not map directly to Ethernet framing, issues can arise when Fibre Channel is tunneled over IP/Ethernet. The basic format of the Fibre Channel frame is shown in Table 3–2. The ordered sets used for the SOF and EOF delimiters indicate where the frame falls within a sequence of frames, as well as the class of service required. The header field contains the destination and source Fibre Channel addresses as well as payload length. The cyclic redundancy check (CRC) is calculated before the data is run through the 8b/10b encoder, with the 4-byte CRC itself later encoded along with the rest of the frame contents. At the receiving end, the CRC is recalculated and compared against the frame's CRC to ensure data integrity.

The SOF delimiter establishes the class of service that will be used for frame transmission, whereas the EOF delimiter may indicate when that class of service may be terminated. Class of service is used to guarantee bandwidth

TABLE 3–2   FIBRE CHANNEL FRAME FORMAT

SOF	Header	Data Field	CRC	EOF
1 word	6 words	0–2112 bytes	4 bytes	1 word

or to require acknowledgment of frame receipt for secure data transport. Storage applications may require different classes of service, but the vast majority of Fibre Channel transactions are performed with class 3 datagram service.

Class 1 service defines a dedicated connection between two devices (for example, a file server and a disk array) with acknowledgment of frame delivery. Class 1 service can be assumed in a point-to-point connection between two devices because there are no other participants to impose bandwidth demands. Class 1 service through a Fibre Channel fabric, however, requires the fabric switches to establish dedicated data paths between the communicating pair. A 16-port switch, for example, could only support 8 concurrent class 1 sessions. Consequently, class 1 is almost never deployed in SAN applications.

Class 2 service avoids the issue of connection-oriented, dedicated bandwidth, but provides acknowledgment of frame delivery. Frame acknowledgment imposes its own overhead, however, and so impacts the efficiency of link utilization. Like class 1, class 2 service is fully defined in standards but is infrequently used.

Ironically, although storage network applications revolve around mission-critical applications that require the highest degree of data integrity, the most commonly used class of service in Fibre Channel is both connectionless and unacknowledged in terms of frame delivery. Class 3 service in Fibre Channel is analogous to datagram service such as UDP/IP in LAN environments. Frames are streamed from initiator to target with no acknowledgment of receipt. In the early days of Fibre Channel adoption, customers balked at the idea of committing their mission-critical data to a datagram type of service. In practice, however, class 3 gained respectability simply because it worked. As a connectionless protocol, class 3 facilitates the efficient utilization of fabric resources because bandwidth is not hoarded by communicators as in class 1. And by eliminating acknowledgments, class 3 service imposes minimal protocol overhead on the link.

The ability of a datagram class of service to transmit and receive data reliably is predicated on a highly stable and properly provisioned infrastructure. The 10^{-12} bit error rate mandated by Fibre Channel standards and the thoughtful allocation of bandwidth for storage network resources enables the use of class 3 service for a wide variety of storage applications. This has significant implications for storage networks based on Gigabit Ethernet, which shares the link integrity requirements of Fibre Channel. For contained switch environments such as data centers, a datagram type of service is viable for stable, high-performance data transfer. This is not the case for potentially congested or lossy implementations, such as wide area switched networks.

Other Fibre Channel classes of service include class 4 for virtual circuits and class 6 for acknowledged multicast applications. As with many other Fibre Channel features that may be supported in fabrics, these are still immature in terms of product implementation and have lacked the engineering focus that Gigabit Ethernet has enjoyed.

Class 3 service requires a flow control mechanism to ensure that a target is not flooded with frames and forced to discard them. Fibre Channel flow control is based on a system of credits, with each credit representing an available frame buffer in the receiving device. If, for example, a disk array has 20 frame buffers, a server could stream 20 frames of a sequence in a single burst before waiting for additional credits to be issued by the array. As the array absorbs the 20 frames, the first in sequence are passed to the FC-2 frame reassembly logic for reconstruction into data blocks for FC-4. As individual frames move up the assembly line, buffers are freed for additional inbound frames. The array issues a credit for each newly emptied buffer, allowing the server to send additional frames.

This frame-pacing algorithm based on credits prevents frame loss and reduces the frequency of sequence retransmission over the fabric. For class 3 service in a fabric, the credit relationship is not end to end between storage devices and servers, but between each device and the switch port to which it is attached. Providing adequate buffers on switch ports is essential for minimizing frame discards. For Gigabit Ethernet SANs, port buffering is also an issue, although the link-level flow control is implemented differently.

3.4.5 FC-3: Common Services

The FC-3 layer has been a placeholder in Fibre Channel standards as the more basic functions of the other layers have been developed. Because FC-3 sits between the FC-4 upper layer protocol and the FC-2 framing layer, FC-3 would contain services that would be performed immediately prior to hand-off to the lower layers. This would include services such as encryption and authentication, although there are currently no such services in Fibre Channel implementations. Arguably, there has not been a lot of incentive to develop such facilities for Fibre Channel, because Fibre Channel SANs presuppose a private, secure environment. Putting storage traffic over metropolitan and wide area networks (MANs and WANs), however, may raise security concerns. This is another area that highlights the advantages of storage traffic over IP, because encryption and authentication tools are readily available to safeguard sensitive storage data.

3.4.6 FC-4: Fibre Channel Upper Layer Protocol

The purpose of engineering a highly reliable physical plant, a rigorous byte encoding scheme, link-layer controls, efficient framing and sequence transmission, viable classes of service, and flow control is, of course, to service the upper layer applications behind which sit end users who are constantly creating and accessing stored data. Although the FC-4 layer standards include support for VI, IP, and other protocols, the most well-developed and most widely used FC-4 protocol is serial SCSI-3 (FCP).

The central task of FCP is to make Fibre Channel end devices appear as standard SCSI entities to the operating system. For host systems, the FCP function is embedded in the Fibre Channel HBA and the device driver supplied by the manufacturer. This allows Windows Disk Administrator, for example, to see Fibre Channel disks as SCSI-addressable storage resources. The operating system does not need to distinguish between storage resources that are direct-SCSI attached, ATA/IDE attached, or SAN attached. If, alternately, Fibre Channel as a storage networking solution had required changes to Windows, Solaris, or UNIX operating systems, it is doubtful that it ever would have been deployed. This is because of the much longer development and test cycles required for operating system revisions and the reluctance of customers to introduce additional complexity into their server environments. Just as FC-0 and FC-1 enabled reliable gigabit transmission of data at the physical and link levels, FCP has enabled a reliable protocol interface to the operating system and supported applications.

As shown in Figure 3–11, the upper layer protocol interface supports standard SCSI mapping for the operating system while maintaining Fibre Channel device address mapping for data destinations in the form of logical unit numbers (LUNs) on the target disks. The Fibre Channel frame header holds the 3-byte Fibre Channel network address, with identifying

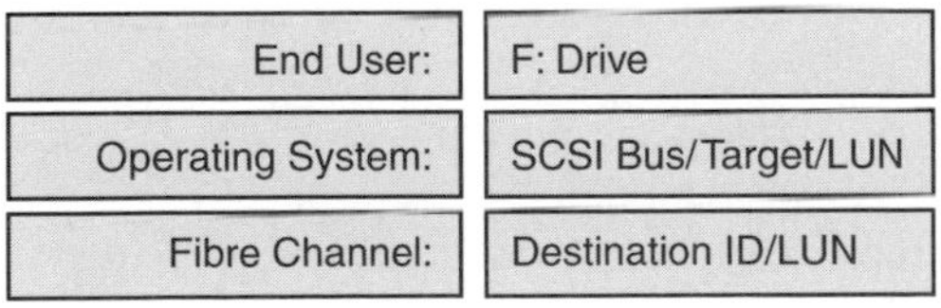

End User:	F: Drive
Operating System:	SCSI Bus/Target/LUN
Fibre Channel:	Destination ID/LUN

Figure 3–11 Perspectives on the Fibre Channel storage target.

LUN information contained in the frame payload. This tiered mapping is, thankfully, transparent to the end user, whose primary interface is through the drive designation assignable through the operating system's file system/volume management interface.

From the standpoint of the operating system, FCP translates standard SCSI commands into the appropriate SCSI-3 equivalents required for block data transfer over a serial network infrastructure. A SCSI I/O launched by the operating system to read blocks of data from disk, for example, would initiate an FCP exchange between the host and target using command frames known as *information units* (IUs). Within the exchange session, groups of frame comprising one or more sequences would be used to transport data from target to host. SCSI commands and responses between the operating system and FCP are implemented through the lower layers as serial SCSI FCP functions, as shown in Table 3–3.

Device drivers for HBAs must translate between conventional SCSI addressing and Fibre Channel device addresses. As a legacy from parallel SCSI, storage devices are identified by a bus/target/LUN triad. The bus is a SCSI chain hung from a specific SCSI port or SCSI adapter card. Multiple SCSI ports on a server require multiple bus designations. The target is a storage device, such as a disk. The logical unit identified by an LUN may represent a logical division of the disk—for example, a disk with two partitions that are accessible from the operating system as drives E: and F:. The device

---

TABLE 3–3   FCP EQUIVALENTS TO STANDARD SCSI FUNCTIONS (FROM AMERICAN NATIONAL STANDARDS INSTITUTE [ANSI] T10 FCP-2)

SCSI Function	FCP Equivalent
I/O operation	Exchange (concurrent sequences)
Protocol service request and response	Sequence (related frames)
Send SCSI command request	Unsolicited command IU (FCP_CMND)
Data delivery request	Data descriptor IU (FCP_XFER_RDY)
Data delivery action	Solicited data IU (FCP_DATA)
Send command complete response	Command status IU (FCP_ RSP)
REQ/ACK for command complete	Confirmation IU (FCP_CONF)

driver of the HBA or storage adapter card must translate this bus/target/LUN designation into a network-addressable identifier so that data can be passed to the appropriate storage target on the SAN. How this is implemented in IP storage environments is examined in the following chapters.

3.4.7 Fibre Channel Topologies

The three topologies supported by Fibre Channel are significant for IP-based storage networks both in terms of legacy support of Fibre Channel SAN segments and for understanding common features that can assist IP storage solutions for faster time-to-market. Different generations of Fibre Channel end devices may be optimized for specific topology protocols. Accommodating these devices via IP storage switch ports will encourage the transition from Fibre Channel SANs to IP-based SANs. In addition, the stability and demonstrated interoperability of Fibre Channel end devices and the FCP protocol enables IP-based storage networks to leverage the intellectual effort that has been vested in these technologies to date.

As shown in Figure 3–12, Fibre Channel supports direct point-to-point connections between two devices (typically a server and a single storage array); a shared, arbitrated loop topology; and a switched fabric. Gigabit Ethernet can support an analogous point-to-point connection as well as switched fabric, but in practical implementation has no shared media option. Fibre Channel point to point was commonly deployed for first-generation solutions, but because it only supports two devices it does not quite qualify as a storage network. Fibre Channel arbitrated loop is similar in concept to

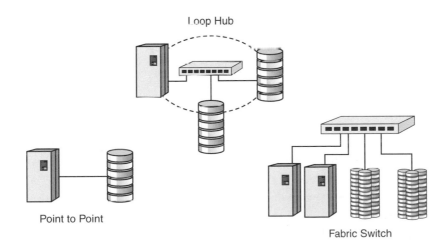

Figure 3–12 Fibre Channel topologies for point to point, loop, and fabric.

Token Ring. Multiple devices (as many as 126 end nodes) can share a common medium, but must arbitrate for access to it before beginning transmission. A Fibre Channel fabric is one or more Fibre Channel switches in a single network. Each device has dedicated bandwidth (200 MBps full duplex for 1Gb switches), and a device population of as many as 15.5 million devices is supported. This large number is strictly theoretical, because in practice it has been difficult for Fibre Channel fabrics to support even a few hundred devices.

Loop and fabric devices may be supported on a single network. A loop hub with six devices, for example, can be attached to a fabric switch port. Each of the devices registers its presence with the fabric switch so that it can communicate to resources on other switch ports. Such devices are referred to as *public loop devices*. They can also communicate with each other on the same loop segment without switch intervention. However, they each must arbitrate for access to their shared loop before any data transaction can occur.

One caveat for loop devices on fabrics is the result of the evolution of Fibre Channel device drivers. Not all loop-capable HBAs or storage devices can support fabric attachment. Such devices are known as *private loop devices*. To support these older loop devices, the fabric switch must provide proxy registration for them so that they become visible to the rest of the network and accessible as storage resources. There are no specific Fibre Channel standards covering this private loop proxy feature, and consequently every switch vendor's implementation is proprietary.

Switched fabrics pose significant issues, many of which are still unresolved. Fabric switches provide a number of services to facilitate device discovery and to adjust for changes in the network infrastructure. Devices register their presence on the switch via a simple name server (SNS), which is essentially a small database with fields for the device's network address, unique WWN, upper layer protocol support, and so on. When a server attaches to the fabric, it queries the SNS to discover its potential disk targets. This relieves the server from polling 15.5 million possible addresses to discover and establish sessions with storage resources. The SNS table in a stand-alone switch may be fairly small, with only 10 to 30 entries. When multiple switches are connected into a single fabric, however, they must exchange SNS information so that a server anywhere on the network can discover storage. The larger the fabric, the more difficult it becomes to update the collective SNS data and to ensure reliable device discovery.

Another fabric issue for large fabrics is the ability to track changes in the network. Fabric switches provide a registered state change notification (SCN) entity that is responsible for alerting hosts to changes in the availability of resources. If, for example, a server has a session with a target array, it can be proactively notified if the array goes off-line or if the path to it through the fabric is broken. Because a Fibre Channel fabric is one large infrastructure, marginal components that trigger repeated SCNs can be disruptive to the entire network.

Management of Fibre Channel fabrics has evolved over time, but has been hindered by the challenges that a new technology faces. Out-of-band management with more familiar Simple Network Management Protocol (SNMP) protocols has enabled device and configuration management, although these are not as mature as the management platforms used by LAN and WAN networking. In-band management over the Fibre Channel links eliminates the need to have a parallel 10/100 Ethernet network for SNMP management, but is vulnerable to link failures. In-band management in Ethernet and WAN networks is predicated on redundant links. If both data and management traffic ride on the same network links, the failure of a single link would simply reroute traffic to available links in the meshed network. For these environments, provisioning redundant links is relatively inexpensive and simplifies network design and management. Achieving this level of redundancy in Fibre Channel networks is both expensive and awkward to implement. Without redundant links for in-band management, however, the loss of a data path may also be the loss of management traffic. Just when management information is needed the most, it would be unavailable.

Probably the most publicized issue for large Fibre Channel fabrics has been the lack of interoperability between vendor switch products. The standard for switch-to-switch connectivity (NCITS T11 FC-SW2) defines the connectivity and routing protocol for fabric switches. Switches are joined to each other via expansion ports, or E_Ports, and share routing information through the Fabric Shortest Path First (FSPF) protocol, a variant of the more commonly used Open Shortest Path First (OSPF) protocol for LAN and WAN networks. Although FSPF itself has not presented an overwhelming engineering challenge, competitive interests among Fibre Channel switch vendors have retarded its implementation. Until recently, dominant vendors have been unwilling to accelerate interoperability, fearing that openess would result in loss of market share. This, in turn, has led to absurd fabric designs simply to achieve higher port counts that could easily be accommodated through vendor interoperability. Some SAN designs have attempted to provide a high port count by deploying stacks of 10 or more 16-port switches, with nearly half the switch ports sacrificed for interswitch links.

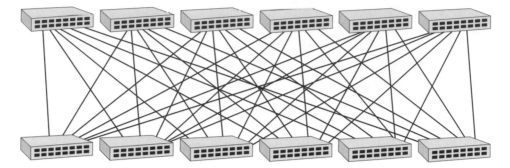

Figure 3–13 An actual vendor example of a higher port count fabric.

The result is a conglomeration of cabling that still results in a blocking architecture if more than one switch-to-switch transaction is started. With switch interoperability, it would be possible to combine high-port-count director-class switches with departmental 16-port switches for a more efficient deployment (Figure 3–13).

One inherent issue for large fabrics is the fact that a fabric is a single network. OSPF in LANs and WANs allows for the subdividing of networks into nondisruptive areas. A disruptive occurrence within a single area does not propagate throughout the entire network. FSPF does not provide this facility. Consequently, as a Fibre Channel fabric grows in population (and importance), it becomes increasingly vulnerable to outages.

Taken collectively, the issues associated with Fibre Channel fabrics are not insurmountable, but will require significant engineering resources to overcome them. The Fibre Channel fabrics that join Fibre Channel end devices have not achieved the level of stability and interoperability already attained by Fibre Channel HBAs, storage arrays, and tape subsystems. This makes the Fibre Channel fabric itself a prime candidate for replacement, which is the stated goal of IP storage solutions.

3.5 Gigabit Ethernet

Gigabit Ethernet owes its existence to the technical innovations of Fibre Channel transport and the historical momentum of Ethernet and IP networking. From Fibre Channel, Gigabit Ethernet has taken the breakthrough technology of gigabit physical specifications, fiber optics, CDR, 8b/10b data encoding, and ordered sets for link commands and delimiters. From Ethernet, it has inherited mainstream status and seamless integration to a vast installed base of operating systems and network infrastructures. Although Fibre Channel has had to struggle for credibility as an emergent technology, Gigabit Ethernet's credibility was established before it was even implemented. Today, 10 Gigabit Ethernet and higher speeds are assumed to be the logical evolution of the technology and of future enterprise networks. In the process, Ethernet is shedding some of its characteristic attributes such as collision detection and shared topology, but is retaining its name.

3.5.1 Gigabit Ethernet Layers

The reference model for Gigabit Ethernet is defined in the Institute of Electrical and Electronics Engineers (IEEE) 802.3z standard. Like 10/100 Ethernet, Gigabit Ethernet is a physical and data link technology, corresponding to the lower two OSI layers, as shown in Table 3–4.

The Gigabit Ethernet physical layer contains both media-dependent and media-independent components. This allows the gigabit media-independent interface to be implemented in silicon and still interface with a variety of network cabling, including long- and shortwave optical fiber and shielded copper. The reconciliation sublayer passes signaling primitives between upper and lower layers, including transmit and receive status as well as carrier sense and collision detection. In practice, Gigabit Ethernet switching relies on dedicated, full duplex links and does not need a collision detection method. Carrier sense multiple access with collision detection (CSMA/CD) is

TABLE 3–4   GIGABIT ETHERNET PHYSICAL AND DATA LINK LAYERS

OSI Reference Layer	Gigabit Ethernet Layer
Data link layer	Media access control (MAC) client sublayer
	MAC control (optional)
	MAC
Physical Layer	Reconciliation
	Gigabit media independent interface
	Media-dependent PHY group
	Medium-dependent interface
	Medium

incorporated into the standard to provide backward compatibility with standard and Fast Ethernet.

Unlike Fibre Channel, Gigabit Ethernet's 8b/10b encoding occurs at the physical layer via sublayers in the media-dependent physical (PHY) group. As shown in Figure 3–14, Fibre Channel layers FC-0 and FC-1 are brought into the lower layer physical interface, whereas traditional 802.3 Ethernet provides MAC and logical link control (LLC; or its offspring, MAC client) to support the upper layer protocols.

To facilitate its integration into conventional Ethernet networks and wide area transports, Gigabit Ethernet uses standard Ethernet framing as shown in Figure 3–15. The preamble and SOF delimiter are followed by the destination (DA) and source (SA) MAC addresses of the communicating devices. Creative use of bytes within the length/type field enable enhanced functionality such as VLAN tagging, as discussed later. The data field may contain as much as 1,500 bytes of user data, with pad bytes if required. The CRC is part of the frame check sequence. Optional frame padding is provided by the extension field, although this is only required for gigabit half-duplex transmissions.

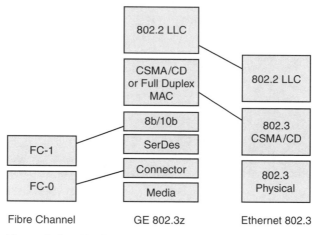

Figure 3–14 Gigabit Ethernet/Ethernet and Fibre Channel.

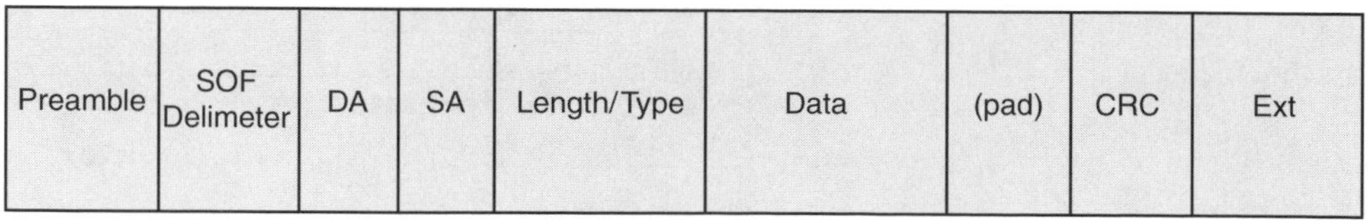

Preamble	SOF Delimeter	DA	SA	Length/Type	Data	(pad)	CRC	Ext

Figure 3–15 Standard Ethernet frame format.

IP over Ethernet is inserted into the data field and provides the network layer routing information to move user data from one network segment to another. TCP/IP provides higher level session control for traffic pacing and the ability to recover from packet loss. Although IP can be carried in other frame formats, link-layer enchancements for Ethernet offer additional reliability and performance capability unmatched by other transports, including Fibre Channel. These include VLANs, QoS, link-layer flow control, and trunking. Collectively, these functions provide a set of powerful tools for constructing storage networks based on IP and Gigabit Ethernet.

3.5.2 802.1Q VLAN Tagging

LANs in a switched Ethernet infrastructure enable the sharing of network resources such as large Gigabit Ethernet switches while segregating traffic from designated groups of devices. Members of a VLAN can communicate among themselves but lack visibility to the rest of the network. Sensitive information (for example, financial or human resource) can thus be isolated from other users, although the traffic is running through a common infrastructure. VLAN tagging was standardized in 1998 through the IEEE 802.1Q committee. An analogous capability is provided in Fibre Channel through a technique called *zoning*. Standards for zoning are still under construction, but only relate to the exchange of zone information by Fibre Channel switches. How zones are actually implemented within a switch is still proprietary. Consequently, there is no direct equivalent to 802.1Q's more open and flexible format.

VLAN tagging is accomplished by manipulating the length/type field in the Ethernet frame. To indicate that the frame is tagged, a unique 2-byte descriptor of hex "81–00" is inserted into the field. This tag type field is followed by a 2-byte tag control information field, as shown in Table 3–5, which carries the VLAN identifier and user priority bits as described later.

TABLE 3–5   IEEE 802.1Q VLAN TAG FIELDS

802.1Q Tag Type Field	Tag Control Information Field		
	User Priority	Canonical format indicator bit (CFI)	VLAN Identifier
81-00 16 bits	3 bits	1 bit	12 bits

The 12-bit VLAN identifier allows for as many as 4,096 VLANs to be assigned on a single switched infrastructure—far more than the number of zones typically offered by Fibre Channel switch vendors.

From a performance standpoint, VLAN tagging is a highly efficient means of segregating network participants into communicating groups without incurring the overhead of MAC address filtering. Intervening switches use the logical VLAN identifier, rather than the MAC address, to route traffic properly from switch to switch, and this in turn simplifies the switch decision process. As long as the appropriate switch port is associated with the proper VLAN identifier, no examination of the MAC address is required. Final filtering against the MAC address occurs at the end point.

All major Gigabit Ethernet switch vendors support the 802.1Q standard. This makes it a very useful feature not only for data paths that must cross switch boundaries, but for heterogeneous switched networks as well. For IP storage network applications, 802.1Q facilitates separation of storage traffic from user messaging traffic as well as segregation of different types of storage traffic (for example, on-line transaction processing) from tape backup. Compared with Fibre Channel zoning, 802.1Q VLANs offer more flexibility and lack the complexity of vendor-specific implementations.

3.5.3 802.1p/Q Frame Prioritization

The 802.1Q VLAN tag control information field allocates 3 bits for user priority. The definition for these User Priority bits is provided by IEEE 802.1p/Q, and enables individual frames to be marked for priority delivery. The QoS supported by 802.1p/Q allows for eight levels of priority assignment. This ensures that mission-critical traffic will receive preferential treatment in potentially congested conditions across multiswitch networks, and thus minimizes frame loss resulting from transient bottlenecks.

For storage network applications, the ability to prioritize transactions in an IP-based SAN is a tremendous asset. Storage networks normally support a wide variety of applications, not all of which require high priority. Updating an on-line customer order or a financial transaction between banks, for example, rates a much higher priority for business operations than a tape backup stream. The class of service provided by 802.1p/Q allows storage administrators to select the applications that should receive higher priority transport and assign them to one of the eight available priority levels. In a multiswitch network, class of service ensures that prioritized frames will have preference across interswitch links. Except for a few proprietary port-based implementations, Fibre Channel currently does not support frame prioritization and thus cannot distinguish between mission-critical and less essential storage applications.

3.5.4 802.3x Flow Control

Flow control at the data link level helps to minimize frame loss and avoids latency resulting from error recovery at the higher layer protocols. In Fibre Channel, flow control for class 3 service is provided by a buffer credit scheme. As buffers are available to receive more frames, the target device issues receiver readys (R_RDYs) to the initiator, one per available buffer. In Gigabit Ethernet, link-layer flow control is provided by the IEEE 802.3x standard. The 802.3x implementation uses a MAC control PAUSE frame to hold off the sending party if congestion is detected. If, for example, receive buffers on a switch port are approaching saturation, the switch can issue a PAUSE frame to the transmitting device so that the receive buffers have time to empty. Typically, the PAUSE frame is issued when a certain high-water mark is reached, but before the switch buffers are completely full.

Because the PAUSE frame is a type of MAC control frame, the frame structure is slightly different from the conventional data frame. Like VLAN tagging, the length/type field is used to indicate the special nature of the frame, in this case hex "88–08" to indicate a MAC control frame. As shown in Table 3–6, this indicator is followed by an opcode of hex "00–01" to define further the MAC control frame as a PAUSE frame. The amount of time that a transmitting device should cease issuing frames is specified by the opcode parameter field. pause_time cannot be specified in fixed units such as microseconds, because this would prove too inflexible for backward compatibility and future Ethernet transmission rates. Instead, pause_time is specified in pause_quanta, with one pause_quanta equal to 512 bit_times for the link speed being used. The timer value can be between 0 and 65,535 pause_quanta, or a maximum of approximately 33 msec at Gigabit Ethernet's 1.25-Gbps transmission rate. If the device that issued the PAUSE frame empties its buffers before the stated pause_time has elapsed, it can issue

TABLE 3–6   IEEE 802.3X PAUSE FRAME FORMAT

Length/Type	MAC Control Opcode	Parameters
88-08	00-01	Pause_time
16 bits	16 bits	16 bits

another PAUSE frame with pause_time set to zero. This signals the transmitting device that frame transmission can resume.

Because PAUSE frames may be used between any devices and the switch ports to which they are attached, and because Gigabit Ethernet only allows one device per port, there is no need to personalize the PAUSE frame with the recipient's MAC address. Instead, a universal, well-known address of 04-80-C2-00-00-01 is used in the destination address field. When a switch port receives the PAUSE frame with this address, it processes the frame but does not forward it to the network.

The 802.3x flow control provided by Gigabit Ethernet switches creates new opportunities for high-performance storage traffic over IP. Fibre Channel class 3 service has already demonstrated the viability of a connectionless, unacknowledged class of service, providing there is a flow control mechanism to pace frame transmission. In Fibre Channel fabrics using class 3, as with 802.3x in Ethernet, the flow control conversation occurs between the switch port and its attached device. As the switch port buffers fill, it stops sending R_RDYs until additional buffers are freed. In Gigabit Ethernet, this function is performed with PAUSE frames, with the same practical result. In either case, buffer overruns and the consequent loss of frames are avoided, and this is accomplished with minimal impact on performance.

The reliability provided by the gigabit infrastructure through data link flow control enables streamlined protocols to be run at the upper layer. For IP storage, the equivalent to Fibre Channel class 3 is UDP. UDP is connectionless and unacknowledged, and thus is unsuited to very congested environments such as the Internet. For contained data center storage applications, however, 802.3x flow control and storage over UDP/IP can offer a reliable and extremely high-performance solution without incurring the protocol overhead of TCP/IP.

3.5.5 802.3ad Link Aggregation

Link aggregation, or trunking, provides higher bandwidth for switched networks by provisioning multiple connections between switches or between a switch and an end device such as a server. Link aggregation also facilitates scaling the network over time, because additional links to a trunked group can be added incrementally as bandwidth requirements increase. In Figure 3–16, two Gigabit Ethernet switches share three aggregated links for a total available bandwidth of 7.5 Gbps full duplex.

Originally, the 802.3ad standards initiative was promoted as a means to provide higher bandwidth for standard 10/100-Mbps Ethernet networks.

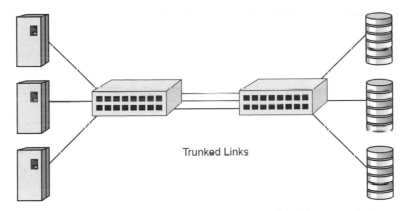

Figure 3–16 Link aggregation between two Gigabit Ethernet switches.

Link aggregation was a means of satisfying higher bandwidth requirements while Gigabit Ethernet was still being developed. As with memory, CPUs, and storage, however, whatever performance or capacity is reached at any given point in time is never sufficient for the increasing demands of users and applications. Consequently, bundled Ethernet links have been replaced with bundled Gigabit Ethernet links, which at some point will be superseded by bundled 10 Gigabit and higher Ethernet links. Replicators, for example, will no doubt require bundled 100 Gigabit Ethernet links.

Link aggregation must resolve several issues to avoid creating more problems than it fixes. In normal bridge environments, the spanning tree algorithm would, on encountering multiple links between two devices, simply disable the redundant links and only allow a single data path. This would prevent duplication of frames and potential out-of-order delivery. Link aggregation must therefore make multiple links between two devices appear as a single path, while simultaneously providing a mechanism to avoid frame duplication and ensure in-order frame delivery. This could be accomplished by manipulating MAC addresses (for example, assigning the same MAC address to every trunked link) or by inserting a link aggregation intelligence between the MAC client and MAC layers. The status of link availability, current load, and conversations through the trunk require monitoring to ensure that frames are not lost or inadvertantly reordered.

In-order delivery of frames is guaranteed if a conversation between two end devices is maintained across a single link in the trunk. Although this is not as efficient link utilization as simply shipping each frame over any available connection, it avoids the extra logic required to monitor frame ordering and to reassemble them before delivery to the recipient. At the same time, additional transactions by other devices benefit from the availability of the aggregated interswitch links, and switch-to-switch bottlenecks are avoided.

Link aggregation as specified in 802.3ad is almost mandatory for IP-based storage networks, particularly when multiple Gigabit Ethernet switches are used to build the SAN backbone. Along with 802.1p/Q prioritization, link aggregation can ensure that mission-critical storage traffic has an available path through the network and that multiple instances of mission-critical transactions can occur simultaneously. This requirement will be satisfied temporarily by the arrival of 10Gb uplinks between switches, but these will inevitably be "trunked" to provide even higher bandwidth over time.

3.5.6 Gigabit Ethernet Physical Layer Considerations

Gigabit Ethernet has borrowed so heavily from the Fibre Channel physical layer that there are relatively few differences between them. Gigabit Ethernet has a slightly higher transmission rate of 1.25 Gbps, compared with Fibre Channel's 1.0625 Gbps. For storage applications, Gigabit Ethernet's faster clock can drive approximately 15 MBps more bandwidth over interswitch links.

Transceivers for Gigabit Ethernet applications may also vary, although some GBICs can interoperate with both Fibre Channel and Gigabit Ethernet transmission speeds. Gigabit Ethernet has introduced support for new cable types for gigabit transport, including category 5 unshielded twisted pair. As shown in Table 3–7, cable distances are comparable with Fibre

TABLE 3–7:   GIGABIT ETHERNET CABLE SPECIFICATIONS

Cable Type	Diameter	Laser Type	Maximum Distance (m)
1000BASE-T	CAT-5 UTP	N/A	100
1000BASE-CX	STP	N/A	25
1000BASE-LX	10 μm	Long wave	5,000
1000BASE-SX	50 μm	Short wave	500
1000BASE-LX	50 μm	Long wave	550

Channel, with the exception of long-wave, single-mode cabling (10 km for Fibre Channel).

3.6 Assumptions for IP-Based SANs

Because it is probable that legacy SCSI, Fibre Channel, and IP-based SANs will coexist for some time, the adoption rate of IP storage solutions will depend on the ability of vendors to supply stable, interoperable, and high-performance products that can accommodate a variety of storage network interfaces.

As the first-generation storage network infrastructure, Fibre Channel has set expectations in terms of storage performance and network flexibility. Although management and interoperability of fabrics may be problematic, stability and performance have at least been achieved for Fibre Channel interfaces on end devices. The onus is therefore on IP storage vendors to accommodate these devices and to ensure the same level of reliability and interoperability for native IP storage interfaces.

Block storage data over IP and Gigabit Ethernet must provide performance equal to or greater than other storage solutions. This is facilitated by functionality inherent in Gigabit Ethernet, including faster transmission speeds (going to 10Gb), link-layer flow control, and link aggregation.

IP storage must also provide enhancements for storage transport unavailable by other means. The more flexible capabilities of VLANs over Gigabit Ethernet and traffic priorization give storage administrators new tools for securing mission-critical transactions in the SAN and for sharing the SAN infrastructure between disparate storage applications.

In terms of management, IP-based SANs benefit from the much wider deployment of sophisticated transport management platforms for enterprise data networks. The merger of storage and networking, however, creates unique requirements beyond network transport management. The integration of network management with storage management is still required to simplify the configuration and management of the SAN, and to reduce administrative overhead.

In terms of interoperability, the greater stability of Fibre Channel end devices and demonstrated interoperability between Gigabit Ethernet switches presents opportunities to combine the best from both worlds to facilitate IP SANs. Native IP storage devices, however, also have to demonstrate both standards compliance and interoperability to achieve acceptance in the market.

3.7 Chapter Summary

Storage Networking Terminology
■ RAID provides performance and data redundancy.

■ RAID 0 stripes data blocks over multiple disks.

■ RAID 1 provides data duplication (mirroring) between two disks.

■ RAID 5 provides striping of data blocks and distributed parity for data reconstruction in the event of failure.

■ RAID levels may be combined—for example, RAID 0 + 1.

■ JBODs are more economical than RAID but have no inherent redundancy or mirroring capability.

■ To maximize performance, software RAID on host systems can be applied against JBOD targets.

■ Tape subsystems may be SCSI, Fibre Channel, or Gigabit Ethernet interfaces.

■ Bridge products can bring legacy SCSI devices into an IP-based SAN.

■ SAN host adapters may include Fibre Channel HBAs and IP storage NICs.

■ IP storage NICs may provide optimized logic for TCP off-loading.

Legacy SCSI Cabling
■ SCSI cabling provides parallel wires for simultaneous transfer of data bits.

■ The maximal SCSI cabling is 25 m.

■ The maximal device population for SCSI cabling is 15 devices on a string.

■ Skew refers to the window of time required to capture all data bits in a parallel transmission.

Network-Attached Storage
■ NAS serves files; SANs provide data blocks.

■ The NAS architecture is comprised of a thin server and attached storage.

- NAS storage may be ATA, SCSI, or Fibre Channel.

- NAS uses NFS or CIFS over IP for file access.

- NAS products are typically marketed as appliances, requiring little configuration or management.

- NAS and IP-based SAN traffic may share a common network infrastructure.

Fibre Channel

- Fibre Channel is a standards-based, layered architecture.

- FC-0 defines gigabit physical layer specifications.

- FC-1 provides data encoding and link-level controls.

- FC-2 defines segmentation and reassembly of data via frames, flow control, and classes of service.

- FC-3 is being developed for common services such as encryption.

- FC-4 is the upper layer protocol interface between Fibre Channel and IP, SCSI-3, and other protocols.

- The most commonly used FC-4 protocol is FCP for serial SCSI-3.

- FC-0 and FC-1 provide the foundation layers for Gigabit Ethernet.

- The 8b/10b data encoding algorithm coverts 8-bit bytes into 10-bit characters.

- Encoding is required to prevent sustained DC states on the gigabit link.

- A proportional representation of ones and zeros is maintained via running disparity.

- Ordered sets are 10-bit characters used for frame delimitation, signaling, and link change notification.

- The maximal payload for a Fibre Channel frame is 2,112 bytes.

- The most commonly used class of service for Fibre Channel is class 3, which is connectionless and requires no acknowledgment of frame receipt.

- Fibre Channel has no standardized encryption or authentication methods.

- FCP is responsible for mapping SCSI devices at the operating system level to Fibre Channel-attached storage resources.

- Fibre Channel topologies include point to point, arbitrated loop, and fabric.

- Fibre Channel fabrics use a subset of OSPF called FSPF for fabric routing.

- The Fibre Channel fabric appears as one integral network.

- Interoperability and management issues for fabric switches have retarded the deployment of Fibre Channel SANs.

Gigabit Ethernet

- Gigabit Ethernet is a data link transport that borrows from both Fibre Channel and conventional 802.3 Ethernet.

- Ethernet framing is used to transport TCP/IP data over Gigabit Ethernet networks.

- 802.1Q VLAN tagging allows segregation of devices on the SAN.

- 802.1p/Q frame prioritization enables mission-critical traffic to be assigned one of eight levels of priority for SAN transport.

- 802.3x flow control provides reliable transport of storage data over connectionless protocols such as UDP/IP.

- 802.3ad link aggregation allows scalability of IP-based SANs with no loss in performance.

- Gigabit Ethernet's transmission rate of 1.25 Gbps provides slightly better performance than Fibre Channel.

- Gigabit Ethernet cabling includes category 5 unshielded twisted pair copper cabling as well as standard multimode and single-mode fiber-optic cabling.

Assumptions for IP-Based SANs

- Storage networks based on IP and Gigabit Ethernet can leverage new functionality for class of service, VLANs, flow control, and trunking provided by Ethernet standards.

- An optimal storage over IP solution accommodates legacy SCSI, Fibre Channel, and native IP storage devices.

- Management of storage networks requires the integration of transport management and storage management.

- Interoperability is a key driver for market adoption.

4 — SCSI Protocol

THE SCSI PROTOCOL performs the heavy lifting of passing commands, status, and block data between host platforms and storage devices. This chapter examines the SCSI protocol apart from underlying transports such as parallel SCSI cabling, Fibre Channel, or IP storage networking.

4.1 Operating Systems and SCSI I/O

One function of an operating system is to hide the complexity of the computing environment from the end user. Management of system resources including memory, peripheral devices, display, context switching between concurrent applications, and so on, are generally concealed behind the user interface. How successfully this is accomplished varies from one operating system to another, but the failure to perform may result in the loss of transient data, reboot of hung applications, reboot of the system itself, and invariably a disgruntled end user. The internal operations of the operating system must be robust, closely monitor changes of state, ensure that transactions are completed within allowable time frames, and automatically initiate recovery or retries in the event of incomplete or failed procedures. For I/O operations for peripheral devices such as disk, tape, optical storage, printers, and scanners, these functions are provided by the SCSI protocol, typically embedded in a device driver or logic onboard a host adapter.

Because the SCSI protocol layer sits between the operating system and the peripheral resources, it has different functional components. Applications, for example, typically access data as files or records. Although these may be ultimately stored on disk or tape media in the form of data blocks, retreival of a file requires a hierarchy of fuctions to assemble raw data blocks into a coherent file that can be manipulated by an application.

The first step in this process is assumed by the file system to which the application is linked via the operating system. A file system creates human-readable abstractions of data in the form of directories, folders, and files. When a user application opens a file, a series of processes are launched that rely on lower layer SCSI commands and controls to transport the appropriate data blocks from storage safely into memory. A translation between file representation and block I/O thus occurs in the file system layer.

Just as the file system presents an abstraction of data to the user application, the physical storage devices are presented as an abstraction to the file system. An E: drive in Windows or a /dev/dsk2 in UNIX, for example, may be a single disk drive, a partition on a larger disk, or a striped array of multiple disks. The file system depends on a volume management function to present sometimes diverse storage devices as coherent and easily addressable resources. Device virtualization turns physical storage into logical storage, and assumes the intricate tasks necessary for placement of data blocks on disks. This file/block translation and mapping function can be as sophisticated as a separate volume management application or as straightforward as an adapter card device driver interface to an operating system disk utility. Windows NT, for example, offers Windows Disk Administrator to assign logical drive names to physical disks. An adapter card's device driver is responsible for making its attached resources visible to Windows Disk Administrator as physical SCSI entities. Windows Disk Administrator is then used to assign logical names to these resources, which in turn are used by the file system to identify potential locations for directories and files.

As shown in Figure 4–1, this hierarchy of logical abstractions descends to the physical world of actual SCSI devices and their connectivity to the host system. Common access methods at the operating system level allow uniform treatment of SCSI devices regardless of their physical attachment to the system. In saving a file, the file system does not need to be concerned with whether the logical drive identifier fronts a direct SCSI-attached unit, a Fibre Channel array, or an IP storage device somewhere on the Gigabit Ethernet network. In each case, the mapping between logical entities and physical storage completes the delivery of SCSI commands between the host system and the appropriate targets to transfer block data.

Regardless of the underlying plumbing, the operating system's view of physical storage is defined by the bus/target/LUN triad inherited from parallel SCSI technology. The bus represents one of several potential SCSI interfaces installed on a host, each one supporting a separate string of disks. The target represents a single disk controller on the string, out of a total of 7 for

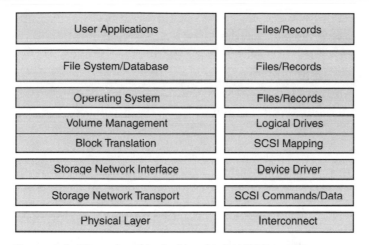

Figure 4–1 Hierarchy of logical-to-physical SCSI mapping.

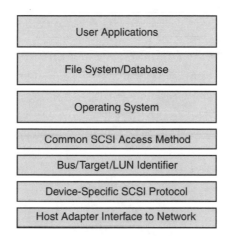

Figure 4–2 SCSI device addressing in relation to the SCSI protocol.

narrow SCSI and 15 for wide SCSI. And the LUN designation allows for additional disks governed by a controller—for example, a RAID device.

The mapping between the bus/target/LUN designation and the logical drive identifier provides the portal between physical devices and the upper layer file system (Figure 4–2). Because Fibre Channel and IP storage are serial transports and have no bus component, the bus identifier may be fabricated for compatibility with the operating system's SCSI nomenclature. Two IP storage NICs in a single server, for example, may have different bus designations to mimic SCSI adapter configurations. How this is implemented is vendor dependent, but the device driver must comply with the operating system's standard SCSI access method.

The bus/target/LUN identifier may be further mapped to the addressing requirements of a specific transport. FCP, for example, maps bus/target/LUN to a device identification (ID)/LUN pair. Consequently, the representation of physical storage has two components. One is directed at the operating system, to establish a familiar, addressable entity based on the SCSI triad; the other is directed at the specific transport, to accommodate the addressing requirements of that topology.

Below this layer, SCSI-3 commands and status are exchanged between initiators and targets to move data blocks. The relationship between SCSI initiators and targets is defined in SAM-2 and various standards documents for specific SCSI-3 implementations.

4.2 The SCSI Architectural Model

The SCSI-3 family of standards introduced several new variations of SCSI commands and a protocol, including serial SCSI-3 and special command sets for streaming and media handling required for tape. As shown in Figure 4–3, the command layer is independent of the protocol layer, which is required to carry SCSI-3 commands between devices. This enables more flexibility in substituting different transports beneath the SCSI-3 command interface to the operating system. In small desktop video editing systems, for example, IEEE 1394 FireWire can be used for high-speed but limited-distance SCSI-3 serial bus transactions to peripheral equipment.

The SCSI architecture defines the relationship between initiators (hosts) and targets (for example, disks) as a client/server exchange. The SCSI-3 application client resides in the host and represents the upper layer application, file system, and operating system I/O requests. The SCSI-3 device server sits in the target device, responding to requests. The client/server requests and responses are exchanged across some form of underlying transport, which is governed by the appropriate SCSI-3 service delivery protocol for that transport, such as the FCP protocol or iSCSI for gigabit serial links. The SCSI-3 protocol that services I/O requests from the host application is thus differentiated from the SCSI-3 transport protocol that actually moves data via the service delivery subsystem.

Because an initiator may have multiple requests pending to a target, the client/server model must accommodate concurrent request/response exchanges and track the status of each. Status and diagnostic functions may be supervised through task management between the two entities. As shown in Figure 4–4,

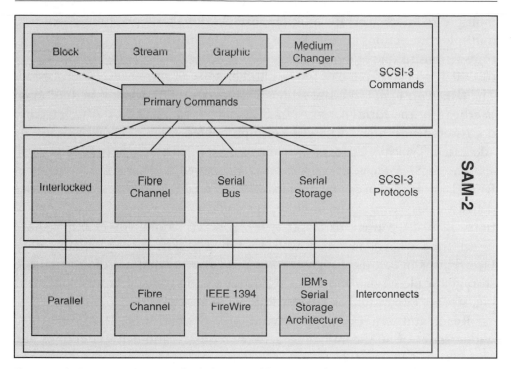

Figure 4–3 SAM-2 SCSI-3 standards functional layers. Implementations such as serial SCSI FCP, iSCSI, and IEEE 1394 come under separate standards initiatives.

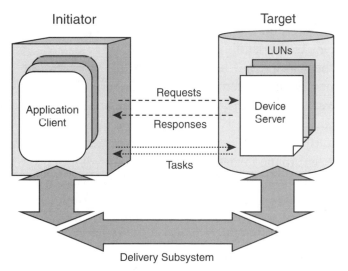

Figure 4–4 SCSI client/server model. The delivery subsystem could be FCP or serial SCSI over IP.

multiple requests generate multiple instances of the application client and multiple transactions for the device server. On the initiator, juggling multiple transactions to one or more targets requires *context switching,* or the ability to switch quickly from one job to another as SCSI responses are processed. The failure to handle multiple threads concurrently may result in additional overhead in the form of retries or SCSI timeouts. The SAM-2 architecture does not define how this is to be implemented, but indicates it must be addressed. Typically, context switching is performed by the host adapter card.

The SCSI-3 architectural model is structured so that the I/O requests from the host system can be serviced without regard to the underlying service delivery subsystem. A single file server could therefore conduct I/O operations against a variety of target types. A server could, for example, have direct-attached SCSI targets as well as serial SCSI targets over a gigabit interface. This is in fact the design of some NAS systems that use direct-attached storage for file serving and serial SCSI over gigabit transports for block serving, storage expansion, or tape backup.

Reads and writes of data between initiators and targets are performed with a series of SCSI commands, delivery requests, and delivery actions and responses. SCSI commands and parameters are specified in the command descriptor block (CDB). The CDB is part of a command frame sent from initiator to target and may be accompanied by data if immediate processing is required. The first byte of a CDB is an opcode that specifies the type of operation the target is to perform. A SCSI write to disk, for example, triggers the creation of an application client that issues a SCSI command request to the target to prepare its buffers for data reception. The target device server issues a delivery action response when its buffers are ready. The initiator responds by sending blocks. Depending on the lower layer delivery subsystem, the blocks may be transported as bytes in parallel (for example, LVD SCSI cabling) or may be segmented into frames for serial transport (for example, serial SCSI over IP). From the standpoint of the application or operating system, the write was conducted as a single transaction. In reality, a single write may cause multiple delivery requests and delivery action exchanges before all data is finally sent to the target, as shown in Figure 4–5.

In a read operation, the SCSI command block reverses the sequence of data delivery requests and acknowledgments, although it is assumed that because the initiator issued the read command, its buffers are ready to receive the first set of data blocks.

The SCSI CDB is the business end of FCP and iSCSI delivery systems. The CDB is encapsulated within FCP IU$ or iSCSI Protocol Data Units (PDU$) and triggers the appropriate read or write operation at the target.

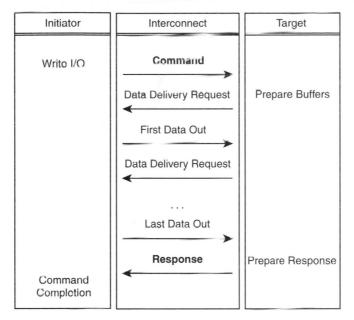

Figure 4–5 A SCSI write operation with multiple data delivery actions to complete a single command/response pair.

In both read and write operations, there is always an opportunity on the part of the initiator, interconnect, and target for things to go wrong. The delivery protocol as implemented in various topologies must be sufficiently robust to accommodate transient delays resulting from queuing, occasional bit corruption (flagged by CRC checks), transaction timeouts, or other mishaps along the delivery subsystem. Particularly for gigabit transports, a stable infrastructure greatly assists the efficiency of the SCSI protocol to move block data with minimal overhead. This is a significant challenge for IP storage, which must invent mechanisms to facilitate block data transport over inherently unstable environments such as WANs.

4.3 Chapter Summary

Operating Systems and SCSI I/O
- Applications view storage resources as abstract representations of the underlying physical devices.

- I/O requests are generated by applications, files systems, and operating systems.

- Logical storage identifiers (for example, the F: drive) are mapped to the SCSI addressing scheme of bus/target/LUN.

- The mapping function is provided by device drivers that support SCSI ports or adapters.

- The supporting SCSI infrastructure may also provide additional mapping between the conventional bus/target/LUN addressing and the address scheme required for that topology.

SCSI Architectural Model

- SAM-2 separates SCSI commands from SCSI delivery protocols and underlying interconnects.

- SAM-2 defines SCSI relationships in a client/server model.

- Initiators are host systems that generate I/O requests.

- Targets are storage devices that process those requests.

- An application client resides in the initiator and is generated for every I/O operation.

- The device client resides in the target device and services requests.

- Multiple instances of the application client may be running concurrently to support multiple outstanding I/Os.

- An I/O is performed through a command/response sequence.

- SCSI commands and parameters are contained in the CDB.

- The CDB is encapsulated within the FCD IU or the iSCSI PDU.

- Multiple data delivery requests and acknowledgments may be exchanged within a single command/response pair.

- The efficiency of the SCSI protocol is dependent on the stability of the supporting interconnect infrastructure.

5 The Internet Protocol

IP ENABLES dynamic routing within complex networks. This chapter provides introductory material on IP addressing and routing mechanisms for readers unfamiliar with IP, and includes examples of how IP networks are configured.

5.1 Layer 2

The OSI Reference Model defines the physical, data link, and network layers as the foundation strata on which higher level functions are built. The physical and data link layers are mandatory for communication between any two devices on the same network segment. A local LAN, for example, may use twisted pair cabling to join three workstations, each provisioned with an adapter card. Copper wire provides the physical layer function, whereas the NICs provide the data link functions. As shown in Figure 5–1, these two layers alone are, theoretically, sufficient for communication between the workstations. Logical link control oversees the orderly transmission of data from the upper layer application to the underlying MAC layer. The MAC layer monitors availability of the physical media. The MAC address in each card gives each workstation a unique identity, so that data sent from workstation A to workstation B does not generate a response from workstation C. And the physical interface on the NIC provides bit encoding and bit transmission onto the wire. This short stack implementation is representative of bit-oriented protocols such as IBM Synchronous Data Link Control.

5.1.1 Layer 2 Bridging

In the absence of a network layer, scalability becomes an issue. As more workstations are added to the LAN, the increased communications load affects overall LAN performance. The first response to this problem was the

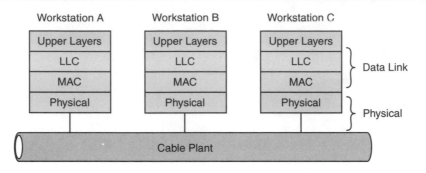

Figure 5–1 Layer 2 stack on a single network segment.

introduction of layer 2 bridges. As shown in Figure 5–2, separate, smaller LAN segments are joined by bridges that monitor the communications on each segment to which they are attached. Because only transactions from one segment to another are forwarded by the bridge, each LAN segment is screened from conversations occurring within other segments. This resolved the issue of performance, at least within an individual LAN segment, and provided limited scalability to larger populations of end devices.

In a bridged environment, each workstation is identified by its unique 48-bit MAC address, typically hard coded by the NIC manufacturer. Although each MAC address is unique, there is no system of address distribution or management throughout the network. A workstation may be

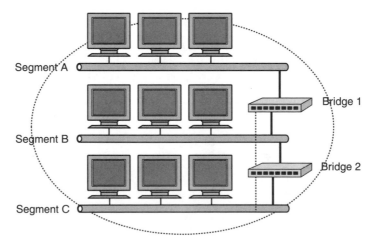

Figure 5–2 Layer 2 bridging brings multiple segments into a single network.

moved from one LAN segment to another, in which case its MAC address now appears in a different area of the network. Until the bridge ports that are listening to the communications on each segment learn of this change, packets addressed to that workstation will be broadcast throughout the network. The additional overhead incurred by broadcasts is the price that is paid for freedom from manual address administration. The random dispersal of MAC addresses throughout the network also makes it difficult to troubleshoot communication problems. A network analyzer may capture transactions between two MAC addresses, but in Ethernet networks there is no indication of where the workstations physically reside. Token Ring dealt with this problem though source route bridging, whereas Fibre Channel addressing uses domain/area/port addressing to identify the segment on which a device sits. As we see later, IP storage leverages network layer addressing to overcome a number of issues associated with link-layer addressing.

5.1.2 Spanning Tree

To facilitate availability, it is possible to have redundant links between bridges and LAN segments. If a primary link fails, the secondary provides an alternate data path. In Figure 5–2, for example, bridge 1 has connections to segments A, B, and C; whereas bridge 2 only provides connections to segments B and C. If all links on all bridges were active, a packet sent from segment A to a workstation on segment C would be forwarded by bridge 1 to both segment B and segment C. Bridge 2 would also forward the packet, resulting in two copies of the same packet being passed to segment C and the destination MAC address. In a complex bridged environment, active redundant links may result in loops through which packets would circulate endlessly (or until predetermined timeout values were reached).

To avoid packet duplication and loops, bridges in an Ethernet network use a spanning tree algorithm to disable redundant links and thus ensure a single data path between all segments. In our example, the redundant link between bridge 1 and segment C would be disabled, forcing all data from segment A to segment C through bridge 2. If the link between bridge 2 and segment C should fail, the standby link on bridge 1 would be activated. Spanning tree enables transparent bridging, because the mechanism for determining data paths is controlled by the bridges themselves, not the end devices.

By contrast, the source route bridging used by Token Ring allows for multiple active data paths between source and destination, but forces the end devices to monitor the routes taken across the bridged network. A routing information field (RIF) in the packet records each bridge crossing as the packet goes from segment to segment. The destination device simply reverses the order of RIF entries to communicate back to the source.

Layer 2 bridging relies on broadcasts of packets for device discovery. A packet addressed to an as-yet-unidentified MAC may be sent to all network segments in search of a response. Layer 2 bridging also creates a single link-layer network that is potentially vulnerable to disruption from any attached segment. An errant workstation, for example, can flood the entire network with packets, causing network failure. Avoiding the overhead of broadcasts and the dreaded broadcast storms was the primary argument for displacing layer 2 bridges with IP routers.

In addition, a single network composed of bridged segments limited the total device population to the number specified by the supporting topology (for example, Token Ring or Ethernet). To overcome both vulnerability to broadcast storms and to allow for higher device populations, it is necessary to have a logical network addressing scheme that simultaneously allows for the separation of networks and controlled communication between them. These criteria have been largely satisfied by IP routing.

5.2 Layer 3–IP

IP has achieved near-universal acceptance as the network protocol of choice for data communication networks. Like Ethernet, this wide-spread adoption has not been the result of exceptional performance or design excellence, but of steady encroachment against competing solutions via availability, lower cost, and open systems orientation. Originally designed to withstand intense network disruptions (such as Cold War nuclear exchanges), IP provides only a best-effort delivery mechanism. On the surface this would make IP unsuitable for mission-critical storage applications, which demand guaranteed delivery of data to disk and tape. In practice, however, adapting an inherently *laissez-faire* protocol to the more rigorous requirements of storage is simply a challenge for engineers and a market opportunity for vendors.

Compared with layer 2 bridging, layer 3 IP networking offers significant advantages for scaling from small to enterprise-class networks and for containing disruptions. As shown in Figure 5–3, IP routing enables communication between separate network segments using a common protocol that is independent of the underlying network topologies.

Unlike layer 2 bridging, each network in an IP-routed environment maintains its own unique address space, which is initially assigned by a network

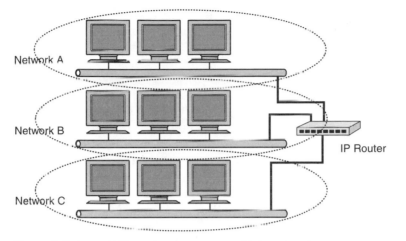

Figure 5–3 Layer 3 IP routing between multiple networks.

administrator. Link-layer broadcasts are therefore restricted to each network, and only traffic that is intended for another IP network is forwarded by the IP routers. Collectively, all networks connected by IP routers may be referred to as an *IP network*. The Internet, for example, is composed of hundreds of thousands of individual networks, each with its own unique IP address space.

5.2.1 IP Addressing

Unlike proprietary networking protocols, IP has evolved in the public realm. The IP addressing scheme therefore assumes that individual end devices will not only have a unique indentity within a particular network, but will be unique globally as well. This assumption has created a conflict between the number of IP addresses still available and the requirements of ever-expanding enterprise networks.

The traditional IP address scheme (IPv4) uses a 32-bit address that is divided into network identifiers and host (device) identifiers. The original IPv4 addressing relied on different classes of addresses to provide address ranges for large and small networks. Class-based addressing has been replaced, for the most part, with a classless address mechanism (described later).

IPv4's 32-bit address space allows for more than four billion unique addresses. A mere four billion, as it turns out, is not sufficient to satisfy the world's demand for IP addresses. Consequently, a new IPv6 enhancement allocates 128 bits for an IP address, for a four billion cubed advantage over the IPv4 total address space. The inadequacy of IPv4 is less a result of its total device support limitations than how the 32 bits are partitioned. As shown in Figure 5–4, the 4 bytes of IPv4 addressing are divided into network and host portions. For convenience, each byte is converted into its decimal equivalent to provide a more readable dotted decimal notation.

Class A uses the first byte to specify networks, and the last 3 bytes for hosts within each network. The class A address allocation allows for 126 different networks, with more than 16.5 million hosts within each network. Class A thus consumes approximately half the total IP host addresses. Because class A address blocks are only granted to governments and very large enterprises that may not actually require 16.5 million hosts, a fair portion of the assigned IP addresses within those blocks may go unused.

Class B has a 2-byte network identifier that, after subtracting reserved bits, allows for more than 16,000 possible networks with more than 65,000 hosts per network. Class B addresses occupy a quarter of the total available IP host addresses, and, like class A, may be allocated to enterprises that do not actually require 65,000 end nodes.

The most dramatic shift in address allocation occurs in class C, which supports more than two million different networks, but with only 254 hosts on each network. Companies or institutions that require a few thousand addresses must therefore request a class B address, which wastes tens of thousands of possible addresses, or enough blocks of class C addresses to support their requirements.

The conventional governing authority for IP address allocation is the Internet Corporation for Assigned Names and Numbers (ICANN). For Internet service providers (ISPs), the Internet Assigned Numbers Authority dispenses blocks of addresses for Internet access. To participate in the public IP network (Internet), each device must have a unique address. Enterprises cannot, therefore, simply assign themselves the most suitable address class for their internal network if they also expect to participate in the Internet. To solve the contradiction between the shrinking pool of available IP addresses and the internal requirements of enteprise IP networks, blocks of

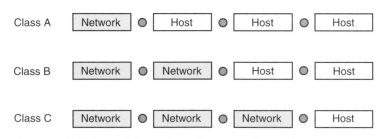

Figure 5–4 IPv4 IP address classes for networks and hosts.

IP addresses have been reserved for private IP networks. These blocks (for example, 10.0.0.0 for class A) can be used by any enteprise as long as those addresses are not exposed to the public Internet. To gain Internet access, a network address translator (NAT) is required to convert transactions originating from private IP addresses into bona fide public IP addresses. The NAT function is typically supplied by an ISP or other access point to the public IP network.

Additional IPv4 address classes include class D for multicast groups, and class E, which is reserved for experimentation.

5.2.2 Subnet Masking

If a company deploys a class B address (private or public), all 65,000 plus potential hosts would appear in the same network address space. It would thus be impossible to segment the network into functional groupings such as engineering, finance, human resources, and so on. To enable convenient subdivisions within a single network, IP addressing includes a facility for creating sub-networks or subnets within an address class. *Subnet masking* refers to the use of host address bits to demarcate individual subnets within the class.

In the class B private network address of 172.16.0.0, for example, 172.16.xxx.xxx represents the network, whereas xxx.xxx.0.0 represents potential host addresses within the network. If no subnetting was implemented, the subnet mask for this network would be 255.255.0.0 in dotted decimal notation, or 11111111 11111111 00000000 00000000 in binary. Bits set to one in the subnet mask indicate the network portion of the IP address, whereas bits set to zero represent hosts.

To create subnets within 172.16.xxx.xxx, host address bits must be borrowed to indicate the presence of subnetworks. If the third byte of the IP address was used to create subnets, a total of 254 usable subnets could be created, each with 254 hosts. As shown in Figure 5–5, the new subnet mask would now be 255.255.255.0 in dotted decimal, or 11111111 11111111 11111111 00000000 in binary.

The advantage of "subnetting" is obvious for enterprise networks that typically have hundreds of separate departments with hundreds or thousands of computers within each department. Subnetting also lightens the load on Internet IP routers, because only the network portion of the address is used to route traffic to a corporate site, while IP routers within the corporate network deal with subnet addressing. A class A address with a subnet mask of 255.255.224.0 could provide more than 2,000 subnets, each with more than 8,000 hosts.

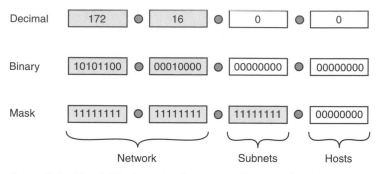

Figure 5–5 Classful "subnetting" on a class B network address space.

Subnetting has proved so useful for enterprise applications that additional implementations have evolved. Variable-length subnet masking (VLSM) enables the creation of subnets within subnets, so that, for example, a regional office that is assigned to a subnet can further subdivide its allocated addresses into smaller functional groups (for example, sales, marketing, administration, and support). Variable-length subnetting was not supported in the original IP Routing Information Protocol (RIP-1) and so required backward compatibility as new routers were deployed. Although variable-length subnetting is an asset for internal network usage, it does not solve the problem of public IP address availability.

With the depletion of class A and class B addresses, expansion of the Internet and new technologies based on IP routing faced a shortage crisis. Classless interdomain routing (CIDR) was created in the mid 1990s as a transitional solution to IPv4 address allocation until IPv6 could be developed. CIDR essentially overturns the notion of fixed IP classes and, like VLSM, offers a more flexible means of demarcating networks and hosts. CIDR ignores the upper bits that identify IP classes and simply indicates the number of bits that should be used for calculating the network portion of the address. The CIDR postfix "/15" appended to a network address of 172.16.0.0/15 would indicate that the first 15 bits of the address should be used to identify the network portion. Because a /15 mask is shorter than the 16 bits normally associated with the class B 172.16.0.0 address, CIDR may not be compatible with earlier NIC device drivers. It is especially beneficial, however, for ISPs in allocating addresses that scale to their customers' requirements.

For all the difficulties associated with IPv4 address allocation, IP addressing offers a viable long-term solution for future storage networks. The deployment of a virtually unlimited IPv6 address space will accompany the widespread adoption of readily available storage as storage network solutions expand from the data center to more consumer-oriented applications. This would be difficult to achieve with the more finite address space and single fabric topology provided by Fibre Channel. In addition, IPv6 standards include QoS and security features that are useful for a wide variety of networked storage solutions.

5.2.3 Address Resolution Protocol

When an IP packet is sent between networks, the header contains the source and destination IP addresses, but no information on the destination's lower level MAC address. Ethernet, for example, uses a 48-bit MAC address for local communication between devices on the same LAN segment. Although a workstation may have both a 48-bit MAC address and a 32-bit IP network address, it cannot receive frames based on the IP address alone. An IP router must therefore be able to associate a specific IP address with the appropriate MAC address to complete delivery. This process is called *address resolution,* and requires a special protocol (Address Resolution Protocol, or ARP) consisting of request and reply packets.

ARP relies on broadcasts that could be potentially disruptive to the LAN. Having received a data packet addressed to the local IP subnet, an IP router would broadcast an ARP request throughout the local LAN segment. The ARP request contains the MAC and IP address of the router (the source), and the IP address of the intended recipient (the destination). Every host on the LAN segment examines the broadcast request and compares the IP address it contains with its own. If there is a match, the host will issue an ARP reply to the router's MAC address and insert its own MAC address as the source of the reply. The router can then resolve the MAC-to-IP addressing and can send the original data packet on the destination LAN segment using the host's proper MAC address.

If this process was repeated every time a packet was received from an external source, the LAN would be flooded with ARP broadcasts and replies. To avoid this situation, each host creates an ARP cache that monitors ARP requests and replies, and builds a table of MAC and corresponding IP addresses. Because a host's IP address may change, either through manual configuration or automatic IP assignment (for example, the Dynamic Host Configuration Protocol), the ARP cache must age the early entries in the cache, typically after 20 minutes after creation. If a router issues an ARP request and receives no valid reply, any IP packets it has buffered for that destination IP address will be discarded.

Hosts such as diskless workstations may not have a local configuration file from which to read an assigned IP address. In such cases, the host may issue a reverse ARP request (RARP) broadcast frame. Any boot server on the LAN segment may respond to the inquirer's MAC address with the appropriate IP address for that station. A similar function is provided by the Bootstrap Protocol (BOOTP protocol), which in addition to the IP address may provide a boot filename, gateway IP address, and so on. BOOTP requests are routable, which provides more flexibility in boot server deployment. RARP requests and replies are not forwarded beyond the local LAN segment.

5.2.4 IP Routing

IP routing relies on layer 3 network addressing for transporting packets between routers, and layer 2 addressing for delivering packets to their final destination on local LAN segments. When an IP router receives a packet from a local Ethernet segment, for example, it strips off the Ethernet header (layer 2) and uses the IP header (layer 3) to make a forwarding decision. At the receiving end, a layer 2 header must be reapplied before the packet can be sent to the appropriate destination IP address. This process allows communication using IP between heterogeneous LAN topologies, as for example, between Ethernet-based and Token Ring-based hosts.

The IP routers themselves must have a means of exchanging information about the IP networks or subnets to which they are attached. Several routing information methods have evolved, including the original RIP and OSPF. RIP-2, which allows for variable-length subnet masks, is a *distance-vector* protocol. As routers exchange information about their attached IP networks, RIP calculates optimal paths through the network based on the shortest number of hops between source and destination. Each IP router represents a single hop. In a meshed network, there may be multiple paths between a source and the destination network. Calculating IP routes based on the fewest number of hops would therefore appear to be the best means to get data from A to B. In reality, the hop count method does not account for the state of the links in the network. IP routers may have different types of links between them, so that one hop is connected by a Fast Ethernet link (100 Mbps), whereas another is connected by a T3 communications link (45 Mbps). In addition, some links may bear more traffic than others, so although there may be fewer hops along a single path vis-à-vis another, packets forwarded along that path may face congestion and may be discarded. The limitations of distance-vector routing encouraged the development of other protocols, including OSPF.

OSPF is a *link-state* protocol. Instead of simply calcuating optimal paths based on the number of hops, OSPF monitors the state of the links to which an IP router is attached and calculates the relative cost of moving data from one point to another based on bandwidth, current traffic load, and other link-dependent conditions. Link-state information is transmitted to neighboring IP routers so that the most efficient data paths can be selected. OSPF also introduces the concept of autonomous areas within the IP-routed network. As shown in Figure 5–6, the OSPF area hierarchy includes autonomous areas of IP routers that are ultimately linked through a common backbone area (area 0). The hierarchical scheme restricts OSPF broadcasts to specific areas, and thus prevents flooding of the entire network with routing information udpates whenever changes occur.

OSPF autonomous areas offer a signficant advantage for IP storage networks over extended Fibre Channel networks. In Fibre Channel, the FSPF protocol does not provide hierarchial areas. Consequently, disruptions in one part of the Fibre Channel fabric can propagate to the entire network. In IP storage networks based on OSPF, disruptions can be contained within a single autonomous area.

Another advantage of OSPF is the ability to accommodate changes more quickly in the network. In network terminology, *convergence* refers to the reestablishment of network connections after a major change has occurred. RIP uses an update interval method that can result in prolonged link failures before new paths are broadcast. In addition, because there are no autonomous areas as in OSPF, convergence time depends on the propagation of routing information throughout the network before stability is achieved. OSPF shortens convergence time by issuing state changes as soon

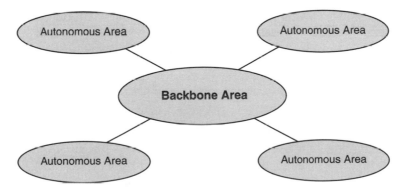

Figure 5–6 OSPF area hierarchy.

as link failures are detected and by restricting via areas the number of IP routers that must be notified of changes.

Other routing protocols, such as Cisco's Enhanced Interior Gateway Routing Protocol (EIGRP), offer additional advantages but impose a vendor-proprietary implementation. Despite the pressure of open systems mentality in the market, a single dominant vendor still has the wherewithal to compel customers to deploy proprietary solutions and thus lock out potential competitors. EIGRP has performance and bandwidth utilization benefits over OSPF, providing that the customer is willing to implement a single vendor network.

RIP, OSPF, and EIGRP are interior gateway protocols that may be used for a single corporate network. As IP routing scales from single network to multiple networks, the IP routing tables maintained by each router may become overwhelmed with entries. To make IP routing in very large internetworks such as the Internet feasible, exterior gateway protocols are required to minimize the load on individual IP routers and yet maximize efficiency for routing between them. The Border Gateway Protocol (BGP4) accomplishes these goals through a path-vector scheme that combines elements from distance-vector (RIP) hop count and link-state (OSPF) protocols. Like OSPF, BGP enables division of the network into autonomous systems, and thus restricts the distribution of routing updates within confined areas. Like RIP, BGP monitors the number of hops from one network to another, although a hop may be an entire autonomous system instead of individual IP routers.

5.2.5 IP Network Example

In the example shown in Figure 5–7, a small IP network is configured with four IP routers. An IP address scheme using 150.176.0.1 and a subnet mask of 255.255.255.0 allows for 256 different subnets with 254 hosts within each subnet. Each LAN segment is assigned its own subnet, as are links between IP routers.

The IP routers in this example are in a fully meshed configuration, with alternate paths between each router pair. The loss of an individual link would therefore result in a reconvergence that would allow routing around the failure.

With a subnet mask of 255.255.255.0, the 256 possible subnets would range from 150.176.0.0 to 150.176.255.0. Allowable hosts within each subnet would range from xxx.xxx.xxx.1 to xxx.xxx.xxx.254, with the xxx.xxx.xxx.255 address within each subnet reserved as a broadcast address.

A workstation on the 150.176.0.0 subnet may be assigned an address of 150.176.0.5, for example, whereas the gateway router for that segment is

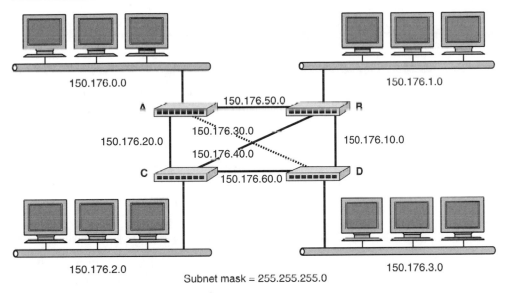

Figure 5–7 A small IP-routed network.

typically assigned the lowest host address for that subnet range—in this instance, 150.176.0.1 . If another workstation on the same subnet wishes to communicate with the 150.176.0.5 workstation, the device driver for the host's interface card will recognize that 150.176.0.5 is on the same subnet. It can then reference its ARP cache to see if there is a MAC address entry for that IP address, or ARP for one if there is not. In either case, no traffic is directed to the IP router because the conversation will occur on the same IP subnet.

If, however, it wishes to communicate with a host with an IP address of 150.176.3.8, the device driver will recognize that the destination address is beyond the local subnet and will forward the packet to the default IP gateway—in this instance, 150.176.0.1.

If the IP router is running RIP, it will have a routing table of destination IP subnets and the metric or hop count to each. In this fully meshed configuration, the routing table for router A will show three different routes between subnet 150.176.0.0 and 150.176.3.0. The longest routes will be through routers A-B-D and A-C-D, with two hops each. The shortest route will be directly from router A to router D, for a hop count of one. With RIP, therefore, a packet from subnet 150.176.0.0 to subnet 150.176.3.0 would be forwarded from router A to router D.

If the IP router is running OSPF, it will calcuate the cost of moving data from 150.176.0.0 to 150.176.3.0 based on the viability of the links it has available. In this example, the dashed line between routers A and D represents a Fast Ethernet link of 100 Mbps. If the other links are Gigabit Ethernet, then the optimal path between the two subnets is actually the one with more hops—for example, A-B-D or A-C-D. The router must then determine other cost factors, such as the current load between the higher speed links or the preferred path values that an administrator has assigned to individual links.

In this example, entire subnet blocks have been assigned to interrouter links. The link between router A and router D, for example, has been assigned to the 150.176.30.0 subnet, with router A's address of 150.176.30.10 and router D's address of 150.176.30.11. Only two of the potential 254 addresses for this subnet are used, wasting 252 addresses. VLSM could be used to subdivide 150.176.30.0 further into a sub-subnet, allowing the unused host addresses to be used elsewhere. In this sample configuration, all the router-to-router links could be assigned to 150.176.30.0, with VLSM used to create small subnets that require only two IP addresses per subnet. A VLSM of 255.255.255.252 would accomplish this.

Because IP routing is not dependent on layer 2 addressing, the different network segments joined by IP routers could be a variety of topologies, including Ethernet, Token Ring, AppleTalk, and so on. Likewise, the links between routers could be based on various transports, including Ethernet, frame relay, point-to-point leased lines, FDDI, or asynchronous transfer mode (ATM). Although each has its own unique framing method, the IP addressing mechanism remains agnostic to the underlying data link and physical transports. As shown in Figure 5–8, a conventional IP router examines only the network layer to make routing decisions, and relies on lower level logic to handle any framing conversions.

In the same IP network in Figure 5–7, routers A and D would route on the basis of IP address, whereas their physical interfaces would accommodate any conversions required between Gigabit Ethernet, Fast Ethernet, or other media types.

5.2.6 IP Routers and IP Switches

Ethernet has maintained its role as the leading LAN topology thanks largely to the development of Ethernet switches. First-generation Ethernet LANs relied on a shared media architecture that severely impacted performance as more devices were added to a single network segment. Because each device had to compete for bandwidth against other devices, scaling networks to larger populations was difficult. Bridging alleviated this situation somewhat,

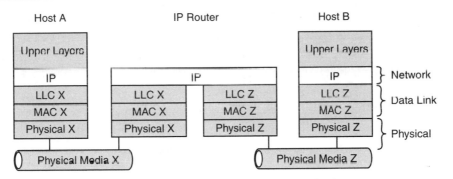

Figure 5–8 IP routing between heterogeneous LAN topologies.

but did not eliminate the potential for network disruptions resulting from broadcasts or erratic end nodes. IP routers allow the segmentation of larger networks into more manageable groups and prevent the propagation of link-level broadcast storms, but do not address bandwidth contention within each attached segment. IP router ports are still too expensive to deploy a single device per port.

Ethernet switches provide link-layer connectivity between multiple devices with dedicated bandwidth per port. In some designs, an Ethernet switch will support multiple MAC addresses on a single port, allowing for the attachment of a small hub or shared LAN segment. Typically, however, an Ethernet switch will support a single device per port, with full bandwidth per device. In the case of Gigabit Ethernet, only one device per port is allowed. From a functional standpoint, the attached device engages in normal carrier sense/collision detection behavior and has no awareness of the switch. If the link to the switch is full duplex, the device's transmit will always be available for communications. So although the device will listen to the carrier before placing data on the link, and will monitor for collision, there is really no need to do so. The Ethernet switch is the only other device on the link. It examines the destination MAC address of the frame and, based on a table of MAC and port addresses, switches the frame to the appropriate destination port.

Ethernet switches are available in port densities of several hundred ports, as well as combinations of Fast Ethernet and Gigabit Ethernet ports. It is possible to build very large networks with high performance per device, with multiple switching decisions being made simultaneously, all based on link-layer MAC addressing. Layer 2 switching is far simpler than IP routing because there are no network address or subnet calculations to perform.

In addition, the Ethernet frame passes intact from source to destination, whereas an IP router must alternately remove and replace Ethernet headers from the frames it handles, as well as examine QoS and other parameters.

Current-generation IP products include layer 3 switches, a.k.a IP switches. What is the difference between an IP router and an IP switch? Mostly, the difference is marketing. IP or layer 3 switches are simply very fast IP routers, which typically accelerate the IP routing function in silicon via ASICs. Like Ethernet layer 2 switches, IP switches may use a *cut-through* switching algorithm that examines only the destination IP address before making a switching decision. Cut-through has the advantage of speed, because the switch does not need to buffer or examine the entire frame before switching. Alternately, a *store-and-forward switch* will buffer the entire frame before sending it to its destination. Store-and-forward switching has the advantage of greater data integrity because a corrupt frame will not be forwarded, but must overcome potential latency resulting from full-frame buffering on frame receipt.

From a marketing standpoint, if the IP router supports homogeneous LAN interfaces (for example, Ethernet to Ethernet), it will be called an IP or layer 3 switch. The word *switch* thus connotes the speed associated with layer 2 switches, which is advantageous for marketing purposes. If, alternately, the IP router supports a variety of interfaces (for example, Ethernet to WAN), it is typically referred to as an IP router. In either case, the decision to forward a frame is based on the layer 3 network address and not, as in layer 2 switching, on the MAC address.

5.2.7 Other IP Considerations

An IP datagram may be as long as 65,535 bytes. Layer 2 transports, however, do not normally handle large frames and will divide an IP datagram into suitable fragments for link-layer transport. Ethernet, for example, has a maximum frame size of 1,500 bytes and will fragment a large IP datagram into smaller units. Fragmentation occurs at the transmitting end, whereas reassembly occurs at the destination.

For IP storage networking, the 1,500-byte limitation of Ethernet versus the 2,112-byte payload of Fibre Channel would appear to give Fibre Channel the advantage in efficiency. Gigabit Ethernet's faster clock rate, however, generally compensates for the difference in frame sizing, giving IP storage comparable performance with Fibre Channel in terms of data delivery. In large block sizes in particular, IP storage over Gigabit Ethernet and IP switching can outperform Fibre Channel switching.

5.3 **Chapter Summary**

Layer 2
- The minimum requirements for communication over a LAN are satisfied by the physical and data link levels.

- Communication between two devices on the same LAN segment use MAC addressing.

- Layer 2 bridging allows for the division of a LAN into segments, passing only the traffic that is destined for remote segments.

- Spanning tree is used by bridges to establish primary paths between multiple layer 2 segments.

- In spanning tree, only one link between two LAN segments can be active.

- Link-layer bridging is succeptible to broadcast storms and network outages resulting from erratic end nodes.

Layer 3—IP
- IP is a layer 3 network protocol that sits on top of the data link and physical layers.

- IP is a best-effort delivery protocol designed to discard packets during congested conditions.

- IP routing enables communication between different networks and/or different segments of a single network.

- IP addressing is based on a 32-bit address field, commonly represented in a dotted decimal notation.

- An IP address has a network component and a host component.

- Traditional IP address classes include class A (126 networks with 16.5 million hosts each), class B (16,000 networks with more than 65,000 hosts each), and class C (two million networks with 254 hosts each).

- Subnet masking is used to divide a single IP address range into small IP segments.

- VLSM allows for the further division of subnets into sub-subnets.

- CIDR was created to overcome IP address starvation, and revises the traditional IP class system.

- IPv6 defines a 128-bit address space to overcome the limitations of IPv4.

- ARP is used to discover the MAC address associated with a particular IP address.

- RARP is used to discover an IP address if the MAC address is known.

- RIP-2 is a distance-vector protocol that calculates optimal routes by the number of hops required to traverse the network.

- OSPF is a link-state protocol that calculates optimal routes by the availability, bandwidth, traffic load, and other factors related to links between routers.

- OSPF's area hierarchy offers advantages for IP storage over Fibre Channel's FSPF protocol.

- Convergence refers to the time required to achieve network stability once a network change has occurred.

- BGP is used by Internet routers to calculate routes between IP-routed systems.

- An IP or layer 3 switch is a marketing term for a fast IP router.

- Cut-through switching begins switching a frame as soon as the destination address is read.

- A store-and-forward switch buffers the entire frame before a switching decision is made.

- An IP datagram will be fragmented for delivery to the underlying transport and will be reassembled at the receiving end before being passed to the upper layer protocols or applications.

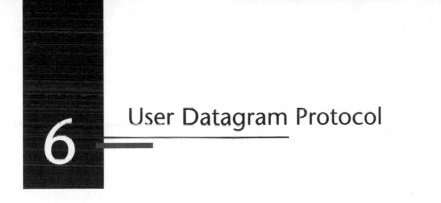

6   User Datagram Protocol

COMPARABLE WITH CLASS 3 SERVICE, UDP provides a connection-less, unacknowledged delivery service to maximize performance over stable networks. The following discussion examines the advantages and disadvantages of using UDP for IP storage.

6.1 Layer 4—UDP

UDP is a streamlined layer 4 transport protocol. UDP provides two services for IP transactions: a port number so that the data payload can be delivered to the proper upper layer application, and a checksum that validates the integrity of the UDP data across the network. Because UDP does so little, it requires few resources on the host system. This makes it an attractive layer 4 solution for applications that require high throughput with minimal CPU utilization. The tradeoff for performance, however, is the risk of data loss. UDP assumes a stable network infrastructure with a low bit error rate, and thus is rarely used in lossy, potentially congested environments such as wide area links.

6.1.1 Connectionless Service

UDP is a *connectionless* transport protocol. When host A sends data to host B, it simply transmits its data without establishing a communications session. If host B is not ready to receive data, the UDP datagram is discarded. This is analogous to making a phone call and, without the pleasantries of a hello or introduction, spewing forth one's important business. UDP also lacks any mechanism for acknowledgment, so there is no way to verify that the data was actually received. UDP relies on upper layer protocols to report missing or out-of-order datagrams. If the underlying network is unreliable, upper layer intervention for recovery will necessarily increase, and the performance advantage of a streamlined transport layer will be lost.

Because UDP lacks an integral flow control mechanism, it requires assistance from the physical network. In Gigabit Ethernet environments, the supporting flow control may be provided by 802.3x functionality in Gigabit Ethernet switches and adapter cards. As discussed in Chapter 3, 802.3x enables a link-layer mechanism for preventing buffer overruns and frame discard. As a receiving device's buffers fill to a preestablished threshold, it will issue an 802.3x PAUSE frame to the sending party. The PAUSE frame contains a counter value that halts transmission for a specified time. When the time has elapsed, the sending device can resume transmission. Link-layer flow control thus enables use of UDP in data center networks based on Gigabit Ethernet switching because both end devices and the interconnecting switches can moderate the flow of UDP datagrams from source to destination.

The lack of acknowledgment capability presents another issue. Similar to its dependency on external support for flow control, UDP must assume that its datagrams were received intact or that upper layer applications will handle delivery failures. On the other hand, because it does not have to wait for acknowledgments, UDP gains a significant performance advantage.

The same rationale is used by Fibre Channel class 3 service. Frames are streamed solely on the basis of a rudimentary flow control mechanism. In the case of Fibre Channel class 3, flow control is implemented via buffer credits (receiver readys), whereas UDP may rely on 802.3x. In practice, acknowledgment of delivery is not required because the network carrying the data is typically a contained, high-speed infrastructure with a very low bit error rate. For storage applications in particular, assumptions that the communicating devices are ready to receive data are usually correct. Both adapter card interfaces and disk controllers typically have sufficient buffering and high-speed processors to accept unsolicited frames. In addition, the storage applications that are driving the data movement have conditioned the lower layers for the transmit or receipt of data. An initiator that has issued a SCSI read from disk, for example, will expect to see frames shortly after the read is issued. In this respect, storage transactions differ significantly from normal user messaging traffic in IP networks. User workstations often receive unsolicited traffic at random (for example, e-mail or unsolicited network messages).

The success of Fibre Channel class 3 service in providing reliable data delivery despite the lack of acknowledgments or sophisticated flow control has established the precedent for UDP/IP for data center storage networking. As with Fibre Channel class 3, however, the caveats of reliable infrastructure and adequate bandwidth allocation apply. Both connectionless implementations require due diligence in SAN design, selection of network components, and quality end systems. Given a stable and properly designed network, however, UDP can offer a significant performance advantage and requires few CPU resources.

6.1.2 UDP Port Numbers

Both UDP and TCP facilitate multiple transactions over IP by assigning port numbers to specific upper layer applications. A port number is a 16-bit integer contained in the UDP or TCP header. A user, for example, may have several Hypertext Transport Protocol (HTTP) sessions open in a Web browser and may simultaneously initiate file downloads. As shown in Figure 6–1, a port number allows the receiving workstation to sort the incoming data frames and to forward the appropriate data to the upper layer application associated with that port number.

In this example, a workstation is running a Trivial File Transfer Protocol (TFTP) application and an SNMP application simultaneously. TFTP is associated with UDP port number 69, whereas SNMP is associated with port 161. Incoming UDP datagrams are sorted by port number and are forwarded to the appropriate upper layer application.

Aside from facilitating concurrent transactions, port numbers may be assigned to standard applications commonly run in IP environments. Well-known port numbers such as 161 for SNMP range from 0 to 1,023. Regardless of the host operating system or platform, datagrams sent to a well-known

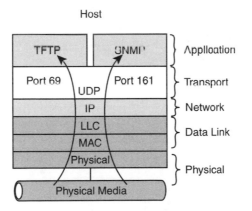

Figure 6–1 UDP transactions for the Trivial File Transfer Protocol and SNMP via port numbers.

port number will be forwarded to a fixed application. In addition to well-known port numbers, a range of registered numbers from 1,024 to 49,151 are maintained by ICANN. The remaining range of port numbers between 49,152 and 65,353 are dynamically assigned as other applications utilize TCP or UDP services. These ephemeral port numbers are active only for the duration of a transaction and then are made available to the pool of private port numbers.

6.1.3 UDP Header

In an IP datagram, the UDP header follows the IP header information and has two components. The UDP header is 8 bytes in length. As shown in Figure 6–2, the UDP header has source and destination port numbers that associate the datagram with specific upper layer applications. The UDP length bytes indicate the length of the UDP portion of the datagram, header plus data. The 16-bit checksum is run against both header and data, and thus provides a data integrity check that the IP header checksum does not.

The duplication of IP address information in the UDP pseudo header allows the UDP layer to verify that the datagram was delivered to the intended destination. Otherwise, this information would be contained only in the IP header, which is removed by the IP network layer before the datagram is passed to the UDP transport layer. Because the UDP header lacks sequencing, acknowledgment, window size, and other parameters, it is quickly processed by the transport layer.

6.1.4 UDP for IP Storage Applications

UDP was designed for low-impact datagram service for applications requiring rapid processing and those tolerant of packet loss. An SNMP management application, for example, would simply reissue an SNMP query if the

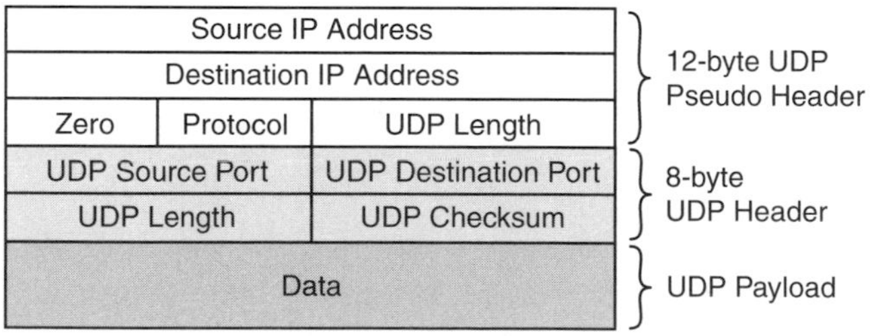

Source IP Address			⎫ 12-byte UDP Pseudo Header
Destination IP Address			
Zero	Protocol	UDP Length	
UDP Source Port		UDP Destination Port	⎫ 8-byte UDP Header
UDP Length		UDP Checksum	
Data			⎫ UDP Payload

Figure 6–2 UDP header and pseudo header information.

destination did not respond within a certain interval. The minimal overhead of UDP, however, allows more compact design for end devices (for example, network devices managed via SNMP) and less network traffic, because no session establishment or acknowledgments are required.

In the more than 20 years since UDP was standardized (RFC 768, 1980), significant improvements have been made in network equipment that, at least for data center environments, have greatly enhanced data integrity at the link layer. The low bit error rate of Gigabit Ethernet systems and 802.3x flow control now enables deployment of UDP-based applications with less concern for packet loss. Until TCP overhead is resolved by off-load engines, UDP is therefore a viable means of enhancing performance for IP storage applications.

UDP's lack of integrated flow control and recovery, however, makes it unsuitable for wide area storage applications and the Internet. Slower WAN links and potential congestion would generate excessive retransmissions by upper layer protocols and thus voids the performance advantage that UDP offers. As we see in the following chapters, a balance between high-performance UDP/IP at the local environment with TCP/IP for wide area crossings offers an optimal solution for a variety of IP-based storage applications.

6.2 Chapter Summary

Layer 4—UDP
- UDP is a streamlined transport layer protocol.

- UDP incurs minimal CPU overhead and offers higher performance.

Connectionless Service
- UDP requires no session establishment prior to data transmission.

- Delivery of UDP datagrams is unacknowledged by the recipient.

- Lack of flow control makes UDP dependent on link-layer services such as 802.3x.

- UDP with 802.3x flow control is analogous to class 3 Fibre Channel service.

- In the event of packet loss, upper layer applications must recover or retransmit.

UDP Port Numbers

- UDP provides identifying port numbers that associate transactions with specific upper layer applications.

- Port numbers for both UDP and TCP are 16-bit integers.

- Assignment of port numbers also enables concurrent applications over a single IP network link.

UDP Header

- The UDP header contains source and destination port numbers, UDP length, and UDP checksum fields.

- A UDP pseudo header contains source and destination IP addresses to validate proper IP delivery.

UDP for IP Storage Applications

- Advances in network equipment enable UDP to be implemented with minimal packet loss.

- A low bit error rate and 802.3x flow control are prerequisites for reliable UDP use in IP storage environments.

- UDP should be restricted to local storage networks, with TCP for wide area links.

- Until TOEs are widely available, UDP can offer optimal performance for local IP-based SANs.

7 Transmission Control Protocol

ALTHOUGH UDP may be suitable for contained, low-loss networks, additional mechanisms are required to preserve data integrity over potentially unusable networks. TCP is required for IP networks that may be subject to congestion, variable bandwidth, and latencies that may result in dropped packets. This chapter examines the main attributes of TCP and TCP's value for IP storage networking.

7.1 TCP

TCP is a *connection-oriented* transport protocol. Instead of simply pushing data from source to destination, TCP first establishes a transmission connection between the communicating pair and imposes a system of datagram acknowledgments to ensure that each transmission arrives intact. TCP also provides a mechanism to recover from packet loss resulting from failures or network congestion. Although UDP requires attention to local network design to avoid burdening upper layer applications with recovery routines, TCP is engineered to withstand lossy environments, and it takes on the recovery task itself. This removes responsibility from the upper layer applications, but adds complexity to the transport.

Because TCP is optimized for potentially congested networks, it is the protocol of choice for wide area communications and is used extensively in enterprise networks and the Internet. The cost for leveraging TCP/IP's data integrity features, however, is measured in performance. Someone has to do the work. In the case of a TCP/IP driver on a host computer system, the CPU must process the TCP routines as datagrams are transmitted and received, resulting in up to 50 to 80% CPU utilization for intensive, high-speed TCP/IP transactions. In addition, the extra transmissions required for session establishment, acknowledgments, and session teardown place more traffic on the network infrastructure. Without transport layer delivery guarantees provided by TCP/IP, however, the potential burden on the network and host CPUs may be even greater, particularly if upper layer applications were forced into constant error recovery and retransmission of larger units of data.

TCP introduces procedures for establishing communications between two network entities, segmentation of messages for handoff to the IP layer, sequence numbers and acknowledgments to track the transmission of bytes across the link, a ramping algorithm to pace the traffic flow, and recovery routines to handle packet loss through the network. Like UDP, TCP uses port numbers to facilitate communications between upper layer applications. The TCP port number and IP address may be combined to create unique identifiers for abstractions known as *sockets*. A socket represents the end point of a TCP session.

7.1.1 TCP Header

The TCP header is typically 20 bytes in length. Whereas the UDP header includes only source and destination port numbers, length, and checksum, the TCP header includes additional fields for sequencing, flags, window size, and options. As shown in Figure 7–1, the TCP header and data compose a TCP segment packaged in an IP datagram.

For connection establishment and acknowledgments, the IP datagram only requires the TCP header with appropriate fields and flags enabled. No TCP data payload is required. The focal point of TCP-based communications is the sequence number. As shown in Figure 7–2, sequence numbers are 32-bit values that follow the source and destination port numbers in the TCP header. Sequence numbers are used to ensure that bytes are delivered to the receiving application in proper order. The acknowledgment number is based on the sequence number for the bytes received in the last datagram plus one for the next expected sequence number.

The 6 bits used for flags provide a compact means to indicate status of the TCP connection or to initiate an action. The urgent or URG bit signifies

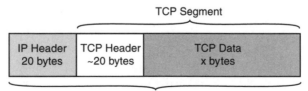

Figure 7–1 TCP segment of an IP datagram.

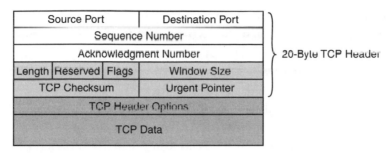

Figure 7–2 TCP header fields.

that the urgent pointer field should be processed so that specific data can be acted on immediately. The acknowledgment or ACK bit is set to indicate that the data identified by the acknowledgment number has been successfully received. The push or PSH bit requests that the sender transmit a segment immediately and alerts the receiving host that data should be forwarded to the upper layer application on receipt. The reset or RST bit is used to reset the TCP connection. The synchronize or SYN bit is used during TCP connection setup to ensure that both parties know the starting point of the sequence numbers they exchange. And finally, the finish or FIN bit indicates that the transmitting host is finished sending data.

The window size field is used for TCP flow control. The window size field is 16 bits, nominally allowing up to approximately 64KB to be transmitted. Because the recipient is responsible for buffering and processing TCP data, it can set a window size optimized for its own processing capabilities.

As with UDP, the TCP checksum is calculated using a pseudo header that includes the source and destination IP addresses as well as TCP header fields and data. Given the greater number of fields to process in each TCP header, the calculation of sequence and acknowledgment numbers, flags to observe, and window size adjustments, it is easy to understand the attraction of TOEs. If this work can be done in silicon on an NIC or a controller, CPU cycles can be spared the constant interruption by transport layer processes. This is the same rationale for the development of VI, although TOEs provide a more seamless integration with existing applications.

7.1.2 Establishing TCP Connections

The creation of a TCP connection between two devices is initiated by an upper layer application. Before an application in one host can actually send data to an application in another, the TCP layers must be synchronized for communication. This initialization of the connection is performed through a three-way handshake between the two parties. In Figure 7–3, this exchange is represented between two hosts acting as a client and a server.

During the first phase of initialization, the initiating host or client sends a TCP header with the SYN flag set. The header indicates the source and destination port numbers (in other words, which application is requested), and an initial sequence number that will be used by the requestor.

During the second phase, the responding host or server returns a TCP header with the SYN flag set and its own initial sequence number. It also acknowledges that it received and has registered the client's initial sequence number by filling in the acknowledgment number field with the client's initial sequence number plus one. The initial SYN sequence from the client thus counts as one sequence number.

During the third phase, the client returns a TCP header with the ACK bit set, and increments the server's initial sequence number by one, putting this value into its own acknowledgment number field. This completes the synchronization of sequence numbers required for the orderly transmission of data between the two devices. Thereafter, the data exchanges between the two hosts will be based on increment and verification of sequence and

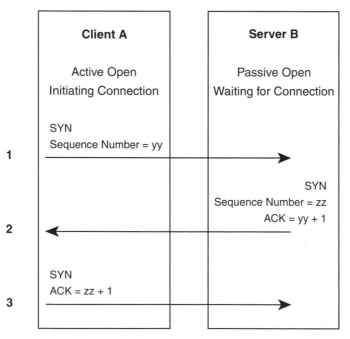

Figure 7–3 Three-way handshake for TCP connection establishment.

acknowledgment numbers to ensure that all bytes of data are properly received and delivered in order.

TCP connections are terminated by the exchange of TCP segments that have the final or FIN bit set. This indicates that no more data will be sent (as in, for example, the completion of a file transfer) and that there is no longer a need to maintain the TCP connection. Resources on both hosts are thus freed for other transactions.

7.1.3 TCP Segment Size

The optional parameters field in the TCP header is used during connection establishment to negotiate the amount of data that may be sent in a single TCP segment. This maximum transmission unit (MTU) option is typically adjusted to accommodate the underlying network to avoid excessive fragmentation. Ethernet, for example, is limited to a 1,500-byte frame per transmission. The optimal TCP segment size should therefore be 1,500 bytes less then IP and TCP header bytes, or ≤ 1,460 bytes in a single segment. In practice, the maximal segment size used by both TCP partners will be the smaller of the two that were advertised during connection setup.

7.1.4 TCP Sliding Window and Congestion Control

TCP is a connection-oriented protcol and thus requires acknowledgment for each TCP segment transmitted. If TCP waited for an acknowledgment before sending the next segment in the queue, however, performance would be adversely affected. To optimize flow control while maintaining acknowledged service, TCP uses a *sliding window* that allows multiple segments to be sent before acknowledgments are received. The window size is negotiated during connection setup and typically reflects the buffering capability of the communicating devices. Larger receive buffers allow more segments to be transmitted en masse before acknowledgments are issued.

If, for example, the window size permits eight segments to be transmitted without acknowledgments, the sending host will transmit all eight segments and then wait for ACKs. If it receives three ACKs, the permissible transmit window will shift to three new segments for transmission while the sender still monitors the five outstanding acknowledgments from the first window position. As each of the remaining five ACKs are received, the window continues shifting to new segments awaiting transmission. The sliding window thus avoids flooding the buffers of the destination device by forcing the transmitter to wait if the maximal number of outstanding ACKs is reached. In Figure 7–4, a window size for three segments is demonstrated. The sliding

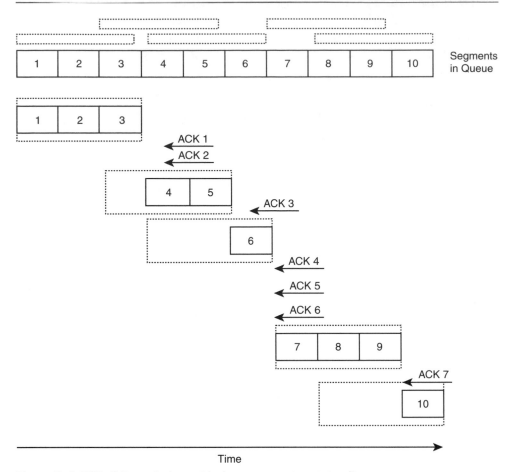

Figure 7–4 TCP sliding window with three segments outstanding.

window scheme provides a base flow control for TCP, but additional routines are required for networks with variable bandwidth and congestion.

Although TCP requires an initial setup between two devices, the logical
connection that is established does not specify which bandwidth is available
for data transport. The underlying network could be a relatively slow WAN
link, an oversubscribed network, or a wide-open switched gigabit infrastructure. Because the network may be unreliable, TCP makes no assumptions
about how quickly it can transmit its data. Instead, it probes the network
capacity by gradually increasing the number of packets sent until congestion is detected or the sliding window value is reached. This ramping algorithm allows TCP to throttle transmissions and adjust for variable network
conditions.

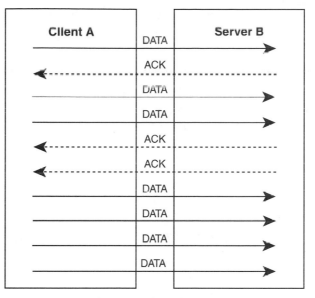

Figure 7–5 TCP slow-start algorithm.

The TCP *slow-start algorithm* (Figure 7–5) tests the rate at which it can inject segments into the network by observing the latency of acknowledgments that are returned by the destination device. The more quickly acknowledgments are received, the more quickly additional segments can be issued. With slow start, a congestion window value (cwnd) is initialized to a value of one segment. As each ACK is received from the destination, the congestion window is incremented exponentially. After the first ACK is received, the congestion window is increased to two segments. When those are acknowleged, the window increases to four segments, and so on, as shown in Figure 7–4.

The sliding window algorithm depends on the buffering capacity of the destination device for how quickly it can process its receive buffers and return acknowledgments. The slow-start algorithm also relies on responses from the destination, but allows the source to limit segment transmissions until confidence in the underlying network is established.

7.1.5 TCP Error Recovery

TCP sequence numbers and acknowledgment numbers enable both sending and receiving devices to monitor the orderly transmission and receipt of data. In a complex IP network, TCP segments may arrive out of order, may be duplicated, or may be discarded by intermediate routers or switches. To complicate matters, TCP is a full-duplex protocol. Applications using TCP/IP transport may be simultaneously transmitting and receiving data over a single connection.

TCP provides multiple mechanisms to deal with the unexpected. Because sequence numbers reflect the exact byte count of transmitted data, they can be used to index back to a point of failure for data retransmission. Likewise, the acknowledgment number carried in an ACK maps to the sequence byte count. The acknowledgment number received by the sending device can indicate whether segments were received out of sequence or not received at all, and which segments need to be reissued.

An IP network may provide multiple paths between source and destination. If individual segments traverse different routes in the network, they may arrive in random order. The TCP layer in the destination host must buffer enough of the inbound segments so that reordering of segments can be performed. If a segment is lost and must be retransmitted, the receiver must also accommodate the tardy data for inclusion into the stream it passes to the upper layer application. In the case of segment duplication, the sequence number plus the destination and source port numbers will reveal the fact that replication has occurred, and TCP will discard the duplicate. All of these techniques make TCP a resilient transport protocol, but also make it top heavy in terms of processing overhead. A stable and well-designed network infrastructure removes some of this burden from TCP (and the CPU that processes it), because although the mechanisms of the recovery algorithms still exist, TCP will not have to perform them very often.

7.1.6 Upper Layer Interface

TCP communications to upper layer applications is accomplished through well-known or dynamically assigned port numbers, as shown in Figure 7–6. The combination of IP addresses and port numbers creates a unique identity for a particular TCP connection and the processes using it. When used in reference to application programming interfaces for network applications, the IP address and port number on each side of a conversation constitute a socket—for example, {tcp, local IP address, local port number, remote IP address, remote port number}.

Because TCP assumes the tasks of orderly delivery of data and error recovery, the upper layer application does not have to incorporate transport-related safeguards. For IP storage applications, rudimentary functions such as SCSI timeout are still required, but the SCSI interface must rely on stable

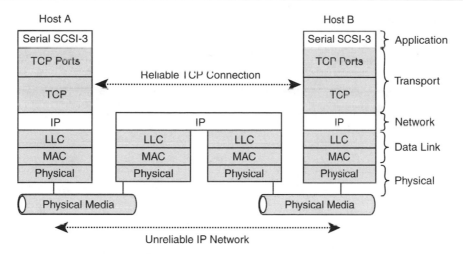

Figure 7–6 TCP end-to-end connection over an unreliable IP network.

data transport at the lower layers. Because TCP ensures reliable transport, minimal disruptions to the upper SCSI-3 layer should occur. This does not mean that the integrity of the IP network is no longer a factor. TCP provides the mechanisms for recovery from errors and for reordering out-of-sequence data, but latency from excessive recovery may quickly percolate up to the application layer. For this reason, the TCP layer itself is no guarantee that storage applications will be immune from poorly designed or oversubscribed IP networks.

7.2 Chapter Summary

TCP

- TCP is a connection-oriented transport protocol.

- TCP initializes a connection between two hosts before data is transferred.

- Data is acknowledged by the recipient.

- TCP provides error recovery and reordering of out-of-sequence segments.

- The TCP/IP stack is CPU intensive for the host system.

TCP Header

- The TCP header is typically 20 bytes in length.

- Source and destination port numbers are used to communicate with specific upper layer applications.

- The ACK flag in the TCP header indicates that acknowledgment numbers are valid.

- The SYN bit is set when a TCP connection is initialized.

- The finish bit is used to tear down a TCP connection when data transfer is complete.

Establishing TCP Connections

- TCP connection establishment is a three-way handshake.

- During connection establishment, both hosts' sequence numbers are initialized to known values.

- Sequence number seeds are constantly incremented to provide unique number ranges for each TCP connection.

TCP Segment Size

- The amount of data per TCP segment is negotiated during connection establishment.

- Segment size is normally set to optimize data transfer over the underlying physical network.

- For Ethernet networks, an optimal segment size is ≤ 1,460 bytes.

TCP Sliding Window and Congestion Control

- Sliding window refers to the transmission of multiple TCP segments before acknowledgments are received.

- The maximal window size is negotiated during connection setup and it reflects the buffering capacity of the communicating devices.

- Receipt of acknowledgments enables additional segments to be sent, up to the maximum allowed by the window parameter.

- TCP slow start prevents TCP from streaming segments onto an unreliable network.

- Slow start monitors the round-trip time through the network via ACKs.

- Slow start initiates a gradual increase in segment transmission rate until the maximal window is reached or network congestion occurs.

- Slow start may impact IP storage applications that use small block sizes.

TCP Error Recovery

- TCP recovery mechanisms provide for retransmission of lost segments, out-of-order delivery, and discard of duplicate segments by the receiver.

- A stable network infrastructure reduces the latency incurred by TCP recovery processes.

Upper Layer Interface

- TCP uses port numbers to communicate with upper layer applications.

- The combination of IP address and port number provides a unique identifier for network application interfaces.

- A TCP socket includes both local and remote IP addresses and port numbers.

- For IP storage applications, network conditions that force TCP recovery mechanisms should be minimized.

8 IP Storage Networking

THE iSCSI, iFCP, AND FCIP PROTOCOLS present alternative means for moving block data over IP networks. For implementation in real products and adoption by real customers, standardization is key. The following chapter discusses the standardization process and examines the technical attributes of each protocol.

8.1 Standards-Based IP Storage Protocols

The development of networked storage solutions based on IP has been driven by both customer demand and vendor initiative. The pull created by customer demand originates in the requirement of enterprise networks to streamline their operations; to reduce acquisition, administrative, and support costs; and to deploy viable storage solutions that do not require extensive training or expertise. The push generated by vendors comes from the usual sources—in other words, to exploit new market opportunities and to increase profitability. The two forces of customer needs and vendor opportunism, however, are not easily reconciled. Since the demise of monolithic IT infrastructures that locked customers into proprietary solutions, customers have embraced an open systems world view. New technologies must be standards based, offer multivendor selections, and have demonstrable interoperability.

These customer expectations naturally throw vendors into a state of angst, because they must now find ways to engineer attractive vendor-specific solutions that are nonetheless open, standards compliant, and interoperable with their competitors. As a consequence, standards development and interoperability testing rarely occur in a pristine, vendor-neutral environment. The commitment to open systems architecture is constantly challenged by the competing interests of technology manufacturers themselves. If proprietary interests are too strong and interoperability is inhibited, market adoption in general may be retarded.

IP storage initiatives have evolved on a foundation of previously established standards for Ethernet and IP. Ethernet is standardized in the IEEE 802.3 standard. Gigabit Etherent is standardized in IEEE 802.3z, whereas 10 Gigabit Ethernet is standardized in IEEE 802.3a. IP-related standards are established by the IETF through diverse Requests for Comment (RFCs) that cover a wide range of protocol and management issues. TCP, for example, was standardized in 1981 in RFC 793, whereas UDP was standardized in 1980 in RFC 768. Ethernet and IP, however, are only half the equation for IP storage networking. IP storage technology must also accommodate previously established standards for SCSI, which is the purview of the NCITS T10 Committee. Because IP storage solutions may also provide gateways to Fibre Channel storage devices, attention must be given to previously established standards for the FCP (NCITS T10) and Fibre Channel transport (NCITS T11).

Standards provide guideposts for technology development, with the ideal goal of product interoperability. The guideposts are not supposed to be moved; in other words, a new technology should not require changes to existing standards. In the case of IP-based storage networking, the two very distinct boundaries of IP internetworking (IETF) and SCSI storage (NCITS) must be brought together without collision or damage to either side. This requires that the IP storage advocates have expertise in both IP and storage technologies, and must avoid inadvertantly knocking over guideposts in their rush to the market. Although IP storage is relatively new, there are already several instances in which some potential conflicts between existing and proposed standards have occurred. This has been primarily the result of the entry of IP networking vendors who, having dominated the data communications world, are still learning the complexities of storage requirements.

8.1.1 The IETF and IPS Work Group

The IETF is a remarkable vehicle for the development of standards and technology. It is international in scope, is open to any interested individual, maintains no formal membership list, fosters common intellectual property, and derives its authority by the collective consensus of the participants and the Internet technical community. Although IETF-generated standards have no government or official stamp of approval, standardized RFCs have tremendous influence, and no vendor wishing to stay in business can afford to ignore them. Vendor data sheets, in fact, often carry long laundry lists of the RFCs they have implemented in their products to build customer confidence in their commitment to open standards. This reflects the authority the IETF has established in the marketplace and the reality that although the customer may in the end buy from only one vendor, the customer nonetheless demands standards compliance should changes be desired.

The IETF has eight functional areas for standards and technology development. These include applications, Internet, operations and management, routing, security, sub-ip, transport, and user services. Each functional area is led by volunteer area directors who monitor the activity of the work groups. Because a single subject area may be fairly complex, multiple work groups may be focused on specific issues. Activities of individual work groups are monitored by work group chairs. In the case of IP-based storage networking, the IPS Work Group was created to formulate protocols for block storage data over IP.

IETF activity in general is supposed to be technology focused and vendor neutral. Lacking the bureaucracy of dues, official membership lists, and prerequisites for participation, any individual can contribute to the technical discussion or submit an Internet draft for review. Although this would seemingly promote trivial submissions, the collective peer pressure by other technologists attempts to discourage abuse of the discussion and review processes.

The real work of standards development occurs in the work groups, typically via Internet mailing lists or reflectors. The IPS reflector (ips@ece.cmu.edu), for example, contains thousands of submissions relating to IP storage issues. Each exchange over a specific technical problem generates a discussion thread that hopefully leads to a solution. In some cases, issues that cannot be readily resolved are, by consensus, shelved for future review. The unspoken social code for the reflector discussions obliges each participant to be current with the subject at hand. There is little tolerance for a new participant who naively raises a point that had been thoroughly discussed and resolved several hundred e-mail messages ago.

During the early phases of standards development, a work group may labor over one or more Internet drafts. As the collective discussion works through the issues associated with an Internet Draft, revised drafts are submitted. The Internet Draft is a work in progress that, if the effort is successful, may become a standardized RFC.

Substantive discussions on working group activity and Internet Drafts are made via reflector discussions and during face to face meetings of the working group participants. Determining consensus on issues may be accomplished through a show of hands or less overt displays, such as humming or other noise making. All decisions are ratified on the working group mailing lists in order to include participants absent from the face to face meetings. Although an IETF working group is composed of individual volunteer technologists such as academics, researchers, end users, consultants and engineers, participants may also reflect the interests of their companies. This creates an underlying contradiction between the vendor-neutral focus of the IETF and the agendas that specific vendors may be pursuing within the IETF. On balance, however, vendor influence is held in check by the collective conscience of the working group and, in some cases, intervention by the working group chair(s) or the Area Director.

The IETF IP Storage working group charter currently includes three main IP storage protocols: Fibre Channel over IP (FCIP), Internet Fibre Channel Protocol (iFCP) and Internet SCSI (iSCSI). In addition, a number of Internet Drafts for management and other issues are being worked, including the iSNS and IP storage Management Information Base (MIB) proposals. In the following sections we review the FCIP, iFCP, and iSCSI protocols, and how each contributes to IP storage networking solutions.

8.2 Fibre Channel Over IP

FCIP is a means of encapsulating Fibre Channel frames within TCP/IP specifically for linking Fibre Channel SANs over wide areas. Among the IP storage protocols under development in the IPS Work Group, FCIP therefore has the least IP content. Instead of a native IP connection between individual storage devices, FCIP provides IP connections between Fibre Channel SAN islands. As shown in Figure 8–1, IP addresses and TCP connections are used only at the FCIP tunneling devices at each end point of the IP network cloud.

The FCIP device could be a stand-alone box, an FCIP blade installed in an IP router, or an FCIP port integrated into a Fibre Channel switch. In this example, the FCIP device is depicted as a stand-alone unit that connects to the IP network on one port and a Fibre Channel switch on another.

Each IP network connection on either side of the cloud is identified by an IP address and a TCP/IP connection between the two FCIP devices. When a Fibre Channel node on one SAN island needs to communicate with a Fibre Channel node on the remote SAN island, the FCIP device encapsulates the entire Fibre Channel frame in TCP/IP and sends it across the IP network. At the receiving end, the IP and TCP headers are removed, and a native Fibre Channel frame is delivered to the destination Fibre Channel node through one or more switches. The existence of the FCIP devices and IP cloud is transparent to the Fibre Channel switches, whereas the Fibre Channel content buried in the IP datagram is transparent to the IP network.

TCP is required for transit across the IP tunnel to enforce in-order delivery of data and congestion control. The two FCIP devices use the TCP connection

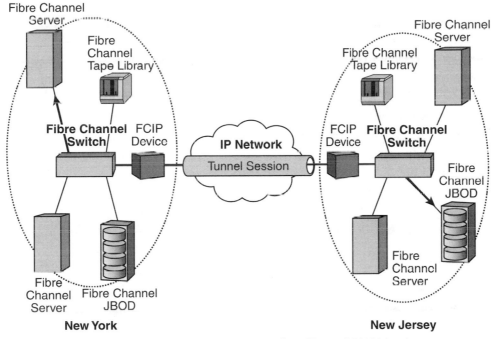

Figure 8–1 FCIP tunneling between two separate Fibre Channel SAN islands.

to form a virtual interswitch link between them and can pass Fibre Channel messages (for example, class F) as well as data.

The FCIP specification makes a few assumptions about the integrity of the wide area link, including a low bit error rate and performance adequate for storage applications such as backup or remote mirroring. It could be a dedicated point-to-point line or some fraction of shared bandwidth provided by a carrier. The WAN link speed could be a relatively slow OC-3 (155 Mps) or fast OC-48 (2.5 Gps), depending on the customer's budget and needs. Line quality, transmission latency, class of IP routers or intermediate switches, bandwidth contention, and other factors determine how much work TCP has to do to maintain data integrity. This in turn determines whether the effects of transport across the WAN link between SAN islands triggers additional recovery mechanisms at the Fibre Channel layer.

8.2.1 FCIP and Timeout Values

Because FCIP provides simple tunneling of Fibre Channel frames, all the rules of Fibre Channel communication are in force. This includes Fibre Channel timeout values that are normally accommodated easily in a well-designed Fibre Channel SAN. The error detect timeout value (E_D_TOV) is used to monitor the orderly flow of frames within a Fibre Channel sequence. If the next frame within a sequence cannot be issued within the E_D_TOV window, a sequence error is generated, resulting in the retransmission of the entire sequence of frames. By default, the E_D_TOV value is ten seconds, although in practice the Fibre Channel fabric switch may establish its own lower E_D_TOV value during port login. A two-second error window is fairly wide for local gigabit networks, but may be activated when spanning between SAN islands over long distances or congested IP networks.

In addition to E_D_TOV, Fibre Channel standards impose a longer timeout value known as the *resource allocation timeout value* (R_A_TOV), also known as the *really awful timeout value* by engineers who have attempted to build large Fibre Channel fabrics. The R_A_TOV is, by default, ten seconds. It differs from the error detect function in that its focus is on the resources (Fibre Channel nodes and switch ports) that have been the victims of communication failures. After a failure, the Fibre Channel resources must not resume operation until all outstanding transmissions up to the detected error are completed. Frames in transit across the fabric must have the opportunity to be delivered or dropped by the fabric. A suspension of ten seconds' duration is an eternity at gigabit speeds, but at least it accomplishes the goal of cleansing the fabric of the effects of a sequence or link service error.

To tunnel Fibre Channel traffic transparently, FCIP must accommodate the E_D_TOV and R_A_TOV windows of Fibre Channel, as well as the TCP retransmission timer values. Because TCP was not originally engineered for gigabit transports, its acknowledgment timeout may be measured in minutes. This creates a potential disconnect between expected performance and recovery between the TCP/IP wrapper and the Fibre Channel payload unless the TCP variables are included in the Fibre Channel boundaries. If, for example, the Fibre Channel layer detected a sequence error and initiated sequence retransmission, TCP might still be attempting to deliver frames that are part of the aborted sequence long after the configured R_A_TOV had expired.

8.2.2 FCIP SAN Interfaces

A major issue for FCIP is how the FCIP bridge devices interface with the Fibre Channel SANs to which they join. FCIP allows for a Fibre Channel backbone (FC_BB) interface as well as the standard fabric E_Port switch interface. Because FC_BB is still under construction, initial implementations have used E_Port connectivity and the Fibre Channel FSPF routing protocol.

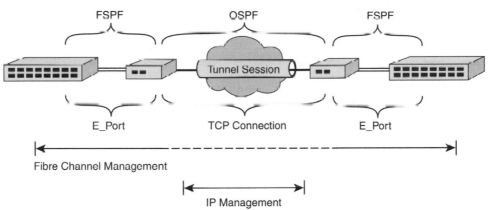

Figure 8–2 FCIP E_Port connectivity and FSPF protocol to each SAN island.

This aligns with Fibre Channel switch standards requirements (FC-SW-2) for building fabrics with switch-to-switch connectivity, and results in the two SAN islands being merged into one logical SAN. From the standpoint of E_Port requirements, the actual distance being spanned is irrelevant as long as timeout values are observed. As shown in Figure 8–2, the two Fibre Channel switches see each other as part of one integrated fabric, exchange SNS information, and maintain their routes to one another as if colocated within a single data center. This transparency is maintained as long as the FCIP tunnel is stable.

What happens if the FCIP tunnel collapses? The Fibre Channel switches on each side of the WAN link will disable the appropriate E_Ports facing the FCIP devices, just as if a fiber-optic cable had been unplugged between two colocated fabric switches. Each fabric switch reestablishes its own isolated SAN island and sends an SCN state change notification to the relevant end nodes that external resources are unavailable. Because each SAN island now has its own principal switch, fabric addressing may be reassigned. Even after the FCIP devices recreate the tunnel between them, however, there is no automatic recovery of the connection between the two remote Fibre Channel switches. The fact that the tunnel has been restored does not automatically prompt either switch to seek out its former partner. Without some intervention by the FCIP devices themselves, the SANs will remain isolated until one of the fabric switches is rebooted. By contrast, in a homogeneous IP network, the IP routers would automatically recover failed links or establish alternate routes through the network.

8.2.3 FCIP Error Handling

Because FCIP is an opaque transport and has no visibility to the content of Fibre Channel frames, it is obliged to pass whatever is generated by one SAN island to its destination SAN without error checking at the Fibre Channel layer. This includes low-level error conditions such as CRC errors, which are passed intact from source to destination, as well as erroneous conditions at the switch routing (FSPF) level. Sporadic errors, for example, that originate on a rogue switch port on one SAN installation can spill onto the other SANs joined by FCIP. The two SAN islands thus have the benefit of communication over long distances, but are also exposed to potential contamination if one SAN island begins generating excessive errors.

FCIP can only assume responsibility for errors generated over the IP network. By FCIP specification, any frame error introduced in the FCIP encapsulation layer would result in the frame being dropped by the receiving FCIP device. This would prevent an IP-generated error not detected by the TCP layer from being propagated on the destination Fibre Channel SAN.

FCIP devices do not perform IP routing or layer 3 switching. Two FCIP devices separated by an IP network will appear simply as TCP end points. Any IP routing required across the cloud is the responsibility of the intervening IP routers or other carrier equipment. The OSPF network shown in Figure 8–2 is thus provided by the IP network infrastructure, not the FCIP devices attached to it.

In the absence of encapsulated Fibre Channel traffic, the FCIP devices maintain active sessions between themselves via TCP keep-alive messages. The TCP keep-alive option may be problematic, because the TCP connection may be dropped even if the TCP end points are healthy. If an intermediate IP router temporarily loses connection as a keep-alive message is sent, for example, the connection between the FCIP devices may be broken even if the router recovers quickly. In addition, although the keep-alive frequency is configurable, the default is two hours. For storage applications, the value needs to be in the seconds or lower range. FCIP devices may also exchange FCIP-specific commands to expedite detection of lost connections. Extended link service (ELS) exchanges allow the corresponding FCIP devices to verify their connectivity and can be used to trigger reestablishment of TCP connections when required.

In all the potential connection error conditions, the FCIP specification forbids retransmitting of FCIP frames from a previous connection once the new connection is reestablished. This prevents frame duplication at the receiving

Fibre Channel device end and thus avoids even lengthier recovery processes or data corruption.

8.2.4 FCIP Flow Control

Because FCIP straddles both Fibre Channel and IP, it must contend with potential congestion originating on either side. A mismatch in line speeds between Fibre Channel and the IP network or an inefficient implementation of the FCIP engine may make the FCIP device itself a bottleneck.

To deal with potential congestion on the IP side, FCIP may leverage established flow control methods for TCP. Although FCIP does not specify a particular implementation, using the standard TCP sliding window would be an obvious choice, including advertisement of a zero window under especially congested conditions at the destination Fibre Channel SAN. If, for example, a receiving Fibre Channel switch does not have sufficient buffering to accept inbound frames from the FCIP device, the FCIP device could "zero window" its partner across the cloud and hold off additional transmission.

Likewise, if a Fibre Channel switch is sending more Fibre Channel frames to the FCIP device than it can process across the IP network, it could manipulate buffer credits to slow the rate of frame transmission by the originating Fibre Channel switch.

Given comparable line speeds on both IP and Fibre Channel sides, normal operation of an FCIP pair would involve both Fibre Channel flow control and TCP flow control mechanisms, particularly for bursty traffic patterns generated by Fibre Channel SAN applications. The worst-case scenarios are therefore presented by inadequate bandwidth across the IP network (requiring Fibre Channel flow control to hold off the sender) and congested conditions on the destination SAN (requiring TCP flow control to hold off the far FCIP device). These mechanisms are mutually dependent, because use of TCP flow control at one end may trigger Fibre Channel flow control at the other.

8.2.5 FCIP Quality of Service

For QoS over the IP network, FCIP may leverage enhancements to the IP header interpretation. The differentiated services architecture (DiffServ) redefines the Type of Service (TOS) field in the IP header to provide a differentiated services code point (DSCP) used for QoS delivery. DSCP defines a per-hop behavior in routers and switches that form the IP network. For example, an IP router may interpret a specific DSCP to mean issue priority frames in the same order as received, and hold back or drop lesser priority frames. Because native Fibre Channel assumes full bandwidth availability, the DSCP field should be set for expedited forwarding to ensure timely delivery across the IP network. The use of DiffServ typically requires negotiation with the providers of the IP network and incurs a premium price for the service. MPLS may also be used to achieve QoS. A review of DiffServs and MPLS is presented in Chapter 11.

8.2.6 FCIP Framing

As shown in Figure 8–3, the FCIP frame is a straightforward encapsulation of the Fibre Channel frame. The Fibre Channel header, SOF, and EOF delimiters; Fibre Channel CRC; and Fibre Channel data are not modified or manipulated by FCIP but are simply carried intact. FCIP uses a Fibre Channel encapsulation frame header that includes identifier fields for the FCIP protocol and version level. The most significant field in the encapsulation frame header is the frame length value, which includes the length of the entire Fibre Channel frame plus the encapsulation header. This can be used to verify the receipt of the entire Fibre Channel frame.

As a receiving FCIP device is handed FCIP frames by the underlying TCP layer, the FCIP device can further verify orderly delivery by monitoring the Fibre Channel EOF and SOF that flank the Fibre Channel frame (Figure 8–4).

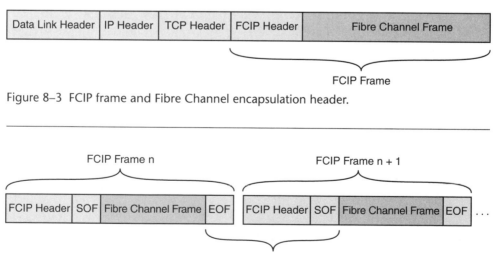

Figure 8–3 FCIP frame and Fibre Channel encapsulation header.

Figure 8–4 Validating proper frame sequencing by monitoring EOF and SOF, and the FCIP frame length.

Validating EOF, SOF, and the FCIP frame length field ensures that the sending and receiving FCIP devices on either side of the IP network are in sync.

8.2.7 FCIP Issues

FCIP is formulated to perform a specific and fairly limited task: to join existing Fibre Channel SANs using TCP/IP transport. From the standpoint of Fibre Channel switch proponents, this is a laudable goal because it preserves native Fibre Channel SANs at the end points. For this reason, the initial offerings by Fibre Channel vendors into the IP space have focused on FCIP tunneling. By preserving a Fibre Channel switch infrastructure, however, FCIP inherits the problems associated with Fibre Channel fabrics in terms of vulnerability to fabricwide disturbances, interoperability, scalability, and management. In addition, because FCIP does not provide a migration path to native IP SANs, its future viability is bound to the fortunes of Fibre Channel. As storage arrays with native Gigabit Ethernet and IP storage stacks come to market, there will be a decreasing requirement for protocols that simply bridge legacy Fibre Channel switches.

These considerations aside, FCIP must address issues common to all tunneling strategies as well as strike a balance between Fibre Channel and TCP/IP requirements. In FCIP's encapsulation scheme, the TCP/IP component ends at the boundary of the Fibre Channel network. Because Fibre Channel frames are shipped through an opaque pipe, IP network management tools cannot penetrate to the level of individual Fibre Channel conversations. This is not the case with iFCP and iSCSI, which can map IP down to the storage end devices. Fibre Channel management likewise has no awareness of the FCIP pipe, which makes it difficult to identify problems that may actually originate within the FCIP transit. Management of FCIP environments thus requires correlation of conditions reported by two different management systems, neither one of which may have the means to pinpoint a problem accurately. A Fibre Channel management platform, for example, may report excessive retransmissions, but, being oblivious to the FCIP tunnel, cannot specify whether the problem originates on the far Fibre Channel switch or within some intervening (FCIP) device.

Finessing both TCP and Fibre Channel timeout values to avoid inadvertant disconnects or errors is also a challenge for FCIP implementations. Providing comparable bandwidth between the two networks helps to alleviate this issue, but FCIP installations, because of budget considerations or vendor limitations, commonly use much slower speed shared WAN links vis-à-vis

Fibre Channel's dedicated gigabit or 2Gb link speeds. Although TCP parameters may be set on the FCIP devices, the ability to massage Fibre Channel timeout values may be limited because of vendor switch design. Link speed mismatch requires additional manual intervention, testing, and reconfiguration until the FCIP solution is properly tuned.

Finally, if no means are provided to recover from a temporary disruption to the TCP connection between the FCIP devices on either side of an IP network, an extended fabric joined by FCIP is always vulnerable to splitting into two separate SAN islands. From a business continuance standpoint, this presents a major obstacle to FCIP-based solutions. For disaster recovery or remote mirroring applications that require wide area connectivity, stability of the SAN interconnect is essential. Rebooting Fibre Channel switches is not normally desirable under any conditions.

8.3 Internet Fibre Channel Protocol

iFCP is a gateway-to-gateway protocol for providing Fibre Channel fabric services to Fibre Channel end devices over a TCP/IP network. Like FCIP and iSCSI, iFCP uses TCP for congestion control, error detection, and recovery. Unlike FCIP, iFCP does not simply join Fibre Channel fabrics over distance, but can be used in place of Fibre Channel fabrics to provide a more integrated IP storage solution. Fibre Channel storage arrays, HBAs, routers, switches, and hubs can be plugged directly into iFCP storage switches. iFCP leverages the work already done by NCITS T10 and T11 on FC-4 FCP and associated fabric services. This enables a faster time-to-market solution and facilitates interoperability with Fibre Channel end devices and storage applications already designed for Fibre Channel SANs. Like iSCSI, iFCP is a protocol stack that can be implemented in an Gigabit Ethernet IP storage NIC, or can be integrated into a storage controller interface. This is advantageous for accommodating both Fibre Channel end devices and native IP storage in a single IP SAN.

8.3.1 iFCP Network Architecture

As shown in Figure 8–5, an iFCP implementation accommodates Fibre Channel end devices by emulating an interface to an expected F_Port (Fibre Channel switch) connection. At the iFCP layer, a Fibre Channel device's 24-bit fabric address is mapped to a unique IP address, providing native IP addressing for individual Fibre Channel initiators and targets. In place of the

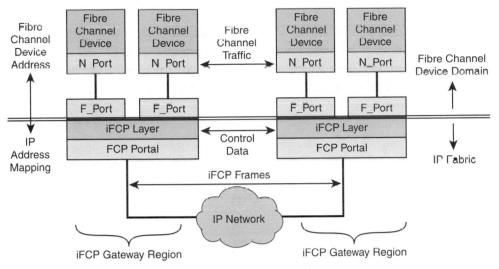

Figure 8–5 A simple IP fabric based on the iFCP protocol.

Fibre Channel lower layer transport (FC-2), iFCP substitutes TCP/IP for reliable transmission over the IP network.

Connectivity to Fibre Channel devices can also be provided through loop (FL_Port) or switch interconnect (E_Port) attachment between an iFCP gateway and a Fibre Channel switch. This feature allows existing SAN islands to be brought into an IP infrastructure, and still provides discrete IP address mapping for individual Fibre Channel devices attached to the Fibre Channel switch.

The IP network in this case could be a WAN or MAN, but could also be a local data center composed of Gigabit Ethernet switches. In the latter case, the IP fabric is a direct substitution for a Fibre Channel fabric and enables the use of more familiar Gigabit Ethernet and IP technologies. This is one reason iFCP did not initially receive a warm reception by Fibre Channel switch vendors. It provides the flexibility of connecting Fibre Channel end devices as well as switches, but can also displace Fibre Channel switches as the preferred interconnect.

A unique contribution of iFCP is the ability to create gateway regions that, while enabling communications between multiple sets of Fibre Channel end devices, also isolate potential disruptions to the troublesome region. The iFCP gateway enables communication between N_Ports across an IP network. Because the gateway itself is handling discrete conversations among the individual Fibre Channel end devices, there is no need for traditional class F Fibre Channel switch-to-switch communication. Those control functions are performed using iFCP and IP methods. Consequently, if an iFCP gateway fronts a gateway region composed of one or more local Fibre Channel switches, Fibre Channel switch-to-switch messages need not be passed across the IP network to other gateway regions. Disruptive behavior within the local Fibre Channel SAN is isolated to that gateway region alone. This ensures the stability of the IP fabric in general, at least with regard to Fibre Channel fabric-inspired disruptions.

Because iFCP performs individual Fibre Channel address-to-IP address mapping, it also overcomes the limitations of FCIP point-to-point tunneling. As shown in Figure 8–6, iFCP enables any-to-any communication over the IP fabric by leveraging standard IP routing.

In contrast to tunneling, iFCP establishes TCP/IP connections between individual Fibre Channel devices. During tunneling, congestion in a TCP/IP connection affects all communications between two SAN islands. With iFCP,

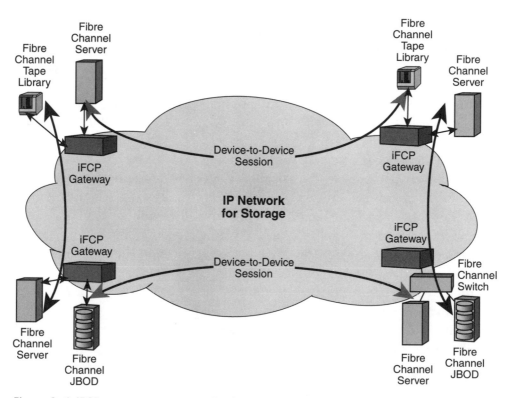

Figure 8–6 iFCP any-to-any communication across an IP-routed network.

congestion may only affect a single communicating pair of Fibre Channel devices.

This strategy provides flexibility in device deployment for WAN, MAN, and local IP SAN configurations, and enables advanced disaster recovery implementations such as data replication between multiple sites. The mechanisms for device discovery and authorization within an extended iFCP network are discussed in Chapter 9.

8.3.2 iFCP Addressing

The iFCP specification defines two addressing techniques for representing the 24-bit Fibre Channel address of end devices: address transparent mode and address translation mode. In address transparent mode, conventional Fibre Channel address rules are followed for assigning unique 24-bit N_Port addresses throughout a Fibre Channel fabric. In standard Fibre Channel, the fabric switch is responsible for issuing a unique N_Port address during fabric login. As shown in Figure 8–7, the Fibre Channel address has three 8-bit components, including the domain ID, area ID, and port ID.

In standard Fibre Channel, each switch in a fabric has an assigned domain ID that, less the reserved addresses, allows for as many as 239 unique domain IDs in a single fabric. This is what determines the theoretical maximum size, in terms of number of Fibre Channel switches, of an extended Fibre Channel network. Each switch has two remaining bytes of addressing (area and port), which provide a 65,000 block of addresses that can be assigned to individual N_Ports as they log in to the switch. The combination of domain ID and concatenated area/port IDs establishes a unique 24-bit identity for each attached Fibre Channel device. The domain ID signifies to which switch the device is attached, and the area/port ID indicates on which switch port the device is connected.

Fibre Channel addressing is deliberately dynamic. If a Fibre Channel end device is unplugged from one switch port and reinserted into a different port, it will acquire a new 24-bit N_Port address. The domain ID component will remain the same (because it is still on the same switch), but the area/port

Fibre Channel N_Port Address

Figure 8–7 Conventional Fibre Channel addressing.

bytes will change. This is done to enable automatic, self-administered addressing in a Fibre Channel network. Although the N_Port address that is used for routing within the fabric may change, the device still has a globally unique identity via its 64-bit WWN. For routing purposes, however, it is much easier to parse a 24-bit field than a 64-bit one.

Fibre Channel N_Port addresses are used within Fibre Channel frames to indicate source and destination addressing. The destination address (D_ID) and source address (S_ID) fields in the Fibre Channel frame header represent the two sides of a transaction. At the receiving end, the frame contents, including the WWN, are processed at the upper layers to verify the integrity of the exchange.

The iFCP address transparent mode accepts the normal Fibre Channel address scheme, which allows it to spoof a conventional Fibre Channel fabric. The penalty for following standard addressing, however, is that each iFCP gateway consumes at least one block of 65,000 addresses, even if only a few are used for active devices. This is the same penalty that Fibre Channel switches impose. In addition, traditional Fibre Channel addressing assumes that the storage network is a single fabric. If additional switches or a separate fabric are added to the network, they must undergo new domain ID assignment and force their attached devices to log in again for new N_Port addresses. This requirement is already creating problems for large Fibre Channel fabrics of 20 or more switches and is imposing lengthy convergence times to stablize the fabric.

To reduce disruption and allow IP-based SANs to scale beyond Fibre Channel limits, iFCP also allows for address translation mode. In address translation mode, an iFCP gateway assigns 24-bit N_Port addresses to its locally attached devices as usual. For local transactions on the same iFCP gateway, the functionality is the same as a Fibre Channel switch. Unlike a Fibre Channel switch, however, the local iFCP gateway also assigns N_Port addresses to remote devices, making them appear as a local resource. The proxied addresses are used only within the bounds of the local iFCP gateway and are not propagated across the IP SAN. The iFCP gateway itself translates between proxied Fibre Channel addresses and actual remote Fibre Channel addresses, substituting the required Fibre Channel D_ID in the frame header for the proxied D_ID as required for remote transactions. Address translation mode requires more processing by the iFCP gateway, but avoids the problems posed by fabricwide addressing. It also allows local SANs to insert into the IP storage network without disruption.

The IP address mapping for network traffic is performed by the iFCP gateway and is included in the IP frame header. As shown in Figure 8–8, the iFCP gateway maintains a lookup table to map N_Port addresses to IP addresses. If address translation mode is used, the lookup table will also include a mapping of proxied (alias) N_Port addresses and remote N_Port addresses.

In this example, the domain component "80" of the Fibre Channel D_ID address tells the iFCP gateway that this Fibre Channel frame is intended for a proxied N_Port address that actually resides somewhere in the remote IP SAN. The iFCP gateway performs an address lookup that produces both the actual N_Port address and its associated IP address. As the iFCP frame is built, the actual N_Port address is inserted into the Fibre Channel frame header, and the IP destination address is inserted into the IP frame header. The trick, of course, is to do this very quickly in silicon and avoid processing latency. During performance testing, iFCP has been demonstrated at gigabit wire speed, even with the overhead of address translation.

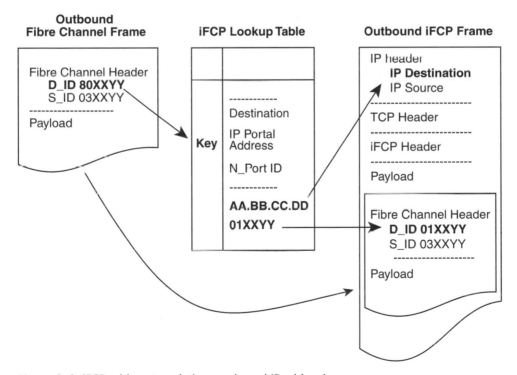

Figure 8–8 iFCP address translation mode and IP addressing.

8.3.3 iFCP Fabric Service Emulation

The iFCP protocol is engineered to support standard Fibre Channel end devices as well as native iFCP devices. Because an iFCP gateway is a direct replacement for a Fibre Channel switch and allows attachment of Fibre Channel N_Ports, it must emulate standard fabric services such as login, SNS registration, and ELS. In addition, the iFCP gateway must intercept Fibre Channel requests such as port login (PLOGI) and must establish the necessary TCP/IP connection with the appropriate destination iFCP gateway.

As shown in Figure 8–9, when a locally attached Fibre Channel device sends a PLOGI to a target, the iFCP gateway must first determine whether the target is locally attached or across the IP SAN.

If the PLOGI is destined for a locally attached device, the iFCP gateway forwards it to the appropriate port. If the PLOGI is addressed to a remote resource, the iFCP gateway will set up a TCP/IP connection to the proper destination iFCP gateway and will send the PLOGI request in an iFCP frame. Another step that may be performed in PLOGI processing is modification of the maximum data field size, which is normally negotiated between two Fibre Channel devices. The iFCP gateway may intercept and modify the proffered maximal data size to be less than 1,500 bytes so that Fibre Channel frames can be more easily accommodated in Ethernet networks without excessive fragmentation.

Interception is also required for standard Fibre Channel SNS queries. An iFCP gateway may have an integrated name server function, or a combination of internal and external name server resources. As covered in more detail in Chapter 9, an external iSNS server may provide name service

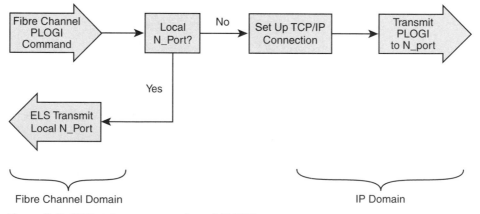

Figure 8–9 iFCP gateway processing of PLOGI.

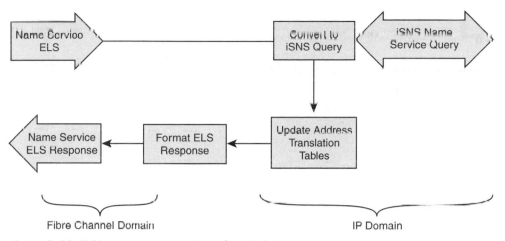

Figure 8–10 iFCP gateway processing of an SNS request.

functions throughout an IP SAN, analogous to DNS servers in IP internetworking. Normally, when a Fibre Channel end device such as an initiator queries a switch SNS service, the switch will return a list of Fibre Channel addresses for available SCSI-3 targets. An iFCP gateway emulates this service, but will internally convert the Fibre Channel SNS request into an iSNS query. When the iSNS server responds with permissible targets, the iFCP gateway records the appropriate Fibre Channel and IP addresses for its own translation table, and formats the SNS response for the initiator. As shown in Figure 8–10, this process allows the iFCP gateway to update the address translation table for further communications (for example, PLOGI) between the initiator and the potential targets.

For all Fibre Channel fabric services, iFCP uses the standardized well-known addresses to which a Fibre Channel end device may send requests. The SNS service, for example, resides at x'FF FF FC' in both a traditional Fibre Channel switch and an iFCP gateway that supports direct attachment of Fibre Channel devices.

8.3.4 iFCP and TCP Connection Control

An iFCP gateway device appears as a Fibre Channel switch to its attached Fibre Channel end nodes. The FCP portal or interface to the IP network, however, does not require Fibre Channel interswitch services or the FSPF routing protocol. Instead, an iFCP gateway will establish TCP/IP connections to other iFCP gateways across the cloud and will use IP routing such as OSPF to navigate the network.

Once they have discovered each other via an iSNS server, the iFCP gateways to the IP network may establish multiple TCP/IP connections between themselves. The TCP connections are managed by TCP link service messages that are exchanged between the iFCP gateways. TCP/IP connections are either bound, meaning active N_Port traffic is passing through the TCP connection, or unbound, in which case the TCP connection is alive but no storage traffic is present. If, for example, an attached Fibre Channel HBA sends a PLOGI to a remote Fibre Channel device, the iFCP gateway will select an unbound TCP connection if one exists, or will establish a new TCP connection for that login session. An unbound TCP connection becomes bound when the iFCP gateway issues a connection bind command to the remote iFCP gateway.

Only one Fibre Channel login session is allowed per bound TCP connection, which separates the traffic between iFCP gateways. The mapping between Fibre Channel addresses and IP addresses, and binding to a dedicated TCP connection via the iFCP gateways ensures that the communication between the Fibre Channel initiator and target will have its own dedicated connection for the duration of their transaction. When the Fibre Channel login session is terminated (for example, the initiator logs out from the target), the TCP connection becomes unbound and available for other Fibre Channel login sessions.

Because iFCP allows any-to-any connectivity in the IP network, an iFCP gateway may have multiple TCP connections to multiple iFCP gateway peers in the network. This provides flexibility in metropolitan or wide area implementations, and facilitates storage applications such as centralized tape backup and content distribution between multiple sites. Additionally, because TCP connections are established between pairs of communicating end devices, each connection's QoS can be tailored to the specific application needs.

8.3.5 iFCP Error Handling

Because iFCP is responsible for both Fibre Channel error detection and TCP/IP error detection, it must monitor Fibre Channel error timeout values such as E_D_TOV and R_A_TOV (as discussed earlier) as well as TCP errors. Compared with FCIP, however, iFCP enables more granular error handling. In FCIP, a Fibre Channel or TCP error may result in a complete disconnect between two Fibre Channel SANs and the loss of multiple Fibre Channel conversations. In iFCP, typically only one communicating Fibre Channel pair may be affected, whereas other login sessions may remain active.

If an individual TCP connection error or Fibre Channel error is not recoverable, the TCP connection supporting the Fibre Channel login session will be dropped and any outstanding frames will be discarded. This will force the Fibre Channel initiator to establish another login session to the target. If the iFCP gateway itself experiences a fatal error (for example, the IP router or switch attached to the network fails), the iFCP gateway will terminate all TCP connections and will attempt to reestablish connection to the destination IP network.

8.3.6 iFCP Security

Securing transactions in an iFCP implementation may be accomplished by several methods. iFCP gateways may be used as a direct replacement for Fibre Channel fabric switches. As with Fibre Channel fabrics, a certain level of physical security is assumed for data center environments. Typically, the Fibre Channel hosts, disks, and tape subsystems are physically colocated. For mission-critical storage applications, the Gigabit Ethernet switches used to connect iFCP gateways should be dedicated for SAN applications and should not be shared for user messaging traffic. Creating a separate network for IP storage thus isolates sensitive storage data in a contained and secure environment. This provides the most elementary form of data security.

Even a secured data center IP SAN, however, may support multiple storage applications for different departments with their own security requirements. Sales commissions statements, for example, should probably not be accessible by engineering personnel. In Fibre Channel SANs, segregation of storage resources is accomplished by zoning. In an iFCP environment, the same function is performed via discovery domains, which (as discussed in Chapter 9) only allow authorized initiators to discover and establish sessions with specific target devices. The secure relationships between assigned initiators and targets can also be enforced with public/private key authentication managed by the iSNS server and implemented within the iFCP gateways.

For overtly exposed IP network links that may be vulnerable to snooping or attack, iFCP can leverage established standard IP and Gigabit Ethernet security methods. An iFCP gateway can use IP Security (IPSec) to enforce authentication and data encryption. The access control lists (ACLs) maintained by IP routers and switches can also be used to police connection establishment. And because storage data now appears as standard IP traffic, third-party firewall and encryption products can be used to "front end" the iFCP gateway's connection to the network and provide virtual private networks (VPNs) for storage traffic. As shown in Figure 8–11, gigabit-speed firewalls may be incorporated into IP routers or may serve as stand-alone units between the iFCP gateway and the IP router interface.

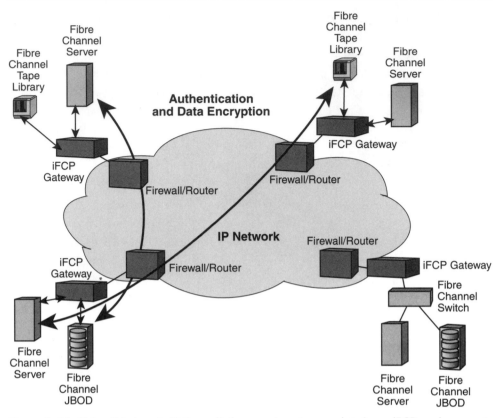

Figure 8–11 Using third-party IP firewalls for securing storage data in an iFCP environment.

Standard off-the-shelf firewall products can immediately provide data encryption solutions for iFCP SANs that are as yet unavailable in Fibre Channel environments.

8.3.7 iFCP Issues

Among the standards track protocols for IP-based SANs, iFCP is the only protocol engineered to support both existing Fibre Channel and native IP storage devices. An iFCP gateway can support Fibre Channel disk arrays as well as disk controllers provisioned with a Gigabit Ethernet interface and iFCP protocol stack. The iFCP standard does not specify support for iSCSI end devices, although vendor implementations may allow for connection of Fibre Channel, iFCP, and iSCSI devices to create a coherent multiprotocol IP SAN.

The iFCP protocol follows Gigabit Ethernet's example of borrowing liberally from Fibre Channel standards to achieve stability and faster time-to-market. Just as Gigabit Ethernet modified some of the lower layer Fibre

Channel architecture to achieve greater efficiency, iFCP has introduced IP-specific modifications such as address translation mode to provide more flexibility for storage network design.

In addition, by leveraging FCP's serial SCSI-3 layer, iFCP adopts a ready-made interface to both operating systems and storage applications. SAN-specific standards such as extended copy are supported by iFCP with no changes. And interoperability with a wide range of Fibre Channel host and storage devices is enhanced because the FCP layer is preserved intact. The tradeoff for these benefits, however, is that the iFCP protocol perpetuates Fibre Channel-specific features even if, eventually, all end devices are native IP instead of Fibre Channel. An iFCP driver for a storage NIC, for example, will still implement WWNs and a 24-bit Fibre Channel address scheme in addition to an IP address.

Whether this Fibre Channel content is really an issue depends on the bias of the vendor or the implementor. If it is transparent to the administrator and facilitates wire-speed performance and interoperability, the preservation of FCP will probably not incite anyone to riot in protest. iFCP complements iSCSI by offering a migration path from Fibre Channel to homogeneous IP storage networks. To the extent that iSCSI can successfully accommodate storage applications and provide functionality beyond FCP, the role of supporting Fibre Channel devices and the FCP layer will decline in importance over time.

Leveraging FCP for IP-based SANs requires extra effort by iFCP to accommodate issues that do not normally arise in pristine Fibre Channel environments. FCP relies on the underlying transport for congestion control. In Fibre Channel, this is provided by the class of service implemented by the transport—for example, ACKs for class 1 and class 2, or R_RDYs for class 3. The iFCP protocol relies on TCP mechanisms to provide the equivalent function, which makes iFCP more suitable for wide area transport. FCP also lacks frame-level recovery, and expects to retransmit an entire sequence of frames if a single frame is dropped. TCP packet monitoring and retransmission enable iFCP to impose a packet-level recovery method underneath FCP's sequence recovery algorithm. FCP also relies on port and node WWNs for unique device identity, and the 24-bit Fibre Channel address for network routing. To make IP-based SANs more scalable than Fibre Channel while still leveraging FCP, iFCP uses IP address mapping and Fibre Channel address translation/proxying. And although FCP on its own lacks authentication, and security functions, iFCP supports layering of secure login, authentication, and data encryption through standard IP methods. Collectively, these enhancements enable the use of a proven serial SCSI-3 layer that accommodates existing Fibre Channel end devices and offers a migration path to native IP SANs.

8.4 Metro Fibre Channel Protocol (mFCP)

mFCP is a UDP/IP variant of iFCP. mFCP shares iFCP's architecture for support of FCP over IP, transparent and translational addressing modes, and accommodation of native Fibre Channel initiators and targets. Unlike iFCP, however, mFCP does not have an integral flow control mechanism such as TCP. Instead, mFCP relies on the link-layer flow control of 802.3x to pace traffic over the IP SAN.

There are several immediate benefits to the mFCP implementation, and several cautionary notes are attached. The most obvious benefit is speed. Like Fibre Channel, mFCP simply streams frames from source to destination. There is no prior connection setup as in TCP/IP, and no transmission ramp to test bandwidth availability. Although Fibre Channel uses buffer credits to control streaming, mFCP uses 802.3x PAUSE frames. Because there are no acknowledgments of frame receipt, mFCP is functionally equivalent to Fibre Channel class 3 service. mFCP assumes that the full gigabit transmission pipe is always available. This may be a correct assumption for a well-designed data center SAN composed of nonblocking Gigabit Ethernet switches with 802.3x support. It cannot be assumed for poorly designed SANs or potentially congested wide area links.

An mFCP implementation also mitigates the issue of TCP overhead on the host CPU. Like FCP over Fibre Channel, mFCP requires minimal CPU cycles. An IP storage NIC with an mFCP stack therefore does not require an auxillary TOE and can be a more economical solution for host systems.

As a connectionless, unacknowledged protocol, mFCP is suitable for data centers and controlled campus or metropolitan storage networks. Having traded connection control for speed and low overhead, however, mFCP would not be appropriate for lossy or congested network segments or the Internet. Speed mismatches between local and remote links or network bottlenecks could potentially result in excessive upper layer error recovery and thus neutralize the benefit of UDP/IP's streamlined transmission and low overhead.

Because mFCP uses iFCP's mechanisms for accommodating Fibre Channel end devices, mFCP storage switches can also directly replace Fibre Channel fabrics. The streaming capability of mFCP products has already demonstrated comparable performance with Fibre Channel, and in transactions based on

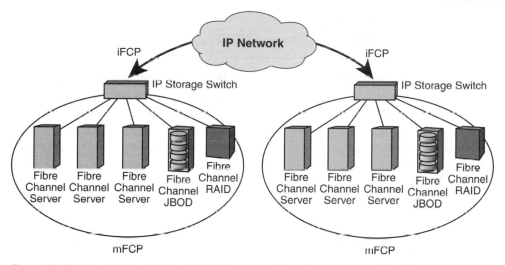

Figure 8–12 Combining iFCP and mFCP protocols for data center and wide area connections.

large block sizes, performance exceeding Fibre Channel switches. This is primarily the result of the relatively faster clock speed of Gigabit Ethernet (1.25 Gbps versus Fibre Channel's 1.0625 Gbps) and efficient processing in silicon.

If mFCP is restricted to the data center or metropolitan boundry, it still requires a solution for wide area links between data centers or remote sites. This may be provided by combining mFCP and iFCP ports, thus enabling the highest performance for the data center or metro SAN via mFCP and the connection control for wide area links via iFCP. Figure 8–12 depicts such a solution.

The mFCP protocol has been submitted via Nishan Systems as an individual contribution to the IETF and thus can be implemented as a nonproprietary solution by any vendor.

8.5 Internet SCSI

FCIP sits at one end of the IP storage spectrum, having the least IP content and the greatest Fibre Channel focus. From the standpoint of IP-based SANs, FCIP is really not so much of an IP storage strategy as a Fibre Channel extension and perpetuation strategy. The iSCSI protocol is the polar opposite of FCIP, having the most IP content and no Fibre Channel element at all. Rather than a migration vehicle from Fibre Channel SANs to IP SANs, iSCSI represents a light switch approach to storage networking that, carried to its logical conclusion, purges Fibre Channel from the notion of SANs. Like iFCP, iSCSI takes IP to the storage end device. Unlike iFCP, iSCSI defines its own serial SCSI implementation for block data transfer over IP networks.

8.5.1 iSCSI Network Architecture

As shown in Figure 8–13, the intent of an iSCSI SAN is to be composed of native iSCSI initiators and iSCSI targets.

Because each host and storage resource supports a Gigabit Ethernet interface and an iSCSI protocol stack, devices can be plugged directly into Gigabit Ethernet switches and/or IP routers. In this respect, iSCSI end nodes appear simply as any other IP entities. As with standard IP implementations, direct connection to the IP network pushes responsibility for connection establishment and integrity back onto the end device, in contrast to Fibre Channel's reliance on intelligence within the fabric switch. Consequently, an iSCSI end device must have additional logic to deal proactively with the SAN. A Fibre Channel switch or iFCP gateway, for example, assumes responsibility for monitoring device status and issuing SCNs. Because iSCSI

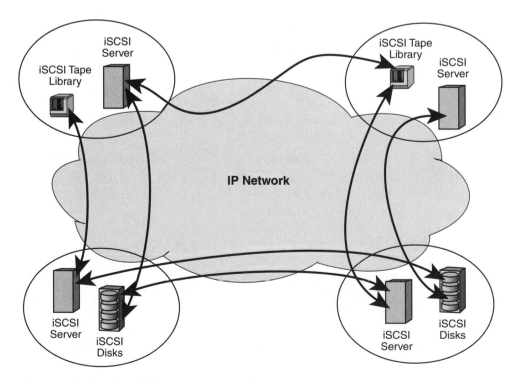

Figure 8–13 A native iSCSI storage network.

does not assume storage intelligence in the Gigabit Ethernet switch or IP router, an iSCSI device itself must have alternate means of dealing with storage-specific phenomena.

8.5.2 iSCSI Protocol Layering Model

As with FCIP and iFCP, iSCSI uses TCP/IP for reliable data transmission over potentially unreliable networks. As shown in Figure 8–14, the iSCSI layer interfaces to the operating system's standard SCSI Access Method (SAM) command set, fulfilling the same function as FCP.

In addition to the normal TCP/IP transport, the iSCSI specification allows for a lower functional level on top of IP to provide services such as IPSec data encryption. The specification also allows for an optional data synchronization and data steering mechanism, which may reside below the iSCSI layer. The purpose of this layer is to ensure in-order receipt of iSCSI data and commands, and to accommodate missing packets as data is written ("steered") directly to application memory. Without such a mechanism, an iSCSI device would require larger buffers and possibly multiple copy operations to store and then reassemble data sequences before they are passed to upper layer applications.

One or more TCP connections are established to support an iSCSI session between initiator and target. TCP connections ensure the orderly transport

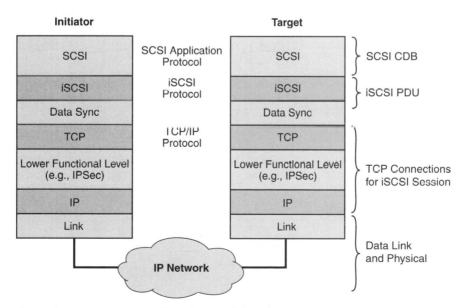

Figure 8–14 iSCSI protocol layering model.

of the SCSI commands, status, and data carried within iSCSI packets known as PDUs. PDUs encapsulate standard SCSI CDBs to convey commands and/or data. At the iSCSI/SCSI boundary, iSCSI's PDUs thus represent a new messaging structure, distinct from the Fibre Channel FCP layer.

8.5.3 iSCSI Address and Naming Conventions

Following the SCSI SAM-2 architecture, iSCSI implements a client/server model. Targets are servers of data, responding to the requests from client initiators for data reads and writes. Because iSCSI represents networked storage, the clients and servers have a network entity identity, which is equivalent to the IP addresses they are assigned. As shown in Figure 8–15, the network entity may contain one or more iSCSI nodes.

The iSCSI node object defines a specific SCSI device within a network entity that is accessible through the network via a network portal. The network portal is the combination of the assigned IP address and the TCP port number. The network entity allows for multiple iSCSI nodes because it may represent a gateway that fronts multiple initiators or targets. Each iSCSI node is identified by a unique iSCSI name that may be manually administered. The iSCSI node name may be as long as 255 bytes.

The separation of iSCSI names and iSCSI addresses ensures that a storage device will have a unique identity in the network even if its location in the network changes. Although the IP address plus the TCP port number will necessarily change if a device is moved to a different network segment, the iSCSI name will travel with the device, allowing it to be rediscovered. In

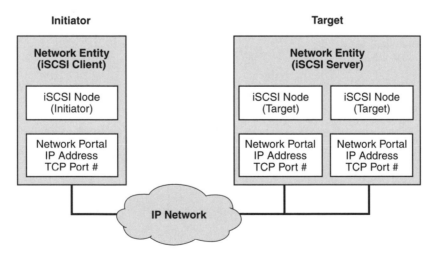

Figure 8–15 Highest level iSCSI name objects.

addition, the iSCSI name is "soft assigned" and remains independent of hardware. This allows, for example, a device driver on a host platform to present a single iSCSI name even if multiple storage NICs are used to attach to the network. Likewise, a target device could have multiple connections to the network for redundant "pathing" and yet be consistently identified as a single entity.

The iSCSI naming scheme is meant to rationalize the discovery process and validate a device's identity during login. The potentially very long 255-byte iSCSI name is therefore not used for routing, which would place an immense burden on parsing engines. Instead, once the IP address and TCP port number are established for a specific iSCSI node, only the IP/TCP port combination is required for storage transactions.

iSCSI naming conventions follow the requirements of the uniform resource names (URN) standard as detailed in RFC 1737. The intention is to create a naming mechanism that provides a unique identity, is scalable, and is human readable. The default iSCSI name is "iSCSI" and it is supplied as a convenience for probing real iSCSI names if the IP address/TCP port number is known. The standard iSCSI name is composed of a type designator and naming authority, followed by the unique identifier assigned by the naming authority. For example, a fully qualified name would have a type of "fqn." The naming authority might be a corporation maintaining a DNS server, "ramjack.com." The unique device name might be "bigarray.research.30221." When assembled as a fully qualified name, the authority field is reversed, yielding "fqn.com.ramjack.bigarray.research.30221" as the full iSCSI name.

In Fibre Channel, the unique identity of a device is provided by a 64-bit WWN, whereas the network address is the 24-bit Fibre Channel address. The WWN convention is also accommodated by iSCSI naming as an IEEE extended unique identifier (EUI) format or "eui." This provides a more streamlined, if less user friendly name string, because the resulting iSCSI name is simply "eui" followed by the hexidecimal WWN (for example, eui.0300732A32598D26).

In either format, the usual uniform resource locator (URL)-type rules apply in that no white spaces and no special characters other than ASCII dots and dashes are allowed. The fully qualified name format, in particular, enables storage resources to be identified by signficant names that are more easily managed by an administrator. The unique identifier component can be a combination of site, department, manufacturer name, serial number, or asset number of any moniker useful for recognizing a storage resource.

In addition, iSCSI provides for alias naming, although an alias is not a substitute for an assigned iSCSI name. The alias option is provided as a convenience for quickly identifying user resources, particularly if iSCSI names have been assigned by a manufacturer or third party and have little relevance to the customer's network naming conventions. Alias names may be exchanged during login and can also be as long as 255 bytes. Management software is typically required to surface these names to the administrator via a command-line interface or management graphical user interface (GUI).

Discovery using iSCSI names is examined in Chapter 9, but, as implied by the structure of iSCSI names, either a distributed or a centralized DNS-type lookup facilitates mapping of iSCSI names required for login to actual iSCSI network addresses. For small IP SANs, the Service Locator Protocol (SLP) may be used for iSCSI discovery.

8.5.4 iSCSI Session Management

An iSCSI session between initiator and target must be enabled through an iSCSI login process known as an *iSCSI login phase*. The login sequence is used to negotiate any variable parameters between the two parties and may invoke a security routine to authenticate allowable connectivity. If successful, the target will issue a login accept to the initiator; otherwise, the login is rejected and the connection is broken.

The iSCSI login exchange uses text fields to negotiate allowable parameters between initiator and target. These fields are associated with keys followed by the values tendered during the negotiations. MaxConnections, for example, is used to establish an agreed to number of TCP connections that will be used during the iSCSI session. The initiator may offer a number for this key of between 1 and 65,000, with the default number of TCP connections being 8. If an initiator's offered range differs from the target's, the lower of the two numbers is used. Text fields are also used to exchange target and initiator names and aliases, as well as negotiated parameters such as security protocol, maximum data payload size, whether unsolicited data is supported, the allowable length of unsolicited data, and timeout values.

Session establishment is potentially complicated by the fact that an iSCSI device may have one or more network portals (IP address plus TCP port number) for attachment to the network and may represent multiple iSCSI targets (for example, disk arrays). As initiators establish SCSI sessions with targets, session IDs are generated to identify individual conversations uniquely between specific iSCSI nodes within the corresponding network entities. An initiator logging on to a target, for example, would include its iSCSI name and an initiator session ID (ISID), the combination of which would be unique within its host network entity. A target, responding to the login request, would generate a unique target session ID (TSID), which likewise, in combination with its iSCSI name, gives that session a unique identity within the network entity in which it resides. A single ISID/ TSID session pair may have multiple TCP connections between them, per the results of login negotiation.

When login is completed, the iSCSI session enters the full feature phase; in other words, normal SCSI transactions. If multiple connections for that session have been established, individual command/response pairs must flow over the same TCP connection. This *connection allegiance* ensures that specific read or write commands are fulfilled without the additional overhead of monitoring multiple connections to see whether a particular request is completed. A SCSI write, for example, would be performed over a single connection until all data was transmitted. Unrelated transactions, however, could simultaneously be issued on their own connections during the same session.

As shown in Figure 8–16, normal SCSI operations for iSCSI are nearly identical to FCP. iSCSI PDUs are used to send commands, status, and data, with ready-to-transmit (R2T) PDUs fulfilling the role of upper layer SCSI flow control between target and initiator. In the SCSI write operation depicted

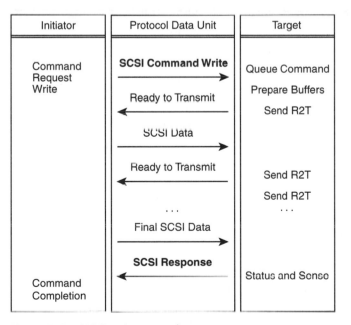

Figure 8–16 iSCSI write example.

here, the R2Ts are issued by the target device as buffers become available to receive more data. At the completion of the write, the target issues status and sense, indicating a successful transaction.

The status of SCSI data transport during reads and writes is monitored through status and data sequence numbers as well as the buffer offset/transfer length fields in the iSCSI PDU. The target paces the flow of data by indicating the amount of data it is able to receive via a transfer length field. In addition, the target can request data blocks in any order by referencing a buffer offset established when the transaction began.

If an initator has outstanding requests to a target and gets no response, it can send the equivalent of an IP ping to the target to verify its status. The iSCSI NOP-Out command with the P (ping) bit set may also include test data that should be returned intact by the target. If the target does not respond, or responds with corrupted or incomplete test data, the initiator may close the connection and establish a new one for recovery.

iSCSI sessions and their associated TCP connections normally remain open, awaiting additional SCSI commands from the upper layer applications. An initiator, for example, typically has assigned disk resources in the SAN, and rarely breaks connection with them unless rebooted. In an iSCSI environment, however, initiator activity may require more TCP connections for some transactions than others, and thus allowance is made for selectively logging out of previously established connections. In some instances, too, it may be desirable to log out of a session and all connections completely (for example, when downing a resource for maintenance). The iSCSI logout command supplies reason codes for terminating sessions or connections within a session, and in the latter case using the connection ID to specify which connection should be taken down. In the event of a connection error, the logout command can be issued on an alternate connection (or a newly established one) to clean up the problematic TCP connection.

8.5.5 iSCSI Error Handling

The SCSI architecture assumes a relatively error-free environment. Direct-attached SCSI devices share a dedicated parallel bus, isolated from network disruptions. A Fibre Channel SAN is predicated on network connectivity, but assumes a very low bit error rate and complete separation from the troublesome messaging network. IP-based SANs may also be deployed on dedicated, low-bit error Gigabit Ethernet networks, but enable use of standard IP networks and WAN links as well. Consequently, the iSCSI specification attempts to accommodate a wide variety of error conditions that may arise from injection of storage data into unreliable network infrastructures including the Internet. Reconciling the requirements of SCSI data with potentially lossy environments has been a major challenge for the iSCSI initiative.

Because iSCSI is a reconstruction of comparable services provided by FCP, it must create its own equivalents of E_D_TOV and R_A_TOV timeout values, and establish boundaries for data recovery. In Fibre Channel, the most granular level of error recovery is the sequence. If a single frame is corrupted, the entire sequence of frames must be retransmitted. The rationalization for this method of recovery is that too much logic would be required to monitor and retransmit a single frame. At gigabit speeds, it is more efficient simply to retransmit the sequence. In the IP world, however, TCP provides packet-level recovery, and this must be brought in line with SCSI block data transport.

One of the primary requirements for iSCSI error handling and recovery is the ability of both initiators and targets to buffer commands and responses until they are acknowledged. In a SCSI write, for example, the initiator should keep data it has just transmitted in its buffer until it has received another R2T from the target, indicating that the previous data has been received and the target is ready for more. At a minimum, iSCSI end devices must be able to rebuild the missing or corrupted PDU selectively for retransmission.

An individual PDU may have missing or inconsistent fields within the frame. This is known as a *format error* and it engenders a reject iSCSI PDU in response. The reject PDU contains an offset indicator for the first bad byte detected in the PDU header.

Another class of iSCSI error covers corruption of data in either the data payload or header content. These are known as *digest* (content) *errors,* and include header digest error and data digest error conditions. These errors also trigger a reject PDU, which in turn initiates recovery of the failed PDU. In the case of a data digest error, a target can request retransmission by manipulating the offset field in the R2T PDU.

The iSCSI command for recovering missing PDUs is the sequence number acknowledgment (or SNACK) PDU. The SNACK will indicate the number of missing PDUs, calculated on the last valid PDU received. In some instances, a hole may appear in a sequence of frames, with valid frames received on either side of the missing PDUs. For efficiency, only the missing PDUs are requested via the SNACK command, with the remaining, already acknowledged PDUs are steered into application memory (if the synchronization and steering layer is available). SNACKs may be issued against both command and data PDUs.

The hierarchy of iSCSI error detection and recovery includes, at the lowest level, detection and recovery within a SCSI task, such as retransmission of a missing or corrupt PDU. In the next layer down, the TCP connection that carries a task may experience an error or failure, in which case connection recovery is attempted via a command restart. Multiple TCP connections may be utilized within an iSCSI session, and thus errors within a session may require reconstruction of connections. And finally, the session itself may fail. Session termination and recovery is normally not required unless all other levels of recovery have failed. It requires closing all existing TCP connections, aborting all queued tasks and outstanding SCSI commands, and restarting the session through login.

8.5.6 iSCSI Security

Because one of the design criteria for iSCSI is its use in untrusted wide area environments, the iSCSI specification allows for multiple security methods to be implemented. Encryption solutions that reside below iSCSI such as IPSec require no special negotiation between iSCSI end devices and are transparent to the upper layers. For other authentication implementations such as Kerberos or public/private key exchanges, the iSCSI login process provides text fields for negotiating the type of security supported by both end devices. If the negotiation is successful, the PDUs exchanged between iSCSI devices will be formatted for appropriate security validation required by the security routine used. As we will see in the following chapters, the iSNS server may assist this process by, for example, serving as a repository for public keys.

8.5.7 iSCSI Issues

The SCSI protocol demands stability, data integrity, and, in current implementations, expects high bandwidth on demand. IP networks, in contrast, are inherently unstable, may drop packets under congested conditions, and have highly variable bandwidth. The TCP layer is meant to deal with the instability and packet loss that may accompany IP, whereas higher speed wide area connections can alleviate bandwidth issues for block storage data. In addition, the internal mechanisms of the iSCSI protocol provide additional monitoring of TCP connections and for recovering from lost or corrupted command and data PDUs.

As an Internet standards initiative, iSCSI must honor existing TCP/IP standards and integrate seamlessly into existing IP-routed networks. As a SCSI variant, iSCSI must comply with existing NCITS T10 standards and integrate into existing operating system environments. In some instances (such as extended copy), iSCSI has used modifications to NCITS T10 standards to accommodate iSCSI-specific functions. Such instances are the exception, however, and in the main iSCSI has evolved between the two pillars of IETF and NCITS, and thus provides a bridge between internetworking and storage technologies.

Unlike iFCP, iSCSI does not define a means of accommodating existing Fibre Channel storage devices in IP networks. Instead of migration or convergence, iSCSI assumes that end devices including hosts, storage arrays, and tape subsystems will be native iSCSI entities. In practice, migration may be provided by iSCSI-to-Fibre Channel gateway products that convert FCP commands, status, and data into their iSCSI equivalents.

For storage networking applications, the iSCSI protocol is dependent on several other technologies to make it more viable than Fibre Channel. Imposing TCP overhead on servers, for example, is unacceptable for storage applications where server CPU cycles are at a premium. iSCSI therefore requires TOEs to minimize processing overhead. Lacking off-load engines, the first iSCSI products to market could only perform at less than half the speed of gigabit Fibre Channel. TOEs greatly assist iSCSI's ability to provide enterprise-class solutions.

In addition, storage applications using iSCSI benefit immensely from 10 Gigabit Ethernet. Ten-gigabit and faster speed Ethernet enables scalable IP SANs that support higher populations of servers and storage devices, and a variety of storage applications that can be run concurrently over the same infrastructure. With TOEs on servers and large data pipes in the network, iSCSI solutions can achieve an enterprise-ready status for IP-based SANs.

8.6 Chapter Summary

Standards-Based IP Storage Protocols

- Customers require standards-compliant products to ensure interoperability and to provide more choices in vendor selection.

- Ethernet standards are developed through the IEEE 802.3 committee.

- TCP/IP-based standards are developed through the IETF working groups.

- SCSI standards are developed through the NCITS T10 committee.

- Fibre Channel standards are developed through the NCITS T11 committee.

- IETF standards are published as RFCs.

- The IETF IPS Work Group is the focal point for IP SAN protocols.

- The three IP storage protocols on standards track include FCIP, iFCP, and iSCSI.

Fibre Channel Over IP

- FCIP is an IP tunneling solution for joining remote Fibre Channel SANs.

- FCIP is a point-to-point solution.

- FCIP encapsulates the entire Fibre Channel frame and makes no alternation to its contents.

- FCIP gateways establish TCP/IP connections over a WAN link to transport Fibre Channel frames.

- FCIP gateways must observe Fibre Channel error detect and resource allocation timeout values.

- FCIP allows connection to Fibre Channel switches via E_Port or FC_BB switches via B_Port.

- FCIP combines two SAN islands into one Fibre Channel fabric.

- Breaking an FCIP connection will result in the reestablishment of isolated SANs.

- Speed mismatch between Fibre Channel and an FCIP-attached WAN link creates flow control issues that may be addressed with a TCP sliding window.

- FCIP solutions require both Fibre Channel and IP management platforms to monitor status.

Internet Fibre Channel Protocol

- iFCP is a gateway-to-gateway protocol for integrating Fibre Channel end devices into an IP storage network.

- iFCP storage switches may replace Fibre Channel switches and may provide direct connection of Fibre Channel end devices.

- iFCP uses Fibre Channel FC-4 serial SCSI-3 on top of TCP/IP.

- iFCP supports any-to-any IP routing of storage data.

- IP addresses are mapped to individual Fibre Channel devices.

- Address transparent mode uses standard Fibre Channel addressing and creates a single fabric.

- Address translation mode manipulates Fibre Channel addressing to optimize address utilization and to minimize network disruption by Fibre Channel switch elements.

- iFCP provides fabric service emulation to translate between Fibre Channel and IP domains.

- iFCP supports multiple TCP connections for concurrent storage transactions.

- Speed mismatch between Fibre Channel and an iFCP-attached WAN link creates flow control issues that may be addressed with a TCP sliding window.

- Security for iFCP implementations may be provided by zoning, public/private keys, and IPSec.

Metro Fibre Channel Protocol

- FCP uses UDP/IP instead of TCP/IP for optimal performance in data center environments.

- mFCP relies on 802.3x flow control to avoid frame loss.

- mFCP and 802.3x provide comparable service as Fibre Channel class 3 at gigabit speeds.

- mFCP should not be used on lossy, potentially congested network segments.

- mFCP and iFCP may be implemented in a single product to provide both local and wide area IP storage networking.

Internet SCSI

- iSCSI follows the SCSI client/server model.

- iSCSI clients reside on host platforms (initiators).

- iSCSI servers reside in disk arrays (targets).

- iSCSI provides its own layer over TCP/IP for block data transport.

- iSCSI assumes that both initiators and targets will have native iSCSI interfaces.

- A data synchronization and steering layer below iSCSI may facilitate writing of data directly into application memory.

- An iSCSI name may be as long as 255 bytes.

- iSCSI naming conventions follow the URN standard and are URL-like in appearance.

- The iSCSI login phase establishes a session with one or more TCP connections between initiator and target.

- The login phase may also negotiate security parameters for the connection.

- The iSCSI full feature phase enables normal SCSI transactions when login is complete.

- iSCSI commands and data are issued via PDUs.

- PDUs are used to encapsulate SCSI CDBs.

- An iSCSI NOP-Out is similar to an IP "ping," and can be used to verify connection between devices.

- Missing or corrupt PDUs may be retransmitted by issuing a SNACK PDU.

- iSCSI error handling includes recovery of individual PDUs, reestablishment of TCP connections, and reestablishment of iSCSI sessions.

- Security may be provided by Kerberos, public key, IPSec, or other methods.

- To provide adequate performance for SANs, iSCSI adapters require TOEs.

- Support for 10 Gigabit Ethernet on switch infrastructures enables new opportunities for enterprise IP SANs.

9 Internet Storage Name Server

FACILITATING DEVICE DISCOVERY and configuration enables SANs to scale from departmental to enterprisewide applications. This chapter discusses the iSNS protocol, which borrows concepts from both Fibre Channel and IP networking to provide device discovery for IP SANs.

9.1 Discovery

In conventional networking, all devices attached to the network are hosts. This implies a peer relationship between networked devices, and requires each host to have sufficient intelligence to discover and communicate with other hosts over the network. Simply plugging devices into a common network does not ensure that they will be able to communicate. A device must be manually configured for the addresses of potential peers, must issue a broadcast or multicast to solicit a response, or must consult a third party such as a directory services entity residing on the network. In the Internet, for example, the DNS enables a host to discover and communicate with other hosts via name/address resolution.

Storage devices that are inserted into a networked environment have unique requirements. Unlike typical networked hosts, storage devices do not initiate transactions, but wait passively for requests from active hosts such as file servers. In terms of device discovery, storage end nodes must somehow register their presence on the network, but it is up to the servers and workstations to initiate the discovery process. In traditional direct SCSI-attached storage configurations, a server can easily discover the storage resources at its disposal by polling the SCSI bus to which the disk arrays are attached. Because the server is the exclusive owner of its direct-attached storage, it can assume that any devices it discovers are available for its use.

In a SAN, by contrast, disk and tape resources may be dispersed across a complex network. Polling through network addresses to discover storage resources may not be feasible. In addition, simply locating a storage resource does not resolve the issue of ownership when, for example, two servers discover the same storage target. Initiators must be able to identify storage resources in the SAN and to determine whether they have permission to access them. SANs therefore require a mechanism to facilitate device discovery and to assign potentially shared storage resources to individual initiators.

The common standards initiative that has been developed for facilitating device discovery in large-scale IP storage networks is the Internet Storage Name Server, or iSNS. The iSNS specification enables discovery of iFCP and iSCSI devices using a common protocol. Because the iSNS protocol borrows from both Fibre Channel and Internet discovery mechanisms, it is useful to understand how much as been taken from each.

9.1.1 Device Discovery in Fibre Channel

As reviewed in Chapter 3, Fibre Channel supports both arbitrated loop and fabric topologies. Arbitrated loop has a fairly finite population of 126 end nodes, compared with the 15.5 million possible end nodes for Fibre Channel fabrics. The number of potential targets an initiator must seek out therefore determines the device discovery process used for each topology.

In an arbitrated loop, an initiator such as a server can simply poll through the 126 possible addresses to solicit responses from potential targets. Walking the address space for 126 possible destinations may be inefficient, but occurs fairly quickly at gigabit speeds. Targets that respond to an initiator's queries verify their presence on the loop and an initiator can thereafter establish sessions (PLOGIs) with each device and begin storage transactions. In some proprietary implementations, a positional map that is generated during loop initialization is used for target discovery. Each active device records its loop address in the positional map, and the map in turn can be used to create an abbreviated address list for session establishment. Although this shortens the process of device polling, not all loop devices support the positional mapping feature.

Walking the address space in a Fibre Channel fabric, however, is unreasonable, even at gigabit speeds. With an address space of 15.5 million, an alternate discovery is required. Fibre Channel standards therefore provide a name service definition to rationalize the discovery process. Whereas in a loop environment the initiator must perform all the work of device discovery, in a fabric this responsibility is shared between the Fibre Channel end nodes and the fabric switches composing the network. A device attached to a fabric switch must first log on to the fabric to obtain a unique 24-bit network address. It then registers its presence on the fabric by logging on to the SNS within the fabric switch. The SNS maintained by each Fibre Channel switch is a small database that contains the WWN, fabric address, class-of-service parameters, and other attributes of each registered device. The most critical entry from the standpoint of device discovery is an SNS object specifying the upper layer protocols that each device supports. For Fibre Channel SANs, the relevant FC-4 upper layer protocol is FCP, or serial SCSI-3.

Because every storage device must register with the SNS, an initiator can simply query the SNS, asking for a list of all devices that support FCP. The address list that is returned from the SNS becomes the polling list for the initiator, which can then send PLOGIs to the listed targets and establish sessions with them. Although the SNS scheme relieves the initiator from having sole responsibility for device discovery, it is predicated on distributed intelligence in the SAN infrastructure. An IP network, by contrast, does not assume that IP routers or layer 3 switches will do anything more than forward packets from source to destination. Discovery mechanisms such as DNS must be added to the network infrastructure as hosts or appliances providing advanced services.

The Fibre Channel SNS streamlines the discovery process but does not dictate assignment of initiators to targets. In some cases, it may not be desirable for a server to discover all possible storage devices in the fabric. An NT server, for example, should not be allowed to discover and establish a session with a UNIX storage array because it would immediately write a signature to the array's boot sector and make it unusable for UNIX hosts. Because the SNS simply responds to initiator queries, an additional mechanism is required to restrict discovery to authorized hosts as part of this access control. In Fibre Channel fabric switches, segregation of devices in the fabric is enabled through zoning. Zoning creates groups of authorized devices that may communicate with each other based on port attachment (hard zoning) or WWN (soft zoning). In some implementations, zoning definitions modify the results of an initiator's query to the SNS so that only those targets in the same zone are reported. Zones must be manually administered, but they are an effective means of isolating storage resources from undesirable initiators.

In addition to SNS and zoning, Fibre Channel provides an SCN function to notify initiators proactively when changes in storage availability occur. Initiators register with the SCN entity with the fabric switch, usually after SNS registration. If new storage resources enter the fabric, the switch notifies any registered (and zoned) initiators so that they can quickly establish sessions.

Because Fibre Channel discovery relies on distributed intelligence in the fabric, scalability to large enterprise-class SANs may be an issue. Each fabric switch maintains its own SNS database. As more switches are added to a single fabric, they must be able to share SNS data so that an initiator anywhere on the network can discover viable targets. When zoning techniques are used to restrict discovery, zone information must also be exchanged between multiple switches. Distributed name service functionality places an ever-increasing burden on switch resources as SANs scale from small SAN islands to enterprisewide fabrics. Network convergence time is thus vulnerable to additional latency as switches generate more complex routing tables and update each other with SNS, zoning, and SCN information.

9.1.2 Discovery in IP Storage Networks

Although Fibre Channel has been forced to pioneer device discovery techniques where no precedents existed, IP-based SANs are able to draw from both IP networking applications such as DNS, SLP, and the Lightweight Directory Access Protocol, as well as Fibre Channel SNS, zoning, and SCN. The iSNS protocol has been submitted to the Internet community as a standards draft, and Nishan Systems has supplied iSNS as open source code to facilitate development of products. iSNS leverages the database objects of Fibre Channel SNS as well as familiar DNS to create a discovery mechanism that can be both distributed or centralized.

Because IP storage solutions may be based on several distinct protocols, iSNS provides support for iFCP and iSCSI. Although each transport protocol has its own unique requirements, each is faced with similar discovery and management problems. Discovery for iFCP and iSCSI may include discovery of gateways, but must also include discovery of discrete storage nodes within an IP SAN.

In comparison with Fibre Channel SNS, iSNS cannot assume that discovery mechanisms are available in every router or switch composing the network. The protocol must therefore be sufficiently flexible and lightweight for distribution over multiple IP storage switches that attach to the network, and must also be able to scale to larger, centralized DNS-style iSNS servers. In addition, iSNS must address discovery-related issues such as zoning and change notification for potentially expansive IP SANs and yet minimize discovery processing requirements for individual IP storage end devices. From a user standpoint, these underlying mechanisms should be transparent, in keeping with the promise of IP storage to reduce management and administrative overhead.

9.2 iSNS Features

iSNS is designed as a lightweight discovery protocol that can be deployed in centralized iSNS servers, IP storage switches, and target devices. Features include facilities for registration, discovery, and management of IP storage resources as well as zoning and state change management. The name registration service enables IP storage devices to register their attributes and address, analogous to the Fibre Channel SNS. Initiators can then query the iSNS to identify potential targets. Zoning functionality is provided by discovery domains, which restrict the discovery of IP storage targets to authorized initiators. And SCN alerts iSNS clients to any change in status of a registered device or reconfiguration of the client's discovery domain.

iSNS discovery domains enable a device to participate in one or more zones. Like Fibre Channel zones, discovery domains must be manually administered, at least for the initial establishment of functional groups within the network. By default, a new device is isolated from the storage network until a management workstation assigns it to a specific discovery domain. This prevents inadvertent access by unauthorized initiators. When a discovery domain has been configured for the device, SCN is used to alert authorized initiators that a new resource has been added to the domain.

iSNS also supports discovery domain sets (DDSs). Analogous to zone sets in Fibre Channel, a DDS can be used to reconfigure an IP SAN quickly for different application requirements. One DDS, for example, could include a tape resource in an NT discovery domain for one configuration, whereas an alternate discovery domain configuration could move the tape device into a UNIX discovery domain.

As shown in Figure 9–1, an iSNS server may reside anywhere within the IP network, accessible by iFCP or iSCSI clients. One or more management workstations are used to configure and monitor the iSNS server, either by the iSNS Protocol (iSNSP) or by SNMP. Because iSNS provides a common resource for a variety of IP storage types, each can register with and query the iSNS server for information relevant to the functionality the device supports. The iSNS server provides the information database for iFCP and iSCSI entities, and can be queried by SNMP or the iSNSP. An iFCP storage switch,

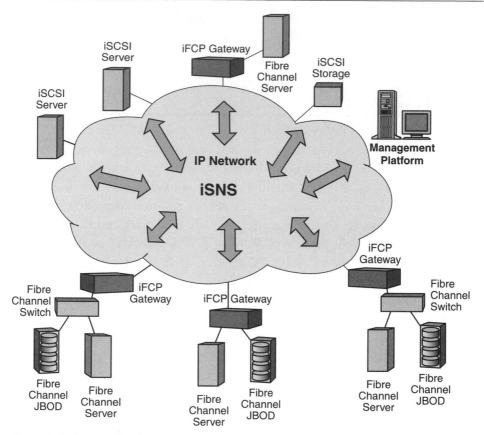

Figure 9–1 A centralized iSNS server for a multiprotocol IP SAN.

for example, could query the iSNS server for the existence of iSCSI storage targets and, if it provided iFCP-to-iSCSI translation, proxy additional entries that would make those resources available to iFCP initiators.

9.2.1 iSNS Discovery Process

The first step in the iSNS discovery process is device registration. Depending on the IP storage device type (iFCP or iSCSI), a device will register its attributes and address information to the iSNS server. The server thus builds a database of iSNS clients that forms the raw material for assignment of discovery domains. In Figure 9–2, devices A, B, and C have registered with the iSNS server. The attributes registered may include the entity type (in this example, iFCP), the unique device identifier (WWN or iSCSI name), the device's IP address, and a bit map signifying the state changes to which this device should be alerted (for example, all events). Because these devices have just registered with the iSNS server, they have not yet been assigned to shared discovery domains. For initiators, this means that no storage resources are visible.

Once devices have registered with the iSNS server, zoning information is supplied by a management workstation. With the appropriate discovery domains defined via management, the iSNS server can notify the clients that a reconfiguration of the network has occurred. As shown in Figure 9–3, this is done via SCN.

In this instance, two discovery domains (DD1 and DD2) have been created. DD1 groups devices A and B in a common zone, whereas DD2 groups B and C. Because device B is a participant in two discovery domains, it will be able to discover both A and C. Device A, however, will only discover device B, or any additional resources that are subsequently added to DD1.

The SCN issued by the iSNS server will prompt any initiators to query the iSNS for available resources. An iSNS response to a query by device A, for example, would return the address and SCSI-3 capability of device B. Device A can then perform a login to device B and begin storage transactions.

The iSNS discovery process is scalable from small departmental SANs to extended enterprisewide SANs that may span regional or national boundaries. Except for the initial creation of discovery domains via management, the iSNS discovery process is automatic and requires no further administration. Network administrators, however, have the flexibility to reassign

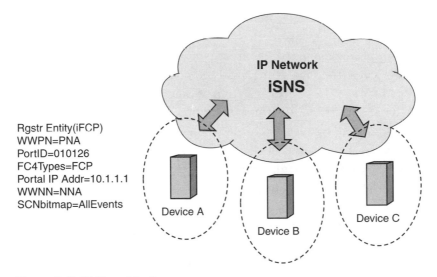

Figure 9–2 iSNS registration.

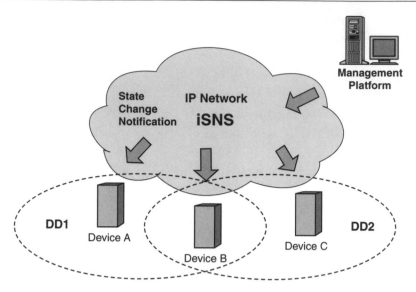

Figure 9–3 iSNS assignment of discovery domains.

resources through reconfiguration of discovery domains and can verify net-work participation through the iSNS information base.

9.2.2 iSNS SCN and Entity Status Inquiry

In Figure 9–3, SCN was used to alert devices to changes in discovery domain configuration. As in Fibre Channel, an SCN is triggered by management instruction or by addition or removal of a device from the storage switch. SCN allows for proactive management of end nodes and enables iSNS to maintain updated information on device availability.

Because the storage switch is directly monitoring the insertion or removal of nodes on its ports, it is immediately aware of changes and can generate change notification. In IP storage environments, however, a native iFCP or iSCSI device may not be directly attached to an SNS-aware switch, but to a standard Gigabit Ethernet switch. A means is therefore required to monitor state changes in devices that may be anywhere in an IP-routed network. For iSNS, this is achieved through entity status inquiry (ESI). A registered device is polled by the iSNS server at preestablished intervals to monitor its avail-ability. If an ESI response is not received after a number of retries, the device is deregistered from the iSNS server and, in the case of target devices, an SCN is issued to interested initiators. The iSNS server can thus maintain an updated database of active devices and can proactively report any changes throughout the IP SAN.

9.2.3 iSNS Objects

iSNS database objects include structures that are broad enough to support a diversity of products, and are specific, when required, for detailed information on a device's attributes. At the top of the object hierarchy is the concept of a network entity. A network entity could be an iFCP gateway or an iSCSI gateway or device. The network entity will have one or more IP interfaces to the network, defined as *portals* in iSNS. The portal object also includes a TCP port number, which in combination with the IP address gives the Portal a unique identity. In this example, the entity ID is a text string formatted as a URL. This string is simply for convenience in assigning user-friendly names to storage resources for administrative purposes. The entity ID may be as long as 255 bytes.

The iFCP object model is somewhat complex, because it defines the iFCP gateway as well as the iFCP storage devices it services. As shown in Figure 9–4,

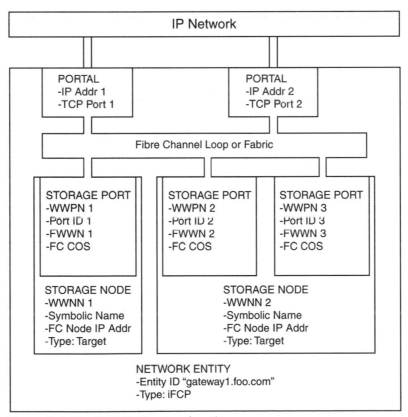

Figure 9–4 The iFCP iSNS network entity.

the network entity for iFCP may be an iFCP gateway with Fibre Channel loop or fabric-attached storage devices. The iFCP storage switch represented by the network entity designation may have one or more portals into the IP network, with unique IP address and TCP port numbers. The iFCP object for iSNS also includes a storage node, representing a disk controller or tape device that may have several Fibre Channel connections (storage ports) to the gateway. The storage node and storage port objects follow traditional Fibre Channel naming conventions, with both node and port WWNs. For discovery, each storage node that represents a disk or tape resource is identified as a target device.

For iSCSI, the iSNS object model includes the network entity, its portal to the IP network, and a storage node object that specifies whether the iSCSI device is an initiator or target. In the case of iSCSI devices, the identifier corresponding to a Fibre Channel WWN is known as a *world wide unique identifier* (WWUI). For discovery, an iSCSI initiator would register its own presence with the iSNS server and, after being notified of a state change of discovery domains, would query the iSNS server for storage nodes with a type of "target" (Figure 9–5).

For both IP storage transport protocols, the iSNS objects enable gateways and devices to register their relevant attributes and addresses and, for

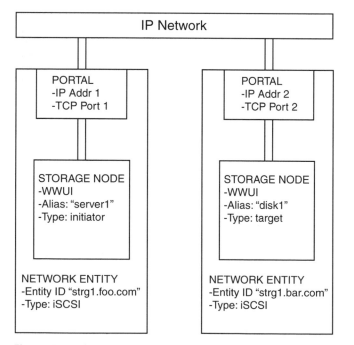

Figure 9–5 The iSCSI iSNS network entity.

targets, to identify themselves as storage resources. For small IP SAN configurations, associating gateways or devices could be accomplished by simple manual configuration or SLP tables. For enterprise-class SANs, however, iSNS provides scalability and minimizes administrative overhead as the SAN population increases.

9.2.4 iSNS Security

One of the central concerns of storage networking solutions is security. Fibre Channel standards for authentication and encryption have been retarded somewhat by the implicit security provided by a non-IP network infrastructure. Because the admission price to Fibre Channel hacking is a $50,000 Fibre channel analyzer, there has been little incentive to integrate security features into fabric switches. Putting storage over IP, however, potentially exposes storage traffic to snooping.

As the central repository of data for device discovery and discovery domain enforcement, the iSNS server is a logical place to host security services. As part of the registration process, for example, an IP storage device could register its X.509 public key certificate with the iSNS server. Once discovery domains are established, the iSNS server can distribute the appropriate public keys between devices in the same domain. As shown in Figure 9–6, the

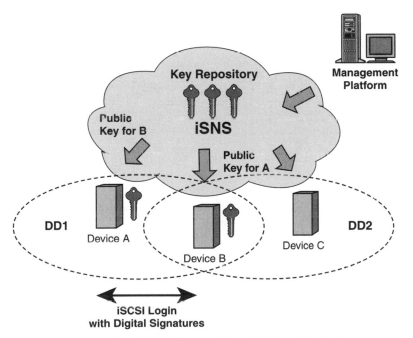

Figure 9–6 Leveraging the iSNS server for public key distribution.

exchange of private keys and digital signatures necessary for device authentication occurs during the login process. In this example, an iSCSI login between initiator and target includes public and private key exchanges to establish secure communication between them. The advantage of public key certificates over other security methods is scalability. Although manual administration (for example, Kerberos) may be suitable for small IP SANs, it is more convenient to leverage public key distribution from iSNS for enterprise-class storage networks.

9.3 Chapter Summary

Discovery

- Discovery refers to the detection of targets by initiators to establish storage sessions.

- Discovery in direct-attached storage occurs by simple polling of the server's SCSI bus.

- Discovery in storage networks requires mechanisms to identify potential targets that may be dispersed throughout the network.

- The discovery process is closely bound to the concept of ownership of storage resources by specific initiators.

Discovery in Fibre Channel

- Discovery in Fibre Channel loop may be accomplished by polling through the loop address space of 126 possible addresses.

- Discovery in Fibre Channel fabrics requires a name service for targets within an address space spanning 15.5 million possible addresses.

- The Fibre Channel SNS is a database of objects maintained by each fabric switch.

- Devices register with the SNS after fabric login.

- Initiators may query the SNS to obtain a list of potential storage resources.

- Fibre Channel zoning is used to segregate storage resources in the SAN.

- Zoning may be combined with SNS to restrict visibility of storage devices.

- SCN is used to notify initiators proactively of adds, moves, or changes in the fabric.

- In an extended fabric, multiple switches must exchange SNS, zoning, and SCN information.

Discovery in IP Storage Networks

- IP storage may borrow from both Fibre Channel and Internet mechanisms to facilitate device discovery.

- iSNS combines Fibre Channel and DNS functions to provide device discovery for iFCP and iSCSI devices.

- iSNS may be centralized in servers or distributed in IP storage switches.

iSNS Features

- iSNS provides device registration, zoning, and state change management for IP SANs.

- iSNS zones are called *discovery domains*.

- Discovery domains may be organized into optional groupings known as DDSs.

- An iSNS server is managed by an external management workstation.

iSNS Discovery Process

- IP storage devices register their attibutes with the iSNS server or entity.

- Registered devices are then assigned to discovery domains.

- Domain assignment is determined via management and is activated through SCN.

- SCN prompts the initiator to query for targets within the discovery domain.

iSNS SCN and Entity Status Inquiry

- An IP storage switch may provide state change information as devices are inserted into or removed from ports.

- Native IP storage devices can be monitored through the ESI.

- If a native IP storage device fails to respond to an ESI, an SCN will be generated by the iSNS server.

iSNS Objects

- iSNS uses objects to register and manage IP storage devices.

- The network entity object specifies the device entity ID and type.

- The portal object specifies the device IP address and TCP port number through which it can be accessed.

- The iFCP and iSCSI device objects include the storage node to identify individual initiators and targets.

- iSNS can scale to large enterprise-class storage networks.

iSNS Security

- The iSNS server may host security services such as public key distribution.

- Authentication keys may be distributed during iSNS login.

- Public key security is scalable to large IP SANs.

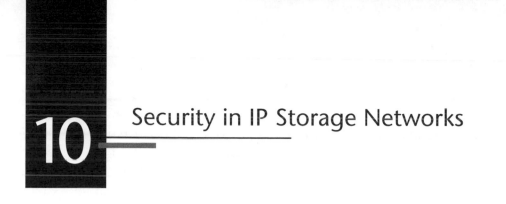

Security in IP Storage Networks

IP NETWORKING has created a variety of ways to safeguard data as it transits the network. This chapter examines the security options available for sensitive IP storage traffic that must traverse untrusted network segments.

10.1 Securing Storage Data Transport

Storage networks typically transport data that is critical to the ongoing operation of the enterprise. Although high-availability server clustering and data backup have been key business continuance drivers for SANs, less attention has been paid to fundamental security issues such as authentication and data encryption. Security issues for storage networks have come to the forefront, however, with the advent of storage over IP. The IP realm, as embodied by the Internet, has notorious security problems simply because of its ubiquity. The internals of IP networking are too well-known and too widely available to prevent even bored teenagers from making mischief with corporate data. The notion of transporting mission-critical storage data over untrusted networks would therefore be unacceptable if auxiliary security methods were unavailable.

The promise of IP storage networking includes the ability to leverage off-the-shelf technology for enhancing data security for SANs. These include firewall products, various authentication and encryption utilities, and VLANs for data center as well as VPNs for wide area applications. These facilities have been unavailable to Fibre Channel SANs because of the incompatibility between Fibre Channel and IP infrastructures. Adapting the FCP to IP transport, as with the iFCP protocol, enables even Fibre Channel end devices to benefit from advanced security utilities developed for IP.

10.2 Security in Fibre Channel SANs

Elementary security for Fibre Channel SANs is enforced by physical separation of networks. Fibre Channel assumes a dedicated network isolated from the user and public network. This separation is guaranteed by use of a unique protocol that is not easily deciphered by mainstream networking tools and by use of Fibre Channel switches that differ fundamentally from standard Gigabit Ethernet switches or IP routers. Because storage traffic and user traffic are physically isolated, access to storage data is restricted. Even supposing a disgruntled user could tap into a Fibre Channel link, a sophisticated analyzer would be required to intercept and decode storage data. The "alien" nature of Fibre Channel vis-à-vis mainstream IP networking is its first line of defense against security violations.

The vulnerability of a Fibre Channel SAN to penetration is exposed not through the Fibre Channel fabric itself but through its management interface. As with most networking equipment, fabric switches typically provide out-of-band management using SNMP over Ethernet. TELNET or SNMP GUIs may provide password protection, but unless the Ethernet network used for management is also isolated from the user network, it is possible to snoop and hack the management interface. Access to fabric management would not give the hacker access to storage data directly, but would allow, for example, a storage resource to be reassigned to a different server. To fill this security hole, some fabric vendors provide in-band management over Fibre Channel links. The tradeoff is that loss of a link may also mean loss of management visibility. Just when management status and diagnostics are needed the most, they would be unavailable.

The typical security concerns of Fibre Channel SANs are not focused on penetration from the outside, but segregation of storage resources within the SAN. If, for example, human resources and engineering share a Fibre Channel fabric, keeping human resource payroll data secure from the prying eyes of engineers is a priority. Fibre Channel enforces basic separation of applications and departments within the SAN through zoning.

10.2.1 Port Zoning

Port or "hard" zoning facilitates grouping of authorized SAN participants based on their physical port attachment. The fabric switch monitors the port-based zones and ensures that only devices in the same zone may communicate. Frames issued to a device outside the authorized zone are discarded, and, depending on vendor implementation, a security violation may be reported to management. If, for example, ports 1, 2, and 8 are in a common zone, the switch will discard any frames originating from port 5 that are addressed to port 8.

Because port zoning does not rely on soft addressing such as WWNs, it cannot be spoofed by manipulating the contents of the frame header. This makes zone enforcement secure, but requires closer attention to device attachment. If a server, for example, is moved from one switch port to another, the zone assignment will stay with the port, not the server. The server would lose its previous zone association and would be unable to communicate with its previously configured targets. In large storage networks with dynamic changes, port-based zoning requires significant administrative overhead.

10.2.2 WWN Zoning

A more flexible zoning mechanism for Fibre Channel SANs uses WWNs instead of port connections to enforce zones. The WWN is unique to every Fibre Channel device and is registered with the fabric during SNS login. The obvious advantage of WWN or "soft" zoning is that zone assignment follows the device, not the port to which the device is attached. A JBOD, for example, can be moved from one port to another without affecting its zone memberships. A further benefit of WWN zoning is the ability to place individual Fibre Channel devices into different zones even if they are connected to a single shared (FL_Port) port. In the JBOD example, different sets of disk drives in the JBOD chassis could be assigned to different zones. WWN zoning is advantageous for any loop segment hung from a fabric switch port and allows much more granularity than port zoning.

WWN zoning, however, can be spoofed, just as source IP addresses can be manipulated to bypass security enforcement. It would be more difficult to generate bogus source WWNs, but it is possible. Consequently, WWN zoning offers more flexibility than port zoning, but it is less secure.

In both port zoning and WWN zoning implementations, it is desirable for zones to extend across multiple Fibre Channel switches in a fabric. The fabricwide zoning specification is detailed in ANSI T11 FC-GS-3. In practical implementation, fabric switches must support a fabic zone server function for exchanging zone definitions. This would theoretically allow a multivendor fabric to share zones and to enforce accessibility of targets by initiators regardless of their location in the SAN.

10.2.3 LUN Masking

Another utility that is useful for secure access to storage provides a zoning capability based on logical units. Normally, when an initiator establishes a session with a target, it will query the storage device to find the logical units to which it can write and read data. The storage controller will respond to the REPORT LUNs command with a list of its LUNs. If multiple servers are accessing a large disk array, however, it may not be desirable for each server to see and (potentially) access all LUNs. In particular, if a large storage array is shared by different departments, the ability to hide certain LUNs would ensure that one department could not access the data belonging to another.

Some HBAs provide a LUN masking utility to restrict visibility of storage. When the HBA first boots, it will naturally discover all LUNs of all storage devices within its zone. An auxiliary utility allows an administrator to parse the LUN list and mark as "masked" any LUNs to which this particular HBA should not have access. When the HBA is rebooted, it will only see its assigned LUNs. The drawback with this implementation is that every HBA has to be configured manually, and the administrator must track all the server/LUN assignments individually.

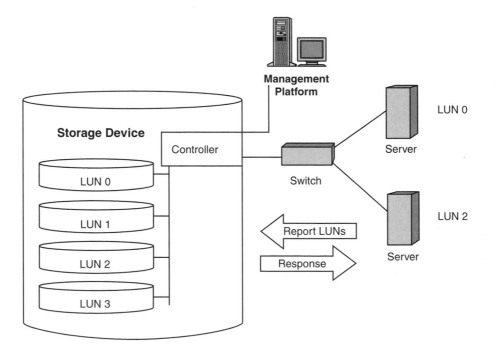

Figure 10–1 LUN masking implemented on a storage controller.

As shown in Figure 10–1, some disk array manufacturers implement LUN masking on the disk controller. This fulfills the same function as the HBA implementation, but likewise requires manual configuration of each disk array to associate individual LUNs with individual servers. In a multivendor environment, the administrator may have to use several different configuration utilities to perform LUN masking on different storage resources.

As yet, no standards specify how LUN masking should be implemented. Consequently, vendors use their own proprietary technique, and this in turn makes it difficult to manage as SANs scale to enterprisewide networks. As we will see, the logical residence for LUN masking functionality is in the storage switches that connect all storage resources. This facilitates more granular and secure storage access even for disk arrays and storage interfaces that do not support LUN masking on their own.

Aside from port and WWN zoning and proprietary LUN masking implementations, Fibre Channel has no integrated security facilitites. The FC-3 common services layer is a placeholder for data encryption and other functions, but these have not been fully formulated or implemented.

10.3 Security Options for IP Storage Networks

Because IP storage networks meld storage and IP networking components, IP SANs must provide comparable services for storage-specific requirements such as zoning and LUN masking as well as security mechanisms common to mainstream IP internetworking. A distinct advantage of IP SAN technology is the ability to leverage sophisticated security utilities for authentication and data encryption. This allows customers to deploy different security solutions that scale from simple zoning to encryption of data payloads. So although IP networking has inherent security exposure, products and utilities are already available to address security concerns.

10.3.1 Discovery Domains

As reviewed in the previous chapter on iSNS, the IP SAN equivalent of Fibre Channel zoning is provided by discovery domains. Discovery domains enforce a baseline security policy by restricting storage access to assigned initiators. As with soft zoning, the discovery domain to which a device is assigned follows the device, not the physical switch port to which it is attached. As storage resources are relocated in the IP SAN, they will remain in the same domain. In addition, DDSs can be used to reconfigure dynamically groups of authorized devices depending on application requirements. If iSNS is implemented in a centralized server, administration of domains is simplified. A single access point provides management visibility of all IP storage resources and their domain configurations.

For accommodation of Fibre Channel devices in an IP SAN, the iFCP protocol also extends discovery domains to individual Fibre Channel storage resources. This enables zoning of Fibre Channel nodes over an extended IP network and could bring Fibre Channel, iFCP, and iSCSI initiators and targets into defined spheres of communication.

10.3.2 LUN Masking

Because LUN masking is independent of the underlying plumbing, it may be implemented for both Fibre Channel and IP storage devices. Just as HBAs and Fibre Channel disk controllers may offer LUN masking as a value-added feature, IP storage NICs and IP-based disk arrays may provide a LUN masking capability for more discrete storage access. If implemented in an IP storage switch, however, LUN masking may be enabled for a much wider spectrum of targets and hosts. Gateway products based on iFCP and iSCSI, for example, could provide granular LUN assignment between existing Fibre Channel storage arrays and iFCP or iSCSI initiators.

10.3.3 VLAN Tagging

As reviewed in Chapter 3, the IEEE 802.1Q standard for VLANs enables individual packets to be associated with designated groups of authorized hosts. The 12-bit VLAN identifier allows for as many as 4,096 VLAN groups or zones within a single network. As a complement to discovery domains, VLAN tagging can be used to enforce traffic separation and prioritization through a switched Ethernet network. VLAN tagging is typically a standard offering for Gigabit Ethernet switches, as opposed to the à la carte option pricing for zoning and other functionality that has become the norm for Fibre Channel fabric switches.

10.3.4 IPSec

The security methods discussed so far have been based on simple segregation of storage resources, either on the basis of operating system, department, or shared storage access. These mechanisms offer rudimentary security, but the data payload in transit across the network is still readable. In addition, if an especially dedicated miscreant found means to spoof a device's identity, it could potentially intercept or copy storage data as it traversed the network.

IP was originally designed for an already-secure military network. It therefore had no inherent security functionality. With the expansion of the Internet and e-commerce applications, however, IP networking now has a diverse set of standard-based security methods to establish authentication between communicating devices and to encrypt sensitive user data.

At the networking layer, the framework for securing IP transactions is known as *IP Security* or IPSec. The IPSec architecture is, as of this writing, defined in the IETF RFC 2401 standards track document *Security Architecture for the Internet Protocol*. IPSec has two main components: authentication of the identity of communicating peers in the network, and data encryption. Authentication is defined in RFC 2402, *IP Authentication Header,* whereas payload encryption is defined in RFC 2406, *IP Encapsulating Security Payload (ESP)*. Because various authentication and encryption methods have evolved over time, IPSec does not specify an individual solution. The specific type of authentication or encryption to be used is negotiated by the end devices or is established by IPSec products, such as firewalls or IP routers with IPSec engines.

An IPSec implementation may use either authentication headers, encapsulating security payload (ESP), or a combination of both. To make storage data undecipherable, an ESP technique must be used. In addition, IPSec provides two types of connections (security associations) for establishing secure communications, as shown in Figure 10–2. In *transport mode,* the security mechanism is enforced at each host. This requires IPSec software or firmware on each communicating peer and a security protocol header immediately following the IP header (for IPv4). In *tunneling mode,* security gateways are the end points of the security association. In this mode, an IP datagram issued from an individual host would be encrypted and wrapped with an additional IP header addressed to the remote security gateway. Tunneling mode generally assumes that decrypted IP datagrams will be served up by the destination security gateway onto the destination LAN segment in their original form. This implies that the local LAN segment is itself secure, either via physical isolation or VLAN configuration.

Authentication and encryption methods are dependent on encryption *keys*. A key is a value that is applied in an encryption algorithm against standard data. The longer the key, the more difficult it is to decipher the newly encrypted data. The data encryption standard (DES), for example, uses a 56-bit key, allowing for as many as 72 quadrillion possible keys that could be applied to a datagram. In a well-publicized challenge, however, a DES-encrypted message was cracked, resulting in a more rigorous "triple DES" implementation. In triple DES, data blocks are passed through three different keys to encrypt them thoroughly.

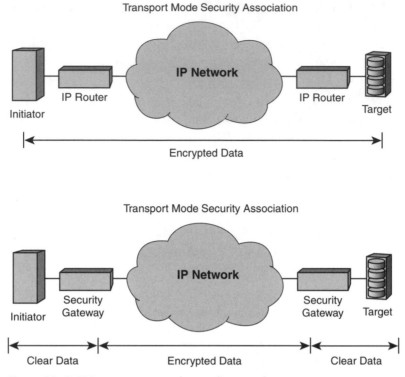

Figure 10–2 IPSec transport and tunneling modes.

Although secret keys such as DES can be used at both source and destination to encrypt and decrypt user data, both sides must have the same list of keys to be used to decipher arriving datagrams properly. Securely exchanging secret key lists is, therefore, an issue. Another approach provided by public key infrastructure (PKI) services uses public and private key pairs for data encryption and decryption. Based on the International Telecommunications Union (ITU) X.509 standard, PKI enables the distribution of public keys over untrusted networks, and relies on the security of individual hosts to maintain control over their private keys. A message that is encrypted by a remote host using one's public key can be decoded locally using one's private key.

PKI resolves the issue of sending public keys across untrusted networks, but for scalability requires central administration and distribution of keys. In addition, authentication between communicating devices requires proof that the public key advertised by an individual host in fact belongs to that host. This proof may be provided in the form of a *certificate* or digital signature—

typically a formatted file that authenticates public key ownership or assignment to a device via a certificate authority.

IPSec can be applied to IP storage networks in a variety of ways. The simplest approach is to install security firewalls with IPSec authentication and encryption between local IP SAN segments and any IP network links that pose potential security risks. Firewall products with Gigabit Ethernet interfaces provide speed compatibility with gigabit IP SANs, although IPSec will naturally engender some latency, depending on vendor implementation. Because the greatest security exposure is typically over WAN links, and WAN links themselves usually incur high latency, the overhead for IPSec processing may not be discernable.

In addition, IPSec may be implemented in IP storage switches and gateways to provide more integrated and possibly higher performance authentication and encryption services. This would also facilitate enforcement of enterprise security policies for local SAN segments as well as wide area or metropolitan configurations.

Finally, IPSec may be implemented directly on storage devices for end-to-end authentication and encryption. As reviewed in Chapter 9, the iSNS server may provide a distribution point for public keys, whereas the IP storage nodes themselves maintain private keys and digital signatures. The iSCSI login also provides for negotiated security services as IP storage devices establish sessions, including key exchanges and Kerberos authentication.

Whether the tradeoff between the additional cost/performance impact of security implementations and safeguarding of storage data is justified depends on the customer's requirements. With attention to SAN design, fairly secure data center IP SANs can be built using discovery domains, LUN masking, and VLANs. Dark fiber or leased lines may provide sufficient security for MAN or WAN storage links. Any shared infrastructure, however, should be implemented with the appropriate authentication and encryption tools. Fortunately for storage network administrators, a wide range of security products for IP networks are available, and they may be deployed to enable secure IP SANs.

10.3.5 Access Control Lists

Gigabit Ethernet switches and IP routers may support policy-based security controls through ACLs. A rudimentary ACL simply specifies a specific IP address or address range that is either permitted or denied access to a destination address. Enhanced ACLs may allow policies based on the type of IP traffic (for example, disallow UDP), as well as specific TCP or UDP port numbers. For example, an ACL may allow two IP addresses to communicate, but may prevent TFTP transactions between them. ACLs require manual configuration via the switch or a vendor configuration utility, but are useful barriers against undesirable access.

10.4 Chapter Summary

Securing Storage Data Transport

■ Security methods are required whenever mission-critical data is transported over untrusted networks.

■ IP storage raises security concerns and also provides off-the-shelf solutions.

Security in Fibre Channel SANs

■ Security of Fibre Channel SANs is typically provided by physical isolation from the messaging network and the use of nonmainstream protocols.

■ Fibre Channel fabrics may be vulnerable to security penetration through management interfaces.

■ Fibre Channel provides zoning to segregate storage resources.

Port Zoning

■ Port zoning is also known as *hard zoning*.

■ Port zoning associates groups of authorized devices based on their physical port attachment.

■ Zone assignments stay with the configured port, not the device.

WWN Zoning

■ WWN zoning is also known as *soft zoning*.

■ WWN zoning associates groups of authorized devices based on their unique 64-bit WWN identity.

■ WWN zoning assignments follow individual devices regardless of switch port attachment.

■ Fabric switches must be able to exchange zone information to enforce zone assignment throughout a complex fabric.

LUN Masking

- LUN masking restricts the logical view of storage resources by initiators.

- LUN masking may be implemented on Fibre Channel HBAs or on storage controllers.

- LUN masking enables a single large disk array to be shared by multiple departments, whereas each only sees its assigned LUNs.

- There are currently no standards for LUN masking.

Security in IP Storage Networks

- IP SANs must provide comparable services with Fibre Channel for basic zoning.

- IP SANs also enable the use of more sophisticated IP authentication and encryption tools.

Discovery Domains

- Discovery domains provide the equivalent service as Fibre Channel soft zoning.

- DDSs may be used to manage multiple zoned configurations per application requirements.

- The iFCP protocol extends discovery domain support to native Fibre Channel end nodes.

- An iSNS server provides centralized management of discovery domains.

LUN Masking

- LUN masking is protocol independent and may be implemented for IP SANs.

- LUN masking may be provided by IP storage NICs, IP storage nodes, or IP storage switches.

- Switch-based LUN masking enables more granular assignment of storage regardless of the capabilities of individual storage devices.

VLAN Tagging

- The IEEE 802.1Q standard for VLANs may be used to supplement discovery domain assignment.

■ VLAN tagging enables separation of storage traffic through a switched IP network.

■ VLAN tagging is a standard feature of most Gigabit Ethernet switches.

IPSec

■ The IPSec framework is described in RFC 2401, *Security Architecture for the Internet Protocol.*

■ IPSec includes authentication of end devices and encryption of user data.

■ Transport mode refers to end-to-end authentication and encryption.

■ Tunneling mode refers to gateway-to-gateway authentication and encryption.

■ Authentication and encryption rely on keys.

■ A key is a variable value applied in an encryption algorithm that processes blocks of data into encrypted output.

■ The DES provides a 56-bit key.

■ Triple DES uses three separate keys to encrypt data blocks.

■ PKI provides public key/private key pairs to facilitate key distribution over untrusted networks.

■ A certificate is a digital signature that verifies ownership of a public key.

■ IPSec may be implemented for IP SANs via firewalls, within storage switches or gateways, or on individual storage devices.

■ The iSNS specification facilitates public key distribution.

■ The iSCSI login process may include negotiated security mechanisms.

■ Shared network segments require some form of IPSec solution to ensure data security.

Access Control Lists

■ ACLs may be configured for Gigabit Ethernet switches or IP routers.

■ ACLs may permit or deny access based on IP address or address range.

■ ACLs may also permit or deny access based on IP traffic type, TCP port number, or UDP port number.

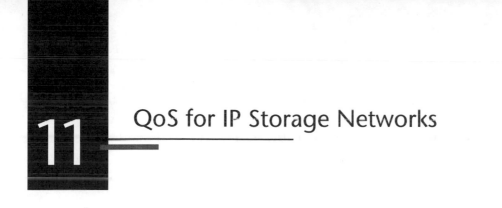

11 QoS for IP Storage Networks

THE ABILITY TO PRIORITIZE mission-critical data is one of the significant benefits of IP SANs. The following discussion examines the options available for establishing QoS policies to ensure data delivery in mixed traffic environments.

11.1 Class of Service and QoS

Without a means of setting data delivery policies, all data within a network infrastructure receives equal treatment. A download of an inconsequential but large graphics file would get the same priority as an on-line transaction processing an update of a critical customer order. Even in the absence of mixed traffic in a shared network, some applications require more strict enforcement of data delivery. In Fibre Channel SANs, for example, the vast majority of applications are run over fabrics using connectionless class 3 service. Class 3 provides best-effort delivery and no acknowledgment of data receipt. The next higher lever of service is class 2, which provides acknowledgment, and above class 2 there is class 1, which provides both connection establishment and frame acknowledgment. The tradeoff for improved class of service is normally performance. Acknowledgment requires additional processing on both ends to monitor frame transmission and receipt.

In the hierarchy of data delivery, class of service is a subset of QoS, although the two terms are sometimes used interchangeably when referring to specific implementations. Class of service typically refers to prioritization of different types of data during transport, whereas QoS may also include higher levels of service such as guaranteed bandwidth and expedited delivery of data. In IP networks, a variety of methods are available for providing different classes and qualities of service. When scaling from low to high service levels, additional requirements placed on network equipment result in greater complexity and cost. As with any advanced service, the customer must determine whether their data deserves the very best or whether it can be reasonably accommodated with the default features provided by the vendor.

Basic class-of-service functionality includes IEEE 802.1p traffic prioritization, the original TOS field in IP headers, and DiffServ for IP networking. Higher levels of quality service include guaranteed bandwidth via RSVP and MPLS for networked environments that may include a variety of transports including IP, ATM, and frame relay. DiffServ, RSVP, and MPLS are still under construction through IETF standards drafts, although vendors have proceeded to implement some functionality in products. To the extent that these advanced implementations actually work and interoperate, they can be leveraged for enhanced services for IP storage networks.

11.2 802.1p Traffic Prioritization

As discussed in Chapter 3, link-layer IEEE 802.1p/Q VLAN tagging includes a 3-bit field for specifying traffic prioritization levels. The 3-bit field allows for 8 levels of prioritization (0 to 7), with 7 representing the highest priority. Not all IP router or Gigabit Ethernet switch products support all 8 levels of priority, but most will provide at least 4 assignable levels.

Class-of-service prioritization is fulfilled through buffer queues. With no class-of-service designations, packets would be forwarded on a first-in/first-out basis through one buffer. Prioritization requires creation of multiple buffer queues so that traffic can be sorted by priority tag. As shown in Figure 11–1, the queues themselves are assigned priority levels so that higher priority queues will receive service before lower priority queues are processed. Typically, packets waiting in the lower priority queues will not be forwarded until the higher priority queues have been emptied.

The packet prioritization and buffer queue relationship allows vendors to implement 802.1Q for a variety of products. Low-end switches, for example, may provide fewer queues and may simply lump 801.2Q levels 4 through 7 into a single high-priority queue while processing levels 0 through 3 as ordinary traffic. High-end switches may provide a full complement of queues to accommodate each packet priority level. Transactions that involve sustained high-priority traffic may starve the low-priority queues, resulting in packet loss if timeout values are exceeded. To avoid this, some vendor implementations also incorporate a weighted round-robin scheduling routine to ensure that low-priority queues are serviced even during periods of high-priority transmission.

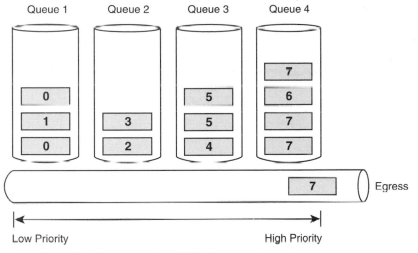

Figure 11–1 Priority queues for 802.1Q tagged packets.

Leveraging 802.1Q for IP storage traffic requires administration of priority levels and support for 802.1Q functionality by all switches within the IP storage network. For native iSCSI end devices attached to Gigabit Ethernet switches or IP routers, the switch vendor's configuration utility (SNMP MIB, GUI, or command-line interface) may be used to assign priority levels. For IP storage switches that support Fibre Channel devices, priority tags may, depending on vendor design, be assignable on a switch port or WWN basis. This allows traffic prioritization for Fibre Channel applications that otherwise would have to contend with other storage traffic. A mission-critical on-line transaction could therefore receive priority against tape backup or other lower priority jobs.

Because 802.1Q support is commonly a standard offering in Ethernet switch products, it provides an economical means to establish efficient link-layer class-of-service policies for different types of storage traffic.

11.3 Type of Service

At the network layer, the IP datagram header includes an 8-bit TOS field that may be used to indicate preference for data delivery class of service. As shown in Figure 11–2, the TOS field is divided into a 3-bit precedence field, a 4-bit field for setting TOS bits, and a single bit that is always zero (must be zero, or MBZ for acronym afficionados). The three precedence bits plus the zeroed bit leaves 4 bits for TOS designation.

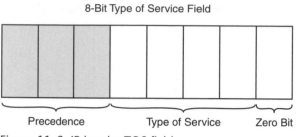

Figure 11–2 IP header TOS field.

Although the 4-bit TOS field could provide 16 different types of service, RFC 1349 defines only five classes of service:

1000—Minimize delay

0100—Maximize throughput

0010—Maximize reliability

0001—Minimize monetary cost

0000—Normal service

Bits may not be set in combination, so only one class of service can be assigned. Recommended values for different IP applications include maximize reliability (0010) for management using SNMP and maximize throughput (0100) for bulk data transfers such as FTP.

Unlike 802.1p, which only associates classes of service with priority queuing (equivalent to minimizing delay), TOS implies a greater sophistication in the routed infrastructure to monitor bandwidth, reliability, and cost. Sudden congestion on a particular link may require a TOS-enabled switch to make a new forwarding decision based on TOS requirements. In addition, applications must have access to the IP header layer to set the appropriate class-of-service bit in the TOS field.

Because of the limited interpretation available for TOS bits in setting different classes of service, the original 8-bit TOS field in the IP header has been redefined by the DiffServ initiative to provide greater flexibility.

11.4 Differentiated Services

As shown in Figure 11–3, DiffServ redefines the 8-bit TOS field in IPv4 (or traffic class octet in IPv6) to enable as many as 64 classes of service to be defined. As specified in RFC 2474 and RFC 2475, class of service is expanded from simple priority labeling to become a policy-based system. Class-of-service forwarding decisions are made at every network node or hop through the network according to per-hop-behavior (PHB) rules.

To provide backward compatibility with IP routers that use the TOS precedence bits, DiffServ defines those bits as class selector codepoints. The higher the numerical value represented by those bits, the greater protection a packet should have against packet discard. For those readers who imagine that pouring through standards drafts is rather monotonous, RFC 2474 offers the amusing observation that "a discarded packet is considered to be an extreme case of untimely forwarding" (page 11). A class selector codepoint of "000" indicates normal traffic that does not receive preferential treatment.

The DSCPs define the various delivery characteristics that should be enforced, but leave the mechanism for fulfillment to specific vendor implementation. The PHB indicated by a particular codepoint may therefore be executed in a variety of methods at different hops as a packet traverses the network. Some IP switches, for example, may use separate output queues with strictly enforced prioritization, whereas others may use weighted round-robin queuing to ensure delivery of nonpriority packets. What matters is that the PHB requirements indicated by the DSCPs are adequately fulfilled by the network router or switch.

A PHB can be used to implement a service level that may include specific requirements for prioritization, packet dropping preference, and bandwidth. Packet dropping rules augment prioritization in cases in which different applications usually have the same level of priority. HTTP and TELNET, for example, may be assigned the same priority under normal network traffic, with HTTP receiving preferential treatment over TELNET under abnormally congested conditions. This allows network administrators to establish class-of-service policies for different applications and still accommodate variations

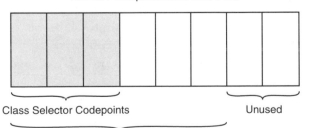

Figure 11–3 DiffServ redefinition of the IPv4 IP header TOS field.

in network conditions. Enforcement of bandwidth requirements may be as simple as selecting optimal routes, or as complex as proactive traffic shaping to ensure bandwidth availability. Joining PHB service indicators into PHB groups allows for class-of-service policies that may include combinations of requirements that are executed simultaneously (for example, guaranteed bandwidth plus low queue delay).

DiffServ PHB definitions include expedited forwarding (RFC 2598) and assured forwarding (RFC 2597). Expedited forwarding is a premium service for mission-critical applications or protocols such as voice over IP that requires consistent on-time performance. It is intended for satisfying low packet loss, guaranteed bandwidth, low delay, and low jitter requirements. Assured forwarding PHB facilitates aggregated packet flows by allowing the administrator to assign bandwidth and buffering guarantees to different traffic types or sources. These policies are useful for fulfilling service-level agreements between network administration and user departments, or between a provider and external customer.

In terms of security for DiffServ implementations, the main consideration is the integrity of the IP header containing the DSCP. In IPSec tunneling mode, for example, the entire IP datagram issued by a host is encrypted and placed within another IP envelop for transit across the tunnel. The original DSCP is thus encrypted along with the rest of the datagram and is invisible to anyone snooping the tunnel. In IPSec transport mode, the IP header DSCP is vulnerable to modification, although even if changed this will not affect data encryption. At the most, the PHB represented in the DSCP could be copied, with rogue packets using the assigned priority to hitch a faster ride through the network. In addition, the PHB on the original IPSec packet could be altered to a lower priority, amounting to a denial-of-service attack. In either case, data integrity would not be compromised, although class of service might.

Support for DiffServ functionality varies by vendor. As shown in Figure 11–4, DiffServ-capable IP routers and switches at boundary areas may set DSCP bits in packets originating from non-DiffServ network segments. This enables policy-based traffic forwarding within the DiffServ realm, even if the local segments treat all traffic equally. It is therefore feasible to leverage Diff-Serv for IP storage networking over WANs and MANs, even if the local IP SANs are not DiffServ enabled. In this example, traffic from host A could receive preference within the IP network, even though the packets it generates are not initially marked for priority delivery.

DiffServs offer more flexibility than 802.1Q prioritization and TOS levels, and less complexity than higher end QoS protocols such as RSVP and

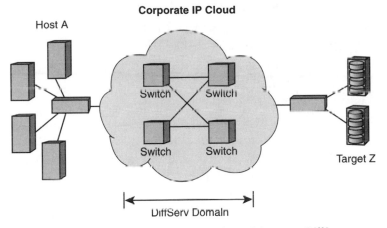

Figure 11–4 A DiffServ-enabled network servicing non-DiffServ segments.

MPLS. The latter, however, provide firmer guarantees of bandwidth availability and priority throughput.

11.5 Resource Reservation Protocol

RSVP is an implementation of Internet integrated services (RFC 1633) and uses a different QoS strategy in comparison with DiffServs. As originally defined in the RFC 2205 standards draft, RSVP may be used to establish QoS levels for application data streams or flows through the network. A data flow is a stream of packets originating from a single IP address/TCP port number and one or more fixed (for the duration of the flow) destination IP address/ TCP port numbers. A digital video multicast, for example, would have a single point of origin with multiple concurrent destinations. Unicast single source and single destination are also supported. The purpose of RSVP is to establish and maintain reserved bandwidth and priority service for the duration of the transaction. Storage applications that would benefit from RSVP include data replication and mirroring, remote backup and vaulting, as well as block-based postproduction video content distribution.

RSVP requires coordination of IP network resources to ensure availability of the requested QoS and to reserve the resulting data path from source to destination. A requesting end node, for example, would send an RSVP request to its local router or switch, indicating the QoS required and the source from which the data flow will be received. The RSVP-capable routers or switches would build the reserved data path using a normal routing protocol and class-of-service mechanisms until the path from source to destination was complete. If at any point a reserved network link supporting the requested QoS criteria cannot be established, the RSVP data path constructed thus far is dismantled. RSVP places considerable responsibility on the network infrastructure, including the authentication of the requesting device.

RSVP assumes sustained sequences of messages or packets that require guaranteed transmission rates through the network. A requesting host defines its requirements in a *flow specification,* which is used by RSVP network nodes to set up the data paths. Currently, RSVP supports data flows based on best-effort delivery, rate-sensitive delivery for applications such as video conferencing, and delay-sensitive delivery for applications such as streaming video. Delay-sensitive traffic would also logically include block SCSI data over IP, whether in the form of streaming video or a streaming tape backup, which must meet delivery requirements to avoid transport or upper layer timeouts. As shown in Figure 11–5, RSVP could be used to establish reserved paths for data replication.

Because RSVP is not universally deployed in IP networks, it must accommodate non-RSVP network segments. This is accomplished through RSVP tunneling across non-RSVP domains. Two RSVP-capable IP routers, for example, may establish a tunnel between them to traverse a network segment composed of ordinary routers. To meet the QoS specified in the RSVP request, however, the non-RSVP portion of the cloud must have excess bandwidth available. Otherwise, the RSVP QoS cannot be fulfilled. RSVP

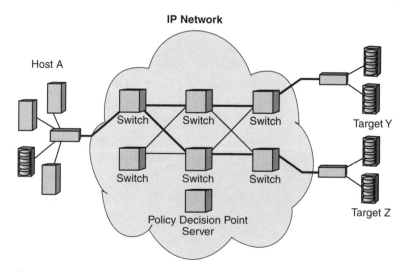

Figure 11–5 Using RSVP to reserve data paths for remote data replication.

tunneling thus has the implicit risk of failure if the non-RSVP routers become congested, because it has no means of enforcing resource reservation through the tunnel itself.

If every host is able to make RSVP requests without supervision, network resources could easily be monopolized. Centralized administration of RSVP requests is enabled by use of the Common Open Policy Service (COPS) protocol (RFC 2748). The COPS protocol facilitates authentication of permissions for RSVP requests through a centralized policy decision point (PDP), typically a network policy server that contains QoS rules for different traffic types. The policy enforcement points for ensuring compliance are the RSVP-capable routers and switches within the network. An RSVP router, for example, would use the COPS protocol to consult the PDP regarding whether a request for RSVP should be granted. This allows network administration to manage network resources and designate the hosts or traffic types that should receive priority in allocating RSVP resources.

The RSVP QoS implementation requires more logic in the IP routers and switches composing the network, reservation requests, and administration between hosts, routers and PDPs, and network management to ensure that RSVP flows do not overwhelm network resources. Once an RSVP data path is established, however, standard IP datagrams can be streamed from source to destination without modification. By contrast, MPLS manipulates IP datagrams within a stream to accelerate flows.

11.6 Multiprotocol Label Switching

MPLS, like RSVP, establishes data paths through the network to speed traffic flows and to enable QoS enforcement. Although RSVP establishes reserved routes based on RSVP requests and exchanges between RSVP-enabled routers, MPLS uses packet labeling. MPLS can be used in conjunction with RSVP to expedite traffic and to fulfill QoS commitments.

The architectural model for MPLS is defined in RFC 3031. The multiprotocol aspect of MPLS does not refer to specific IP protocols, but to interoperability between various transports, including IP, ATM, frame relay, and switched optical networks. The label switching aspect of MPLS resides somewhere between layer 2 and layer 3, or, according to some vendor literature, is a fusion of layer 2 and layer 3. The advantage of label switching is that routing decisions can be made more easily on the basis of the label values as opposed to traditional next-hop routing tables. In conventional IP routing, each router must examine the network layer information in an IP packet and make a next-hop routing decision based on routing information tables built via OSPF or RIP. In MPLS, the network layer of a packet is examined only once, as the packet enters the network. As shown in Figure 11–6, the edge MPLS router (label switch router or LSR) applies a label (header) to the packet and sends it to the next LSR. Thereafter, next-hop forwarding from router to router is done on the basis of labeling, with the label finally removed from the packet as it exits the last-edge MPLS router.

In traditional IP routing, the network address is used for routing table lookup and next-hop forwarding. Through a complex network, traffic flowing from a number of sources may arrive at a router and, based on routing algorithms, may be forwarded to a specific next hop in the network. Although the received packets may represent very different applications and ultimately different host destinations, if they share a common next-hop decision they may be considered to be a single class of traffic. MPLS uses the term *forwarding equivalence classes* (FECs) to refer to this commonality, and associates FEC grouping with specific label assignment. At the entry point to the MPLS network, the packet header and network address are examined. The packet is assigned to an FEC via a label or header, and the label follows the packet as it transits the network. The value represented in the label is not static, but is revised hop by hop by subsequent LSRs to complete the network path. A Label Distribution Protocol (LDP) is used between LSRs to negotiate binding of FECs to specific labels.

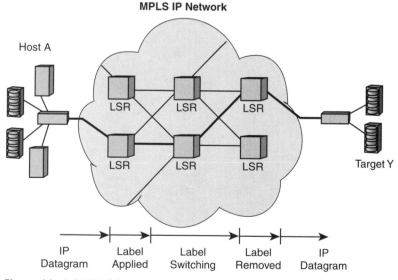

Figure 11–6 MPLS label switching.

Because labels are applied and removed only by LSRs, MPLS is transparent to the end nodes benefiting from expedited service. Depending on vendor implementation, label assignment may be based in part on class-of-service codepoints specified by the DiffServ field in an IP header, so that the label switch route through the network reflects delivery characteristics required by the sending device.

Aside from fast routing and improved QoS, MPLS provides a means to switch IP datagrams quickly in ATM and optical networks that lack layer 3 network routing capability. This will provide more flexibility for IP storage transport as well as high-speed optical, switched networks which are deployed for MANs and WANs.

11.7 Chapter Summary

Class of Service and QoS

- Class of service is required to give preferential treatment to data as it transits the network.

- Class of service refers to prioritization of different traffic types.

- QoS includes class-of-service features as well as bandwidth allocation and timely delivery guarantees.

- Class of service includes 802.1p link-layer prioritization, IP header TOS bits, and DiffServ.

- QoS includes bandwidth allocation via RSVP and MPLS.

- Standard class-of-service and QoS mechanisms can be leveraged for IP storage networking.

802.1p Traffic Prioritization

- The IEEE 802.1p standard is a link-layer method for assigning priority to a frame.

- A 3-bit prioritization field provides 8 levels of service (levels 0–7) with level 7 representing the highest priority.

- 802.1p is enforced through buffer queuing in IP switches.

- Different priority queues may be used to sort frames with different levels of 802.1Q prioritization.

■ Weighted round-robin queueing algorithms ensure that low-priority queues are serviced even during periods of high-priority traffic.

Type of Service

■ The 8-bit TOS field in an IP header may be used to establish required delivery characteristics.

■ TOS classes of service include options based on delay, throughput, reliability, cost, and normal treatment.

■ Only one type of TOS may be selected per IP datagram.

Differentiated Services

■ DiffServ uses the TOS field in IPv4 packets to provide more flexible class-of-service offerings.

■ DiffServ enables policy-based traffic prioritization.

■ Forwarding decisions are made on the basis of PHB rules.

■ Six bits of the TOS field are used to indicate the DSCP or PHB.

■ Satisfying PHB requirements is left to the specific vendor implementation.

■ Expedited forwarding is provided as a premium service for mission-critical applications.

■ Assured forwarding enables bandwidth and buffering guarantees for aggregated traffic.

■ DiffServ may be combined with IPSec for data encryption.

Resource Reservation Protocol

■ RSVP establishes guaranteed bandwidth for data flows.

■ A data flow is a stream of packets from a source to one or more destination IP addresses.

■ RSVP-capable routers build a reserved data path through the network in response to an RSVP request from a host.

■ The requesting host indicates the preferred class of service via a flow specification.

■ RSVP supports data flows based on best-effort delivery, rate-sensitive delivery, and delay-sensitive delivery.

■ Delay-sensitive applications may include block data streaming for video or streaming backup.

■ An RSVP tunnel may be created to span network segments that do not support RSVP services.

■ Administration of RSVP requests may be enabled by COPS.

■ A PDP is typically a server attached to the network that maintains a QoS database.

■ Policy enforcement points are COPS entities in RSVP-capable switches and routers.

Multiprotocol Label Switching

■ MPLS uses labels to expedite traffic through the network.

■ A label may be a header inserted in front of a standard IP datagram.

■ MPLS is designed to work in IP, ATM, frame relay, and optical networks.

■ An MPLS-capable router is referred to as an LSR.

■ An edge LSR applies a switching label to an IP datagram as it enters the network.

■ The MPLS label is removed before the IP datagram is delivered to the destination LAN segment.

■ FEC refers to groups of packets with common next-hop requirements.

■ Labels are bound to FECs through LDP between LSRs.

■ Labels may be assigned on the basis of class of service indicators in the DSCP field.

■ MPLS is transparent to the IP end nodes.

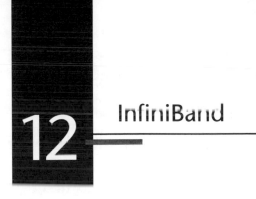

12 InfiniBand

ALTHOUGH IP STORAGE is reshaping the san infrastructure, InfiniBand promises to alter radically the servers attached to the SAN. This chapter provides an overview of the InfiniBand architecture and discusses the integration of InfiniBand servers with IP SANs.

12.1 InfiniBand Architecture

InfiniBand represents a major renovation of server architecture and server I/O to peripheral devices such as storage. Originally two separate initiatives (Next Generation I/O from Intel and Future I/O from IBM, Compaq, and Hewlett-Packard), InfiniBand standards are currently being driven by the merged InfiniBand Trade Association (IBTA). The problems InfiniBand is addressing stem from the increasing divergence between CPU processor speed and the ability of the I/O bus to support concurrent high-speed transactions. The 66-MHz PCI bus or 133-MHz peripheral component interconnect extended (PCIX) bus designs in current server platforms are increasingly inadequate for gigahertz and higher multiprocessor servers. The InfiniBand architecture intends to replace the standard bus with a switch matrix, patterned after Fibre Channel and Gigabit Ethernet switching.

As with SCSI bus limitations, the server bus has inherent limitations in terms of device support and distance. Extending a high-speed bus to accommodate higher populations of adapter cards is difficult without inadvertantly creating timing and skew issues. In addition, the bus is a shared architecture. Contention for bus access by high-speed adapters may affect performance, whereas failure of a single adapter card can cause the bus to crash. Lack of scalability has hindered the server manufacturers' ability to leverage much higher performance CPUs and interprocess communications (IPCs) for multiprocessor and clustered environments.

Replacing the traditional bus with a switch matrix is a radical departure from conventional server architecture and enables radically new relationships between CPUs, memory, and server I/O. InfiniBand introduces the concept of a channel adapter (CA) as a means of decoupling memory queueing, memory protection, and I/O protocol processing from the CPU. By assuming these tasks, the CA off-loads the CPU and distributes intelligence to the InfiniBand fabric. InfiniBand host channel adapters (HCAs) service the CPU, whereas target channel adapters (TCAs) provide InfiniBand connection to external peripherals and networks. As shown in Figure 12–1, InfiniBand assumes a switch infrastructure to join HCAs and TCAs.

The InfiniBand specification calls for an initial switch matrix based on 2.5-Gbps links (known as 1X), with a road map for 10 Gbps (4X) and 30 Gbps (12X). InfiniBand uses a four-copper wire or two-fiber-optic lead cabling scheme with distance support limited to 17 m for copper and 100 m for fiber-optic cabling. For 10-Gbps support, InfiniBand requires 16 copper wires or 8 fiber-optic leads per link, whereas 30 Gbps would require 48 copper wires or 24 fiber-optic leads per link. InfiniBand cabling thus resurrects a buslike cable scheme to achieve higher speeds. This unique cabling plant implies close proximity of servers, switches, and TCAs, and requires gateways such as routers or InfiniBand-to-Gigabit Ethernet devices to reach beyond the server cluster.

Communications over the InfiniBand fabric are performed through virtual lanes (VLs). A VL represents a pair of receive and transmit buffers on a port, with each VL providing its own flow control. Each port or link may support as many as 15 VLs for data and one for management. The different

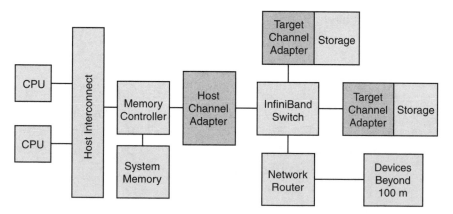

Figure 12–1 InfiniBand server architecture based on the IBTA model.

data streams originating from an HCA are mapped to VLs and are multi-plexed into a single serial stream for transport over the link, and are then separated at the receiving end.

Segregation of resources is provided by partitioning. Hosts may share a common partition as in, for example, server clustering or IPC applications. Hosts may also be partitioned into the equivalent of zones with their own external resources. Overlapping partitions are allowed to facilitate different application requirements.

With a new switch matrix connecting servers to servers and servers to external resources, InfiniBand proposes a new protocol for direct memory-to-memory communications between devices. The InfiniBand protocol is primarily intended as a subnet protocol, reflecting its server-centric focus, and not a networking protocol comparable with IP. For subnet transactions within a cluster group, InfiniBand uses 64-bit addressing. For external transactions between InfiniBand subnets, 128-bit IPv6 addressing is used. This enables InfiniBand traffic to integrate more easily into mainstream IP networking via IP routers with optional InfiniBand interfaces or InfiniBand-to-IP gateways. As shown in Figure 12–2, traffic within an InfiniBand subnet is data link switched from source to destination, whereas off-subnet traffic is routed using network-layer addressing.

In InfiniBand parlance, upper layer applications are *consumers*. Consumers, as may be expected, are divided into privileged and user level, with privileged consumers having access to the HCA and system memory manipulation.

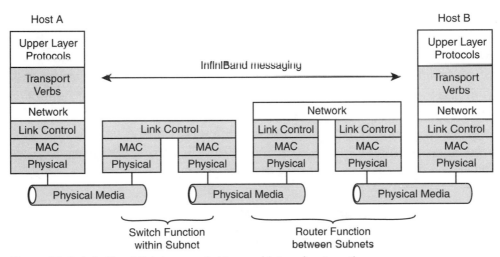

Figure 12–2 InfiniBand link-layer switching and intersubnet routing.

Consumers communicate with the transport layer through verbs that are used to create, modify, or delete memory address points or to establish queue pairs within the HCA for data transport. On receiving data from an upper layer application, the transport layer segments the data into packets that can vary from 256 to 4,096 bytes in length. Packets contain a globally unique identifier of the destination, and are given route information by the network layer. For intrasubnet traffic, the data link layer appends a local identifier to the packet before it is handed off to the physical layer. Despite the new names assigned to established processes, this may sound very familiar.

Communcation between InfiniBand servers and devices is accomplished through messages. Messages may be RDMA read or write operations that provide high-speed data transfer without the load and store overhead characteristic of shared buses. Messaging is also used to establish connection setup between CAs before data transfer begins.

For security, InfiniBand assumes that the subnet of servers and devices will be secured through physical isolation. Although a system of authorization keys are defined, the keys themselves are passed through InfiniBand messages and thus could be easily discovered by anyone sniffing the subnet. Management and access keys are therefore only useful as a first-line defense against inadvertent configuration changes or device assignment. In terms of security facilities available in IP networking, InfiniBand security needs much more work.

QoS for InfiniBand is also under construction. The service-level mechanisms can be used to assign traffic to specific VLs for bandwidth availability. In addition, partitioning of servers and resources into working groups protects a partition from the effects of bandwidth consumption by other partitions. The underlying assumption in the superficial treatment of QoS is that bandwidth availability is not a pressing issue. This is probably a safe assumption to make until InfiniBand solutions are deployed in production environments.

Given the comprehensive set of engineering challenges that InfiniBand poses, the rollout of InfiniBand servers will be focused on server-specific applications such as parallel processing and server clustering. The switching and network components as well as viability of InfiniBand-based storage will be driven by the rate of market acceptance of new server platforms.

12.2 InfiniBand and Storage Networking

Because InfiniBand is a complete revision of conventional I/O, InfiniBand servers cannot directly access the installed base of storage devices. Storage arrays with SCSI, Fibre Channel, or Gigabit Ethernet require an intermediate gateway, both to translate between different physical media and transport protocols and to convert SCSI, FCP, and iSCSI data into InfiniBand format.

One solution is to provide a CA that can accommodate PCI and PCIX adapter cards, including HBAs and Gigabit Ethernet NICs. Such accommodation is almost a certainty, because it would be unreasonable to expect customers to "forklift" their current peripheral, storage, and networking investment to benefit from InfiniBand server clustering performance. The migration from PCI-based servers to InfiniBand servers will be facilitated by backward compatibility with the installed base currently servicing enterprise networks.

Another solution is offered by TCAs, which bring SCSI and other devices into InfiniBand at the edge of the subnet. Just as Gigabit Ethernet-to-SCSI bridges can leverage SCSI disks and tape subsystems for IP storage, InfiniBand-to-SCSI bridges can provide connectivity to storage resources that otherwise would be unreachable. These may be specialized bridge products with dedicated connections, or intelligent storage switches that provide any-to-any connectivity between InfiniBand, SCSI, Fibre Channel, IP storage, and IP internetworking. The latter simplifies deployment for the administrator, who would rather not support mulitple boxes for disparate technologies.

The native solution for InfiniBand storage is being worked through NCITS T10 in the form of a Serial RDMA Protocol (SRP) over VI initiative. This protocol must accomplish serial SCSI mapping comparable with FCP and iSCSI, with the added task of moving block SCSI data directly into system memory via RDMA. As with FCP and iSCSI, SRP must establish a login routine between initiator and target, query LUNs, and support SCSI commands, data, and status over a serial link. For SRP, the channel and messaging mechanism of InfiniBand replaces Fibre Channel's exchange and iSCSI's TCP connections. SRP may assist integration of IP storage with InfiniBand, however, by providing a structured serial SCSI equivalent that facilitates mapping between the two protocols.

Considering the difficulties associated with reengineering the server architecture to abolish the conventional bus architecture, InfiniBand proponents have put more developmental effort into server design and protocols. Server I/O for storage has received less attention, although major storage vendors are anxious to leverage the performance advantages that InfiniBand promises for high-end enterprise applications. The gating factor for InfiniBand storage is not the developmental priorities of the server manufacturers, but the commitment by storage manufactures to provide InfiniBand interfaces. Because these vendors are already supporting SCSI, Fibre

Channel, and IP storage interfaces, the decision to implement an additional interface will be driven by market demand and advantages over other solutions.

For systems and storage administrators, the diversity of new offerings from technology providers can be overwhelming. There is little benefit to high-performance servers if they cannot attach to networked storage, and no one can wait until a new technology delivers all of its own pieces required for a coherent implementation. InfiniBand adoption will therefore be dependent on intelligent storage switches that can provide connectivity to SCSI, Fibre Channel, and IP storage.

In addition, although almost everyone would be glad to see the conventional bus go away, it's not clear that InfiniBand will ever dominate the data center switch infrastructure. By the time InfiniBand switch products based on 2.5 Gbps are deployed, Ethernet would already have delivered 10-Gbps performance. Raw speed may not fix the server bus problem, but it will be difficult to justify InfiniBand switching as a new infrastructure when mainstream transports are much faster and, via intelligent storage switches, can provide InfiniBand gateway ports as well. If Infiniband is deployed at comparable 10-Gbps bandwidth, this will make it easier to match 10-Gbps Ethernet to 10-Gbps Infiniband for high-speed applications, but will still require CAs to bridge between server clusters and the rest of the network.

12.3 Chapter Summary

InfiniBand Architecture

- InfiniBand replaces the traditional server bus with a high-speed switch matrix.

- InfiniBand protocols enable direct data placement in memory via RDMA.

- HCAs provide memory queueing, memory protection, and I/O protocol processing tasks.

- TCAs enable connection to external peripherals such as storage.

- InfiniBand switching provides 2.5 Gbps per link.

- High speeds are achieved by bundling additional copper or fiber-optic pairs.

- InfiniBand cabling has limited distance support, with 17 m for copper and 100 m for fiber optics.

- Communication paths over InfiniBand links are established by VLs.

- A single link may support as many as 15 VLs for data and one for management.

- InfiniBand offers partitioning as a means to zone resources.

- A local InfiniBand grouping is refered to as a *subnet*.

- Subnet communications are performed via data link switching.

- Intersubnet communication is based on IPv6 addressing and network routing.

- Upper layer applications are known as *consumers*.

- InfiniBand has limited security and QoS support.

InfiniBand and Storage Networking

- InfiniBand requires gateways for connectivity to SCSI, Fibre Channel, or IP storage resources.

- Specialized bridges may provide InfiniBand-to-SCSI connectivity.

- Intelligent storage switches may provide any-to-any storage connectivity.

- SRP is being developed as a native InfiniBand serial SCSI-3 protocol.

- Native InfiniBand storage deployment will be driven by storage vendors and market demand.

- InfiniBand switching must compete with 10-Gbps Ethernet for control of the data center.

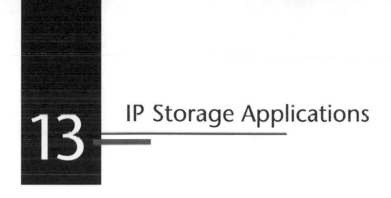

13 IP Storage Applications

AS NEW IP STORAGE PRODUCTS come to market, customers have additional options for solving storage problems. The following application studies provide examples of how existing SCSI, Fibre Channel, and IP storage products can be combined to deliver integrated IP SAN solutions.

13.1 IP Storage in Data Center Applications

Storage network solutions have steadily penetrated enterprise networks to address a wide variety of application issues. SAN adoption has occurred primarily in the larger data center environments where technical resources and budgets are available to meet increasing storage requirements. Traditional direct-attached SCSI storage, however, continues to ship in large volume. This may not mean that other enterprises are content with the limitations of conventional SCSI, but may simply indicate that they lack the budget and the expertise to deploy and support SANs based on Fibre Channel technology. By minimizing the Fibre Channel component in SANs, IP storage networking may accelerate the adoption of networked storage. Using familiar switched Etherent infrastructures and existing network administration and support, more enterprises can leverage the benefits of SANs while minimizing the pain that typically accompanies new-technology deployment.

Although enterprise storage networks may support a wide variety of concurrent applications, SAN solutions have been most successful when they are targeted at resolving specific problems. Solution providers, for example, typically do not market SANs as a generic high-speed infrastructure, but package product sets that address specific customer needs. High availability may be packaged as a solution set that includes recommended server models, adapter cards, storage switches, storage devices, and supporting software. Storage consolidation may be packaged as a certified solution of storage array, storage switch, and recommended storage adapters for the customer's host platforms. A tape backup solution set may include a recommended tape subsystem sized to the customer's storage capacity needs, a storage switch, and qualified host adapters and software. It is not uncommon to see a data center with multiple unconnected SAN islands, each representing a specific application need, and often rack mounted inches from each other.

This segregation of SANs based on application requirements has been reinforced by the slow progress of interoperability between Fibre Channel switches. Solution providers themselves often discourage interconnecting SANs, fearful that an untested fabric configuration will disrupt the specific solution they have installed. Because IP storage relies on mainstream Ethernet switching for connectivity, this is an area in which IP storage can rationalize SAN deployment and create a more integrated approach to data center storage networking.

The following application studies will review the major applications that are natural targets for storage networking and will show how different IP storage solutions can be used as complements to or replacements for Fibre Channel components. Anticipating that customers may have mixed environments of traditional SCSI and Fibre Channel storage, examples will demonstrate how these may be combined into a working IP SAN solution. In addition, where appropriate, the IP storage products shown here are depicted generically to avoid "obsoleting" the example. Vendors are constantly introducing new configurations and functionality into products, so the focus here is on basic features and protocols required to support the configurations shown.

13.1.1 Server Clustering

High availability of applications and data has been a central issue for enterprise networks, especially as mission-critical applications and data have migrated from highly reliable mainframe systems to less reliable server platforms. The tradeoff for the reduced cost and greater flexibility offered by servers is the additional requirement for redundancy in the event of server failure. The $7 \times 24 \times 365$ operation characteristic of Internet-based e-commerce and global enterprises has aggravated the need for data availability and has spawned new software and hardware solutions.

SAN technology is an enabler for high-availability server clustering. Small two-node clusters may be built with direct SCSI-attached storage, but networked storage is required for larger multinode configurations. Server clustering has two basic components. First, clustering software is required so that servers may monitor the status of individual servers within the cluster and assume their tasks in the event of failure. Depending on the supplying vendor, clustering software may trigger a failover when a server suffers a catastrophic failure, or may failover when a particular hardware or software component within the server fails. Status between servers is exchanged through a heartbeat protocol, essentially compact keep-alive messages passed over IP.

The second major clustering component is the SAN that joins the clustered servers to common disk resources. One or more disk arrays are normally partitioned into logical units, with each server in the cluster assigned to separate logical units. If an individual server fails, a server in the cluster would map to the failed unit's LUNs and continue operation. With more sophisticated software, a server cluster could share logical units simultaneously. This requires lock handling so that files are not inadvertantly overwritten. Sharing of storage resources requires connectivity between the collective initiators and their targets. In Fibre Channel SANs, this is provided by HBAs, Fibre Channel switches, and Fibre Channel storage interfaces. IP storage offers several means to share resources, depending on the components the customer wishes to integrate.

In Figure 13–1, a server cluster based on an IP SAN infrastructure relies on existing Fibre Channel storage.

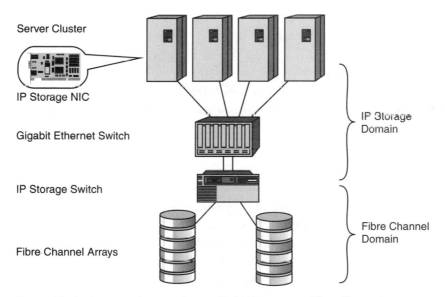

Figure 13–1 A server cluster using an IP SAN to access Fibre Channel storage arrays.

In this example, Gigabit Ethernet NICs with either iFCP or iSCSI proto-col stacks allow direct attachment to a Gigabit Ethernet switch for block storage access. The IP storage NIC may also have a TOE and specialized logic for SCSI processing. With the appropriate storage NIC, the same con-nection used for block storage may also be used for clustering heartbeat mes-sages, whereas Fibre Channel-based clusters typically require an external Ethernet connection for heartbeat. Because Fibre Channel storage does not allow direct Ethernet attachment, an IP storage switch is needed to convert Fibre Channel to Gigabit Ethernet. "Trunked" links between the Gigabit Ethernet switch and the IP storage switch provide higher bandwidth for con-current server access to storage. In this example, the two Fibre Channel stor-age arrays would be adequately serviced by a two-line trunk.

The IP storage switch may be provided in various configurations. Some vendors only provide fixed Gigabit Ethernet and fixed Fibre Channel port configurations, whereas others allow Gigabit Ethernet or Fibre Channel attachment on any port. In the latter instance, the port design must accom-modate both the 1.25-Gbps speed of Gigabit Ethernet and the 1.0625 Gbps of Fibre Channel. Some GBICs support both speeds.

The IP storage protocol used also depends on vendor implementation. Because the iFCP protocol uses Fibre Channel serial SCSI-3, less conversion is performed by the IP storage switch sitting between the Fibre Channel end device and the iFCP storage NIC. An iSCSI IP storage NIC would require conversion from Fibre Channel serial SCSI-3 to iSCSI serial SCSI-3. Whether this would have a performance impact is vendor dependent. Because this example depicts a contained data center environment with no lossy wide area segments, it would also be possible to run the mFCP protocol for higher performance. The mFCP protocol uses UDP/IP and thus requires no TOE. If mFCP is used, the Gigabit Ethernet switches should have 802.3x flow con-trol enabled to prevent buffer overruns.

The diagram shown in Figure 13–1 fulfills the basic requirements for server clustering. If a single server fails, other servers in the cluster have access to its data. In this configuration, however, each server has only a single data path to the IP SAN, as does each disk array. For full redundancy, duplicate Ethernet switches and IP storage switches should be used, as shown in Figure 13–2. This fully redundant configuration accommodates the failure of any single link within the SAN and enables data access even if a entire switch fails. In addition, if the two storage arrays shown represent a pri-mary and secondary disk mirror, redundancy extends to the data block level as well.

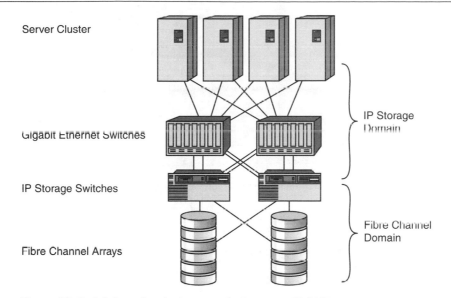

Figure 13–2 A fully redundant server cluster on an IP SAN.

Several variations on this theme are possible. The Ethernet switch shown in Figure 13–1 could be a director-class, high-availability switch. In this case, a single Gigabit Ethernet switch may be used instead of the two shown in Figure 13–2, with redundant links from each server connected to different switch blades. In addition, the Gigabit Ethernet switch and IP storage switch functions may be combined in a single unit. As shown in Figure 13–3, IP storage switches are used to connect the server cluster to storage. Because the server connectivity is still Gigabit Ethernet and IP, heartbeat messaging is accommodated as well.

The advantage of using larger Gigabit Ethernet switches is scalability. Director-class Gigabit Ethernet switches fulfill the same function as director-class Fibre Channel switches in providing a high-performance switched back-bone capable of supporting fan-out to high populations of storage devices and hosts.

Because Gigabit Ethernet is used as the SAN interconnect, scaling to large server cluster configurations can be accomplished without the complexities of an extended Fibre Channel SAN. For Fibre Channel switches, each server cluster must either be a stand-alone entity or must be part of a single physical fabric. As stand-alone clusters, each cluster must be managed separately. As a single extended fabric, disruptions on one part of the fabric could affect the entire fabric. In an IP SAN configuration, all server clusters can be

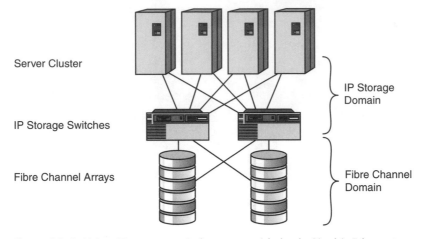

Figure 13–3 Using IP storage switches to provide both Gigabit Ethernet and Fibre Channel connectivity.

part of one network (facilitating management and connectivity), whereas potential disruptions are isolated to individual cluster segments. The iFCP protocol, for example, proxies fabric attachment for Fibre Channel storage and hosts while maintaining separation of assigned groups of devices. The iSNS server function can be used to assign discovery domains as well as to enforce public key authentication to ensure that only designated servers are grouped into the appropriate clusters. As shown in Figure 13–4, multiple server clusters can be configured into a single IP SAN while maintaining cluster integrity and common management.

As IP storage interfaces become available on high-performance storage arrays, server clustering configurations can migrate from Fibre Channel to native IP storage targets. Figure 13–5 depicts a server cluster with access to both Fibre Channel and native IP storage.

For customers who have already deployed server clusters with Fibre Channel HBAs and who wish to leverage the benefits of IP SANs, IP storage switches that accommodate both Fibre Channel initiators and targets may be used. As shown in Figure 13–6, IP storage switches can be deployed for both server and storage access. This configuration allows the customer simply to replace a Fibre Channel fabric with an IP fabric with no changes to the end nodes themselves. It also facilitates management and extensibility of the SAN using well-understood Ethernet and IP technologies. Additional servers may be added to the cluster using IP storage NICs. To date, only the iFCP protocol supports native IP mapping for Fibre Channel hosts.

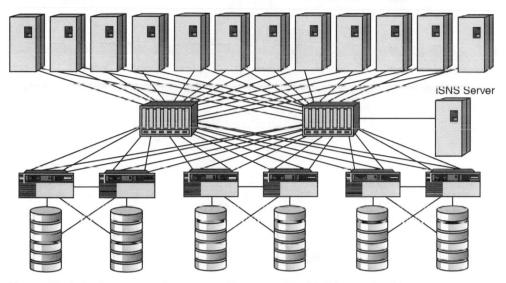

Figure 13-4 Scaling server clusters on a IP storage Gigabit Ethernet backbone.

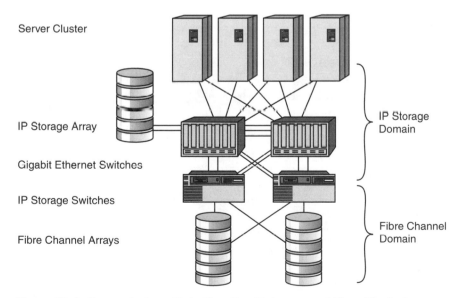

Figure 13-5 Server cluster with both native IP storage and Fibre Channel arrays.

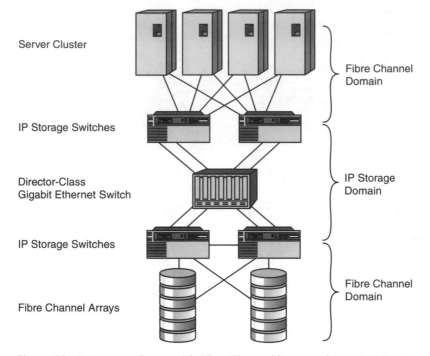

Figure 13–6 A server cluster with Fibre Channel hosts and targets joined by an IP storage network.

A much-neglected area for server clustering is the accommodation of direct SCSI-attached storage and hosts over a storage network. IP storage bridges that provide support for both initiators and targets can leverage the distance, performance, and scalability of IP SANs while still preserving customer investment in legacy SCSI devices. As shown in Figure 13–7, a SCSI SAN for server clustering provides the same benefits of Fibre Channel SANs without the additional cost of HBAs and Fibre Channel storage. Because the SCSI hosts are connected to the IP SAN via parallel SCSI cabling, an external Ethernet or Fast Ethernet LAN connection is required for cluster heartbeats. This configuration puts advanced high-availability solutions into the hands of customers who, as a result of budget or support constraints, have not yet implemented SAN solutions. They also gain the benefit of nondisruptive addition of storage resources, a critical issue in high-availability operations that cannot be resolved by conventional direct-attached SCSI.

At some future point, native IP and Gigabit Ethernet interfaces will displace Fibre Channel as the default offering of solution providers, resulting in certified solutions based exclusively on IP. Figure 13–8 depicts a

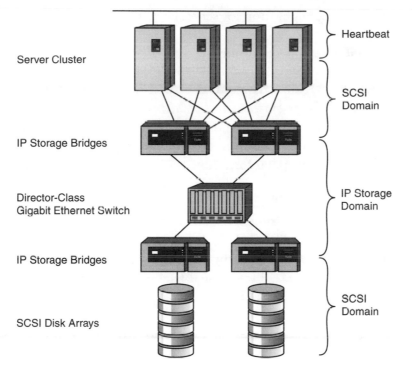

Figure 13–7 A server cluster with SCSI hosts and targets joined by an IP storage network.

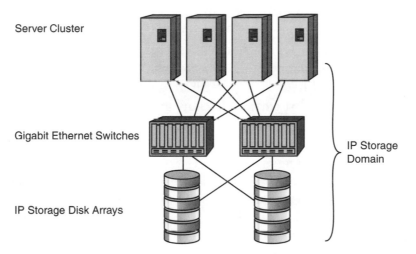

Figure 13–8 Server clusering with end-to-end native IP storage networking.

pristine IP storage configuration for server clustering, minus any Fibre Channel component.

Because one of the prime directives of InfiniBand is to facilitate server clusters, IP storage networking must eventually service InfiniBand hosts as well as native IP or Fibre Channel hosts. As discussed in Chapter 12, integrating InfiniBand server clusters into IP SANs will require TCAs to bridge InfiniBand to Gigabit Ethernet and IP. TCAs may be stand-alone bridge products or may be embedded into intelligent storage switches that provide ports and protocol conversion for InfiniBand and IP-attached storage.

13.1.2 Local Tape Backup

Securing disk data by periodic backups to tape is a universal problem and has been one of the main drivers for SAN adoption. As data storage has grown from gigabytes to terabytes, simply allotting sufficient time for backup is a pressing issue. In traditional backup scenarios, file and application servers are prompted to initiate scheduled backups by a dedicated backup server. Backup traffic is passed over the LAN between the file server and the server hosting a tape subsystem. For Fast Ethernet LANs, the sudden influx of streaming backup files can overwhelm backbone resources. Gigabit Ethernet LANs may be less impacted by backup streams, but still face the issue of user traffic and storage data sharing the same network.

The separation of backup traffic from the messaging LAN is known as *LAN-free backup*. The creation of a separate network to support server backup was implicit in Fibre Channel topologies. Fibre Channel is a distinct transport and is not normally used to support end-user messaging. Consequently, creating a separate network dedicated to block storage data movement was enforced by Fibre Channel's divergence from mainstream LAN protocols and infrastructure. The concept of LAN-free backup, however, is not bound to Fibre Channel. Any separate gigabit transport that supports block storage data and segregates backup streams from the user LAN will do. IP storage protocols and Gigabit Ethernet can also be deployed for LAN-free backup, with the advantage of leveraging familiar Gigabit Ethernet switches and transport management software.

In the example shown in Figure 13–9, a LAN-free backup solution is constructed with IP storage switches and Fibre Channel storage. Block storage access to the IP SAN is provided by IP storage NICs connected to conventional Gigabit Ethernet switches. Depending on vendor implementation, the IP storage protocol may either be iFCP or iSCSI. Access to shared storage is provided by IP storage switches that convert Fibre Channel to the

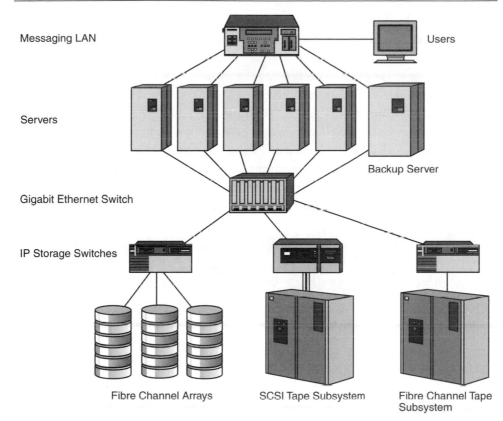

Figure 13–9 LAN-free tape backup on an IP SAN.

appropriate IP storage protocol. Tape subsystems may either be SCSI attached through IP storage bridges, or Fibre Channel through IP storage switches. As with traditional backup, a backup server schedules each server for backup, with the backup data path now established by the IP SAN instead of the user network.

This configuration provides the flexibility to incorporate different types of host and storage connectivity, depending on customer requirements. Fibre Channel hosts may also be accommodated by IP storage switches running the iFCP protocol. SCSI-attached storage may be introduced via IP storage bridges. Tape subsystems with Gigabit Ethernet and IP storage stacks may be connected directly to the Gigabit Ethernet switches providing the IP SAN backbone.

This configuration is also highly scalable. Tape backup streams typically consume 10 to 20 MBps of bandwidth. Multiple streams may therefore be run over a single gigabit link, with hundreds of links provided by the switched Gigabit Ethernet infrastructure. Tape libraries that support multiple tape drives and high-speed robotics within a single enclosure can provide high-performance backup and terabytes of capacity for large storage networks.

A customer may elect to create a separate network for backup traffic simply by configuring VLANs within the Ethernet network. This is facilitated by 10-Gbps uplinks between Ethernet switches, because potential bottlenecks can be avoided. Director-class Gigabit Ethernet switches offering hundreds of ports can be "VLAN-ed" between user and storage network needs, thus providing the segregation of sometimes sensitive traffic. As shown in Figure 13–10, a backbone infrastructure can simplify deployment of both storage and users in a single physical network that still accommodates the objectives of LAN-free backup.

In Figure 13–10, the dashed lines represent VLAN assignment for user traffic whereas the solid lines represent IP storage traffic. The servers are shown with dual NICs installed, based on the assumption that the customer will still want a dedicated IP storage NIC for block storage data in addition

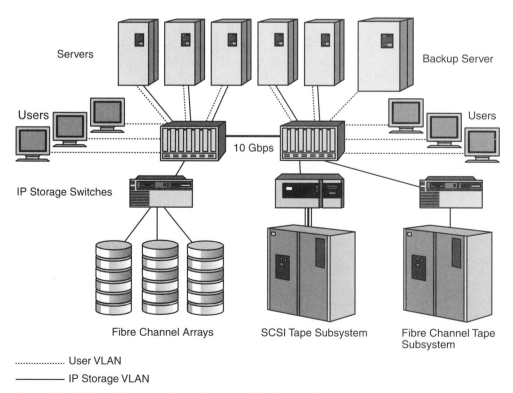

Figure 13–10 Logical separation of user and backup traffic through VLAN configuration on a IP SAN.

to a standard Gigabit Ethernet NIC. Theoretically, a single optimized NIC could provide both block storage over IP and standard TCP/IP messaging support.

Whether used as a dedicated physical network or a VLAN configuration as shown, an IP storage network uses the iSNS protocol to ensure authorized access to shared tape resources by multiple servers. Because iSNS supports DDSs, it is possible to have dynamic zone changes synchronized with tape backup scheduling. A tape subsystem, for example, could be in a discovery domain with one or more servers for the duration of a scheduled backup, and could then be placed in a different discovery domain to oblige the next scheduled servers. DDSs thus enable access to the shared tape resource only when required and prevent inadvertent access by other servers.

LAN-free tape backup over an IP SAN can also be provided by SCSI hosts and disk arrays. As shown in Figure 13–11, SCSI storage may be direct

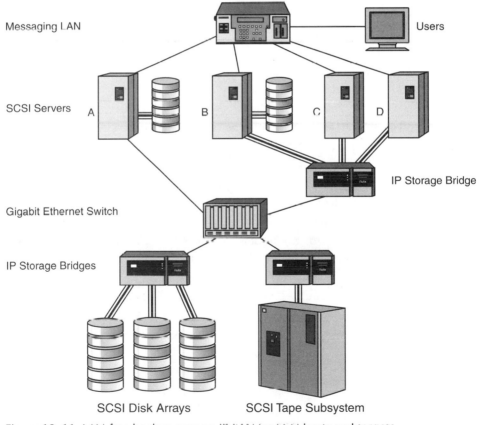

Figure 13–11 LAN-free backup over an IP SAN for SCSI hosts and targets.

attached to SCSI hosts, or centralized on the IP SAN via IP storage bridges. In this example, hosts A and B maintain their direct parallel SCSI connection to local storage, whereas hosts C and D have SAN-attached SCSI storage. Host C's connection to the IP storage bridge also gives it access to SAN-attached storage and the tape subsystem. Host A is provisioned with an IP storage NIC, and thus likewise can back up its direct-attached storage to SAN-attached tape. In every case, SCSI hosts can participate in LAN-free backup and can enjoy the benefits of high performance and traffic separation. Decoupling SCSI storage from SCSI hosts brings the added benefit of storage centralization and dynamic addition of storage as capacity requirements increase.

This scenario also facilitates migration. IP storage hosts, Fibre Channel hosts, Fibre Channel storage, Fibre Channel tape, and native IP storage and tape may be introduced over time without disrupting or displacing the customer's legacy SCSI investment. In addition, the IP SAN infrastructure enables integration of server clustering and other SAN applications for concurrent operation in the storage network.

As native IP storage and tape devices come to market, new installations may be based on unadulterated IP SAN components. This assumes the homogeneity of IP storage networking, whereas most enterprise environments include a fair population of legacy devices. Figure 13–12 shows an IP SAN with a uniform deployment of IP hosts, storage, and tape subsystems.

As noted previously, VLANs may be used to create a single physical network for this configuration while still allowing segregation of user and tape backup traffic.

In all the cases presented, when a backup server instructs a file or application server to launch a backup, the backup data path is from storage to server to tape. During the backup routine, the server repeatedly reads from disk and writes to tape, and thus must be interrupted whenever the tape subsystem is ready to receive more data. As CPU processor speeds have increased, utilization to handle the backup interrupts has become more of an annoyance than a severe drain on CPU resources. Nonetheless, in the spirit of separating servers and storage into a peer network, it is desirable to remove the server from the backup process and free CPU cycles for user requests.

The mechanism for establishing server-free backup is provided by a set of SCSI commands known as *extended copy* or *third-party copy*. Extended copy allows a third-party device to assume the task of reading from disk and writing to tape on behalf of a server. By taking the server out of the backup data path, the third-party copy agent provides another step for

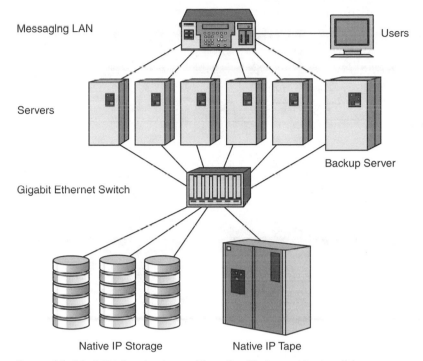

Figure 13–12 LAN-free backup with native IP storage hosts, disk arrays, and tape.

removing traditional dependencies between servers and storage, and enables greater intelligence in the SAN.

A third-party copy agent can be provided by any SAN device with processing power, buffers, and appropriate microcode to implement SCSI extended copy commands. There has been considerable debate over where the third-party copy agent should reside. It can be embedded in a tape or disk controller, in a SCSI bridge, in a storage switch, or simply in a black box connected to the SAN. Because many tape libraries support SCSI interfaces, vendors may implement third-party copy agents in SAN-to-SCSI bridges. And because storage switches play a central role in connectivity, third-party copy agents may be supported in them as well. For IP SANs using conventional Gigabit Ethernet switches as interconnects, third-party copy will generally be supported on bridge products, although director-class IP storage switches that serve both as Gigabit Ethernet switches and gateways are also a logical residence.

As shown in Figure 13–13, server-free tape backup may be implemented on an IP SAN using an intelligent third-party copy embedded in a Gigabit

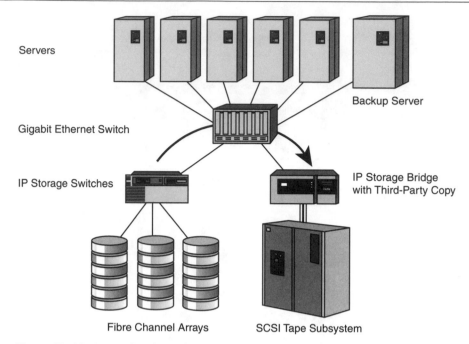

Figure 13–13 Server-free/LAN-free tape backup using a third-party copy agent in a Gigabit Ethernet-to-SCSI bridge.

Ethernet-to-SCSI bridge product. In this example, use of the iFCP storage protocol facilitates interoperability with existing backup applications and third-party copy implementations. To accommodate iSCSI, the extended copy standard must be amended to allow long iSCSI name designations. In addition, because previous versions of backup applications may have been written specifically for the FCP protocol, iSCSI-compatible versions must be used. These caveats aside, third-party copy is a useful means of off-loading servers from mundane backup tasks and it enhances the value of SANs in providing comprehensive backup solutions.

Local tape backup may include individual departments with a few servers or data centers with extensive server farms. To reduce administrative costs, enterprise networks may wish to consolidate tape backup operations by bringing multiple departments into a single SAN. The investment in larger tape libraries can be amortized over different cost centers in the enterprise whereas fewer administrative personnel are required to manage centralized backup. Extending this economy to remote sites is discussed later, as well as strategies for remote vaulting and disaster recovery.

Gigabit Ethernet and IP storage can make significant contributions to reducing total cost of ownership. Although the initial investment in IP storage switches and IP storage NICs may be comparable with Fibre Channel products, the ability to leverage standard Gigabit Ethernet switches and IP for the SAN backbone facilitates installation and reduces ongoing support costs.

13.1.3 Storage Consolidation

Consolidation of storage resources is another key driver for SAN technology. The problems posed by dispersed storage are manifold. Most enterprises have experienced some degree of spontaneous, unplanned growth. When a department begins to run out of storage capacity or needs a new application installed, the solution is typically to install new servers with direct-attached storage. The servers themselves may simply be provided as a means of furnishing additional storage, which is the case as long as servers are the exclusive owners of attached storage. Over time, this reactive approach to storage results in the growth of hundreds or thousands of servers and fragmented, overprovisioned storage capacity. Administration is required to manage the servers themselves, to keep operating system versions and applications current, upgrade memory and adapter cards, and install new bus adapters for additional storage devices. Storage administration is also required to monitor capacity, install and format new arrays, configure volume management, and configure and schedule tape backups. The overall result is high administrative overhead, duplication of applications and data, underutilization and overutilization of storage capacity in various areas, shrinking real estate to house the growing family of servers and storage, inability to rationalize tape backup processes, and ultimately vulnerability of the enterprise to data loss resulting from unmanageable growth.

The obvious solution, as any vendor of high-end disk arrays will confirm, is to consolidate storage resources via very large-capacity enterprise-class storage arrays. These are typically marketed with high-availability features such as disk mirroring, redundant interfaces, power supplies, and fans as well as "phone home" self-diagnostics and 7×24 service. The considerable price tag is justified on the basis of total cost of ownership, mission criticality, and protection of the corporation's valuable data assets. Consolidation of storage enables consolidation of storage management, meaning fewer administrators per terabyte of data and tighter control over the enterprise's data. Storage consolidation over a SAN also alters the server-to-storage ratio, because greater storage capacity can be provided by fewer server platforms.

Storage consolidation also facilitates the management of applications by reducing the need for duplicate copies and licenses. In the anarchy of distributed storage, multiple copies of the same application are often dispersed over multiple storage devices. Systems administrators may not be able to identify where duplication exists. This has spawned new storage resource management applications that walk the network to locate duplication of applications and data, and pinpoint over- and underutilitized disk resources. By forcing applications and data onto centralized storage, unnecessary duplication can be eliminated.

Because the driving rationale behind storage consolidation is reduced total cost of ownership, it has a natural ally in IP storage networking. Administrative overhead for the SAN itself is reduced by leveraging IP network personnel to deploy and manage the SAN infrastructure. Network managers already familiar with IP network management tools, Gigabit Ethernet switch configuration, VLANs, traffic prioritization and traffic-shaping techniques, and IP security mechanisms can be recruited to support the storage network.

As shown in Figure 13–14, storage consolidation can be phased in to support the consolidation of legacy storage as well as high-end disk arrays.

In this example, the customer's legacy SCSI disks are consolidated via an IP storage bridge product. Physical consolidation on an IP SAN enables SCSI storage to be added or removed in a nondisruptive manner and allows the administrator to assign disk resources to servers through SAN management software. The newly introduced, large-capacity storage array may be SCSI, Fibre Channel, or native IP attached to the IP SAN. In this example, a Fibre Channel high-capacity array is brought into the IP SAN through an IP storage switch. As in the server clustering discussion, hosts may attach with IP storage NICs, Fibre Channel HBAs, or legacy SCSI adapters.

Storage consolidation, local backup, and server clustering may be combined with other storage applications in a single enterprise-class IP SAN. Support for concurrent storage applications requires attention to SAN design, particularly in assigning storage resources into functional groups and in allocating sufficient bandwidth so that applications do not suffer performance loss as a result of contention. Functional groups for IP SANs can be enforced through the iSNS discovery domain configuration. Bandwidth allocation is facilitated by the IEEE 802.3ad link aggregation standard. As shown in Figure 13–15, a complex data center IP SAN can support multiple concurrent applications by intelligent use of link aggregation on Gigabit Ethernet and IP storage switches.

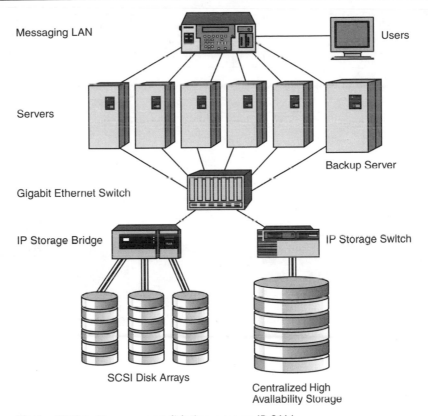

Messaging LAN

Users

Servers

Backup Server

Gigabit Ethernet Switch

IP Storage Bridge

IP Storage Switch

SCSI Disk Arrays

Centralized High
Availability Storage

Figure 13–14 Storage consolidation over an IP SAN.

Link aggregation allows the SAN designer to provision bandwidth where it is most needed and thus avoid potential bottlenecks. This technique may be complemented with traffic prioritization, both at the link layer with IEEE 802.1Q and via DiffServ for layer 3 switches.

Reduced administrative costs are an essential component of IP SANs. This does not mean that storage administration, volume management, or other storage-specific applications are not required. Regardless of SAN infrastructure, management of storage will always have its own unique requirements. What IP SANs eliminate in terms of administrative costs is the need for specialized skills to configure and maintain a fabric. The benefits of storage consolidation would not be realized, after all, if the entry costs included even more technical expertise than the customer required previously.

Storage consolidation may be complemented with storage virtualization. Storage virtualization turns physical storage resources into logical storage

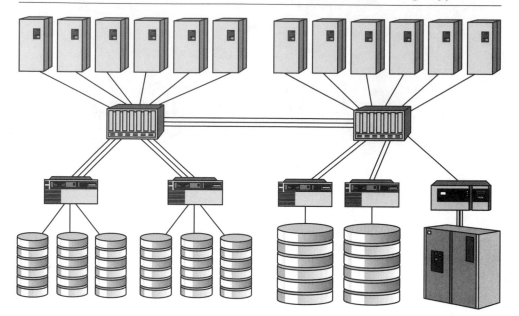

Figure 13–15 Leveraging IEEE 802.3ad link aggregation for high-performance data center applications.

resources, and thus offers the ability to consolidate multiple physical storage devices into a single, more manageable virtual device. As virtualization technology matures, it may offer more automated functionality. Ideally, a virtualization engine should recognize when new storage is added to the SAN and dynamically allocate it when needed. Currently, virtualization products require manual administration to create and assign virtual storage entities, and they are sometimes no easier to administer than traditional physical storage.

13.2 IP Storage for Remote Applications

Most modern enterprise networks have metropolitan, regional, or global network segments. Remote offices and regions may be serviced through dedicated leased lines, shared MAN or WAN services, or via VPNs on the Internet. Existing MAN and WAN links are usually based on Gigabit Ethernet (MAN) or IP over WAN transports such as point to point, frame relay, or ATM. This existing infrastructure enables storage applications to extend beyond the data center, either leveraging current links (when bandwidth and security allow) or by using the same MAN and WAN services to establish new links for storage traffic.

Because of the inherent distance limitations of Fibre Channel, auxillary equipment is required to drive Fibre Channel traffic beyond 10 km. Dense Wave Division Multiplexing (DWDM) allows native Fibre Channel frames to span longer distances, as long as 100 km or more depending on vendor implemenation. Native Fibre Channel extension, however, is also dependent on the buffering capabilities of fabric switches. As shown in Figure 13–16, port buffering capacity directly affects the total round-trip distance that can be supported. In this example, a Fibre Channel switch with 32KB of port buffers could sustain full link utilization up to approximately 15 km in each direction (approximately 30 km round-trip). This limitation is the result of the number of frames that could be held in the port buffer while waiting for acknowledgments from the receiving end. Beyond approximately 15 m in each direction, link utilization falls dramatically, with 50% utilization at approximately 30 km in each direction and continued decline as the round-trip distance is extended. This is the result of the number of frames that are in transit over the link and is also affected by the bandwidth of the remote connection. Fibre Channel switches were not engineered for metropolitan or wide area extension. By contrast, an optimized IP storage gateway with 250 MB port buffering can sustain full link utilization beyond 100 km in each direction full link utilization over longer distances. Straight Fibre Channel extension using DWDM is therefore suitable only for shorter distance metropolitan applications. In addition, because native Fibre Channel extension assumes that only Fibre Channel frames will be used, it cannot integrate into existing IP network infrastructures.

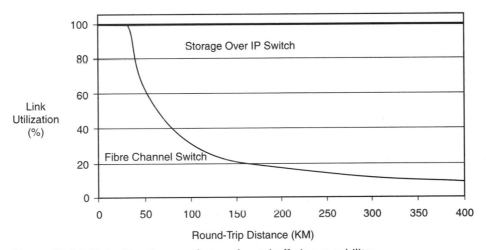

Figure 13–16 Link utilization as a factor of port buffering capability.

For integration of SAN applications into existing metropolitan and wide area IP network services, IP storage protocols and gateways are required. As discussed in Chapter 8, the three standards track protocols for block storage data over IP are FCIP, iFCP, and iSCSI. From the network perspective, these appear simply as additional TCP/IP traffic. From a storage perspective, the mission-critical nature of storage data requires advanced services from the network, including transport management, security, and QoS guarantees. These enhanced services are available through products based on established IP standards or standards proposals that are embedded in IP switches, routers, and auxillary products. As for which IP protocols and products should be used, that depends on the ability of vendors to provide competitive solutions at a reasonable cost, and their ability to demonstrate competency in real-world applications.

13.2.1 Remote Backup

As with tape backup issues in the data center, rationalizing tape backup processes for dispersed networks can simplify administration and enforce data security policies that are otherwise difficult to control. With sufficient equipment and personnel, backup at each remote site is entirely possible. Site-based backup, however, results in duplication of effort and costs, and may still not guarantee that proper backups are performed. For enterprise networks with multiple remote sites, each with their own servers and storage, consolidation of backup to a central location reduces administrative overhead and enables the use of larger, high-performance tape libraries to accommodate multiple backup windows.

As shown in Figure 13–17, a remote tape backup configuration over IP can support mulitple branch office SANs for consolidated backup, even if the remote sites have different generations of servers and storage. Site A may have Fibre Channels hosts and storage that were previously connected by a small Fibre Channel arbitrated loop hub. To facilitate remote backup, the loop hub is replaced by or attached to an IP storage switch that supports both Gigabit Ethernet and Fibre Channel connectivity. This also enables new servers with IP storage NICs to be introduced over time. The IP storage switch at site A is connected by Gigabit Ethernet to an IP router, which in turn provides IP connection to the cloud. In the case of a MAN that supports native Gigabit Ethernet connections, the IP router is not required. The IP storage switch can insert directly into the MAN.

In site B, a local SAN is already built using a Fibre Channel switch. The Fibre Channel switch either could be replaced by the appropriate IP storage

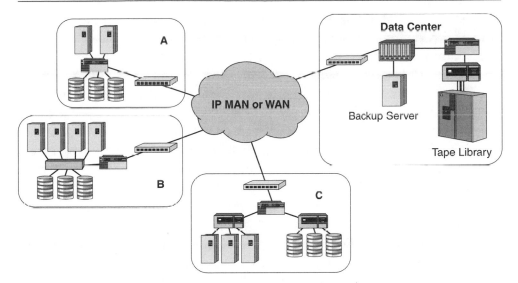

Figure 13–17 Remote tape backup with IP storage switches and gateways.

switch or, as shown in the diagram, could be left in place. To provide conversion from Fibre Channel to IP storage, an IP storage switch is installed. It, in turn, is either connected to an IP router or connected directly to a Gigabit Ethernet MAN.

Site C was originally a stand-alone server configuration with direct-attached SCSI storage. In this case, an IP SCSI SAN is created by placing hosts and storage on Gigabit Ethernet-to-SCSI bridges. The bridges are connected to an IP storage switch for introduction into the IP MAN or WAN. Depending on vendor implementation for the IP storage switch, each site could have a mix of SCSI, Fibre Channel, or IP hosts or storage.

At the data center site, backup traffic is received from the network and is forwarded to an IP storage switch. The IP storage switch can support attachment to the centralized tape library either through direct connection (Gigabit Ethernet interface and IP storage protocol stack), Fibre Channel, or via a Gigabit Ethernet-to-SCSI bridge product.

In each instance, it is assumed that the IP storage switch can support a gateway function for connection to the IP cloud. For storage data, this means deep buffers to accommodate long distances and TCP/IP for session control over the network. Some products provide gateway ports as an option, whereas others offer dedicated gateway units optimized for WAN connectivity.

From a network design standpoint, the selection of WAN link speed depends on the number of concurrent backup streams that should be supported.

Link speed availability is also determined by the MAN or WAN provider's equipment. A circuit switched lease line for storage applications would be, at a minimum, a T3 line providing 45 Mbps. Although not suitable for disk mirroring or high-speed backup, a T3 offering less than 5MB of bandwidth may be sufficient for sequential backup of remote sites, particularly if incremental rather than full backups are performed. Higher performance is available through ATM/SONET networks. An OC-3 link at 155 Mbps could support a full backup stream to a high-performance library at approximately 15 MBps. An OC-12 service at 622 Mbps could support three or four concurrent tape streams at approximately 15 MBps each. And an OC-48 link at 2.5 Gbps would allow trunking of multiple Gigabit Ethernet pipes for 12 to 15 concurrent backup streams, depending on tape library performance and the customer's budget. For MAN services based on Gigabit Ethernet, half of that number could be supported. Because wide area connectivity is priced according to bandwidth and distance requirements, concurrent backups for a widely dispersed network can be very expensive. As always, cost must be balanced against benefit. Financial institutions that have both business and legal requirements for safeguarding data via tape backup have been the first market opportunity for IP-based remote storage backup.

Multisite remote tape backup is supported by the FCIP, iFCP, and iSCSI protocols. As a variation on Fibre Channel extension, FCIP requires Fibre Channel SANs at each remote site, plus individual tunnels between each remote site and the data center. iFCP and iSCSI products provide more flexibility for both local SANs and WAN connectivity. The iFCP solution has the added benefit of directly replacing Fibre Channel fabric switches as shown in site A, while simultaneously providing gateway access to legacy devices.

In addition to consolidating tape backup at a central site, IP SANs can leverage MAN and WAN connectivity for remote vaulting. Backing up data to tape provides protection against the loss of data on disk. Once the data is secured on tape, however, the next step is to secure the tapes themselves. In many data centers, this is accomplished simply by boxing up tape cartridges and transporting them off-site. In the event of a fire or other data center catastrophe, the tapes and the data they contain are still available for restore operations. It would be much more convenient, though, to back up to a secure remote site and forego the boxing and trucking of tapes. IP SANs not only replace manual methods, but enhance data safeguarding by enabling tape vaulting to more remote (and hopefully more safe) locations than would be feasible through manual transport.

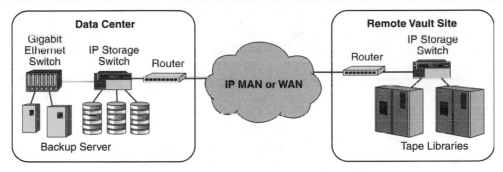

Figure 13–18 Remote tape vaulting using IP storage switches with gateway support.

Figure 13–18 depicts a remote tape vaulting application between a data center and off-site backup facility. As in the previous example, a variety of storage hosts, disks, and tape subsystems may be supported, depending on vendor selection for IP storage switches and gateways. The greater the distance and higher the throughput between the data center and vaulting site, the greater the buffering capacity that is required on the IP storage gateway device or port.

Remote tape vaulting may either replace or supplement local tape backup. In addition, the vaulting strategy may include hierarchial storage management to copy tape archives subsequently onto optical media for long-term storage. Most optical libraries support a SCSI interface, and thus can be incorporated into this configuration through a Gigabit Ethernet-to-SCSI bridge product.

13.2.2 Remote Mirroring

Like remote backup and vaulting, remote mirroring applications may be used to safeguard data at a geographical distance from a primary data center. Remote mirroring has other benefits as well, including data replication for application development and faster recovery for business continuance should the primary site fail. Data replication enables programmers to have a current copy of real-time transactions and data against which revisions to applications can be tested. This accelerates development time and minimizes disruptions when new applications are brought on-line. Business continuance via mirroring avoids the lengthy restore operation required for tape and reduces lost business resulting from outages. Customers, particularly on the Internet, have little patience for downtime and quickly go elsewhere when their requests cannot be met.

Disk-to-disk data mirroring has a significantly higher bandwidth requirement than tape backup. A tape backup subsystem may only be capable of 10 to 20 MBps of throughput. A disk subsystem may run at near link speed of 80 to 95 MBps, depending on the application. For remote mirroring, an IP storage solution must be sized to the bandwidth and latency requirements of the application to avoid loss of data synchronization and the mirror itself. Typically, T3 and lower link speeds are inadequate for mirroring applications. An OC-3 link at 155 Mbps may also be too slow, whereas an OC-12 at 622 Mbps may be suitable for applications that only require updates to records in an established database. Disk-intensive applications, however, may require full Gigabit Ethernet speeds for MANs or OC-48 (2.5 Gbps) for WANs to sustain synchronization between remote disk pairs.

As shown in Figure 13–19, primary and secondary disk arrays are connected over an IP SAN using either Gigabit Ethernet MAN or IP WAN service. For MAN connectivity less than 100 km, the IP storage switch may connect directly to a Gigabit Ethernet service, making the IP routers shown unnecessary. The IP storage switch may connect to Fibre Channel or native IP disk arrays, or to SCSI storage via a Gigabit Ethernet-to-SCSI bridge. Hosts, likewise, may be Fibre Channel, native IP with IP storage NICs, or SCSI through the appropriate bridge product. Remote mirroring is a high-end enterprise application and normally uses high-availability storage at both sites. Although storage virtualization vendors have promoted use of their software and JBODs to create cheaper mirroring solutions, the economy has not been quite so dismal as to displace the more expensive high-availability arrays. Either site may be configured with redundant pathing between servers and disk, redundant IP storage switches, and redundant links into the cloud, depending on the customer's confidence level and budget.

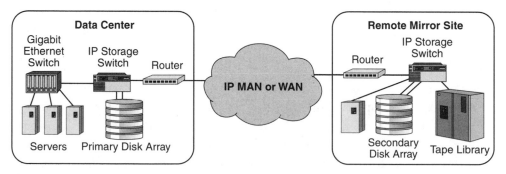

Figure 13–19 Remote mirroring via an IP SAN.

Remote mirroring may also be combined with tape backup for hierarchal storage management. In this example, mirrored data is subsequently backed up to tape for archiving, providing an additional level of data security should the primary or secondary array (or both) fail. This configuration may be duplicated for other mirroring applications, such as EMC's Symmetrix Remote Data Facility (SRDF)

13.2.3 Symmetrix Remote Data Facility

SRDF enhances the remote mirroring strategy by enabling high-availability storage arrays to use each other for data replication. SRDF can be configured for unidirectional mirroring (active/passive) between primary and secondary disk arrays, or bidirectional mirroring (active/active) between two peer sites. In the latter case, an enterprise may have two active data centers that use each other for disaster recovery backup or data synchronization.

Figure 13–20 depicts both active/passive and active/active SRDF implementations.

A peer-to-peer SRDF looks substantially the same as the configuration shown in Figure 13–19, except that data traffic flows in both directions simultaneously as each disk array updates its remote partner. In addition, both sites would have tape backup facilities so that both disk copies could be

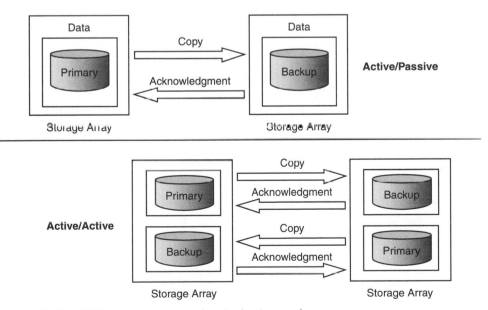

Figure 13-20 SRDF active/passive and active/active modes.

secured to tape. It should be noted that other vendors of high-end storage arrays have similar solutions for peer-to-peer mirroring, following EMC's lead.

IP SANs enable SRDF-like configurations to span much longer distances than supported by Fibre Channel extension. As in conventional remote mirroring, bandwidth for MAN or WAN connectivity must be properly sized to accommodate the maximum data throughput requirements between peer sites.

13.2.4 Disaster Recovery

Disaster recovery may combine elements of both remote backup and remote mirroring to accommodate multiple data centers or remote sites. A disaster recovery strategy must define the geographical distance that is sufficient to guarantee business continuance in the event of catastrophe, and how quickly the disaster recovery site should assume full production.

Disaster recovery implementations may be as sparse as a remote tape vaulting solution, or as sophisticated and expensive as a full duplication of mainframes, servers, and storage at geographically dispersed sites. Prior to the availability of IP storage solutions, disaster recovery policies for server-based applications were constrained by the distance limitations of Fibre Channel extenders. A 15-mile separation may be suitable for disaster recovery installations between New York and New Jersey, but 15 miles is probably not adequate for bridging all the fault lines in the Bay Area. IP storage enables much longer distances between primary and disaster recovery sites while accommodating a variety of bandwidth requirements from relatively slow T3 to higher speed OC-48 and more services.

A disaster recovery solution may include duplicate data center facilities as well as centralized backup or mirroring for regional sites. As shown in Figure 13–21, a disaster recovery site may provide services for the main production center as well as regional and district offices. Because iSCSI and iFCP are routable protocols within the IP WAN and are not dependent on tunneling, this configuration provides greater flexibility for introducing additional sites into the disaster recovery scheme and for providing any-to-any connectivity. The production site in the diagram, for example, includes a Gigabit Ethernet MAN segment for joining metropolitan resources into the production center. Programming staff, for example, could be housed in a different part of the metropolitan area and have high-bandwidth availability to the data center, and their product would be secured at the disaster recovery site.

As in the previous examples, IP storage switch and bridge products may support a wide variety of SCSI, Fibre Channel, and native IP devices. Disas-

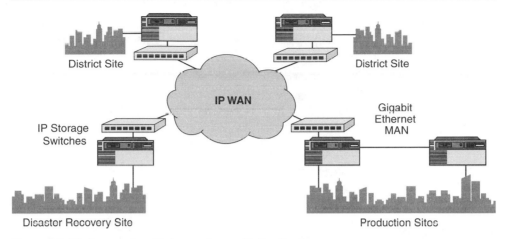

Figure 13–21 Leveraging IP storage for multisite disaster recovery.

ter recovery planners can thus focus on their central objectives without the contraints that simple Fibre Channel extension or tunneling impose.

13.2.5 Content Distribution

Centralized distribution of Internet content to locally based Web cache servers minimizes wait time on the Internet and thus reinforces customer allegiance to specific Web sites. Caching of content is accomplished by installing servers at the edges of the Internet, in close proximity to local service providers. As a query is made to a specific URL, the request is redirected to the cache server closest to the customer, resulting in a much faster response time than if the content was routed through the Internet from a central source. The altruistic benefit is that less traffic is generated within the Internet infrastructure. The real benefit is that the customer is less temped to click over to the competition.

Although some Web content is fairly static, e-commerce applications may require daily or hourly refresh of information posted to the cache network. For efficient block transfer of data from a central location to dispersed targets, IP storage provides support for IP routing, multicast, security, and QoS mechanisms. As shown in Figure 13–22, a central host can be configured to send updated content to multiple cache servers using IP storage protocols and products.

Although it is inadvisable at this point to commit sensitive corporate data to the Internet for remote tape backup or other storage applications, this is one application that is quite well suited for data transport over the Internet itself. To safeguard Web content in transit within the Internet, authentication

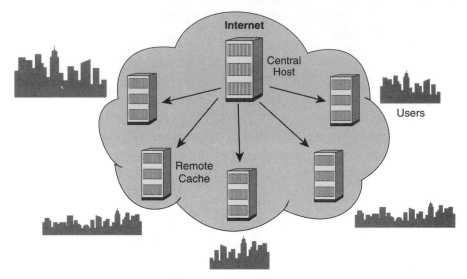

Figure 13–22 Content distribution using IP storage for block data transfer.

via iSNS security and data encryption can ensure that content arrives intact. With the appropriate IP storage products, the edge cache servers may have SCSI, Fibre Channel, or native IP storage.

13.3 Chapter Summary

IP Storage in Data Center Applications

- SAN adoption has occurred primarily in larger data centers.

- IP storage networking can accelerate SAN adoption by simplifying installation and administration.

- SANs are typically deployed as packaged solutions for specific applications.

- Data centers may have multiple separate SANs, each focused on a particular application or department requirements.

- Large-scale enterprise SANs have been hindered by lack of fabric interoperability.

- IP storage solutions based on conventional Gigabit Ethernet switching facilitate enterprise-class SANs.

Server Clustering

- Server clusters provide high-availability access to applications and data.

- Clustering software may provide failover on failure of a specific component or application or failure of an entire server.

- SANs provide common access to storage for clustered servers.

- IP storage switches in a server cluster may support SCSI, Fibre Channel, or native IP servers and storage.

- The iFCP protocol can be used to support Fibre Channel hosts in a server cluster.

- Director-class Gigabit Ethernet switches can provide a highly available IP storage backbone.

- Use of Gigabit Ethernet enables highly scalable server clusters supporting hundreds of devices.

- Gigabit Ethernet-to-SCSI bridges allow the creation of SCSI SANs for server cluster configurations.

- A homogeneous IP storage solution for server clustering requires native IP storage hosts and targets.

Local Tape Backup

- Tape backup is a universal problem shared by all data networks.

- LAN-free backup is the separation of backup traffic and user messaging traffic via a SAN.

- LAN-free backup on an IP SAN may accommodate a variety of hosts and storage interfaces including SCSI, Fibre Channel, and native IP.

- A separate network for backup traffic may also be constructed by use of a VLAN configuration on a common physical network.

- 10-Gbps Ethernet uplinks facilitate VLANs for both storage and messaging traffic.

- iSNS may be used to enforce segregation of resouces through discovery domains.

- DDSs enable flexible assignment of shared tape subsystems to different servers during backup.

- Server-free backup removes the server from the backup data path.

- An extended copy (third-party copy) agent is required to perform reads from disk and writes to tape without server intervention.

- Backup applications that use extended copy should be updated to support iSCSI naming conventions.

Storage Consolidation

- Consolidation of storage resources simplifies administration and reduces total cost of ownership.

- Migrating data to high-availability storage helps avoid unnecessary duplication of applications and data.

- IP storage helps reduce administrative overhead for the SAN.

- Dispersed SCSI storage can be consolidated through Gigabit Ethernet-to-SCSI bridges.

- Server clustering and storage consolidation may be combined in a single IP SAN to facilitate high availability.

- IP SANs do not eliminate the issues associated with storage management.

- Storage virtualization may be combined with storage consolidation but requires more sophisticated mechanisms for automatic storage configuration.

IP Storage for Remote Applications

- Enterprises with dispersed networks require support for long distances to integrate storage applications.

- Fibre Channel extenders using DWDM enable Fibre Channel SAN interconnect at distances less than 100 km.

- Fibre Channel switches were not designed for wide area applications and may only have buffering capacity for full link utilization less than approximately 15 km.

- Optimized IP storage gateways can sustain full link utilization over 100 km.

- Wide area IP storage transport requires TCP/IP for session control and larger buffers for long-distance support.

Remote Backup

- Consolidation of backups to a central site reduces administrative costs.

- IP storage solutions allow mixed environments of SCSI, Fibre Channel, and native IP devices to engage in centralized remote backup.

- FCIP requires Fibre Channel SANs at each remote site.

- iFCP storage switches can replace Fibre Channel fabrics or loops.

- iSCSI and iFCP facilitate flexibility deployment of remote backup solutions via IP routing.

- Remote vaulting is used to avoid physical transport of tape cartridges to off-site locations.

- Remote vaulting may supplement or replace local tape backup.

Remote Mirroring

- Remote mirroring may be used to secure a copy of data at a geographical distance from the data center.

- Data replication via remote mirroring may be used for application development and testing.

- Remote mirroring facilitates business continuance by eliminating time-consuming restores from tape.

- Remote mirroring may require much higher bandwidth than remote tape backup.

- Typically Gigabit Ethernet MANs or OC-48 (2.5-Gbps) WAN links are used for high performance remote mirroring applications.

- IP storage facilitates remote mirroring by using established IP network equipment and management.

Symmetrix Remote Data Facility

- SRDF enables storage arrays to serve as both primary and backup resources.

- SRDF active/passive mode provides conventional remote mirroring.

- SRDF active/active mode enables two remote disk arrays to act as mirrors for each other.

■ IP SANs enable much longer distance support for SRDF-like applications than Fibre Channel.

Disaster Recovery

■ Disaster recovery strategies may include elements of remote backup and remote mirroring.

■ IP storage enables long-distance support for disaster recovery.

■ Multiple data centers and regional sites can be incorporated into a disaster recovery solution based on IP storage networking.

■ IP storage switches and bridge products enable a wide variety of hosts and storage devices to be included in a comprehensive disaster recovery plan.

Content Distribution

■ Web cache servers accelerate response time via colocation with local service providers.

■ User requests to a central URL are redirected to the nearest cache server.

■ Cache servers must be periodically refreshed with updated content.

■ IP SANs enable block data transport for content distribution.

■ IP SANs may provide multicast, security, and QoS features to facilitate content distribution.

■ With the appropriate IP storage switch and bridge products, a variety of cache servers and storage can be accommodated.

14 Conclusion

ALTHOUGH PROMISING NEW SOLUTIONS, new technologies often have their own problems to resolve. As discussed here, the success of IP SANs has a number of dependencies, including standardization, interoperability, and resolution of processor overhead issues.

14.1 Great Expectations

The value proposition of IP storage networking is that it will simplify and lower the cost for acquisition, deployment, and management of shared storage solutions by integrating block storage data into mainstream IP networking. For customers who already have acquisition channels for IP switches and routers, skilled IT staff well-versed in IP networking, and IP network operation centers to monitor the enterprise network, IP storage presents an appealing solution.

New technology introductions are typically accompanied by marketing and promotional campaigns that attempt to capture customer attention by making bold claims of features and benefits. The Gartner Group has been kind enough to objectify the cycle of new-technology hype as shown in Figure 14–1.

As shown in Figure 14–1, the introduction of new technology is followed by a sudden ramp in customer expectations, driven by vendors who are eager to gain mindshare and who consequently may exaggerate product capabilities and product availability. Fibre Channel, for example, was aggressively marketed long before basic stability had been achieved. IP storage was likewise introduced as a panacea for all sorts of storage network issues before real capabilities could be demonstrated.

As early adopters begin working with early market products, the air gradually leaks from the inflated expectations that were fostered by vendors.

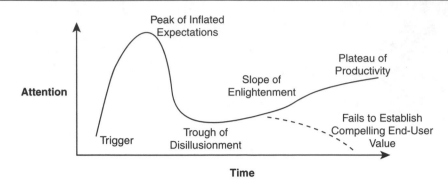

Figure 14–1 Gartner Group new-technology hype cycle.

This may result in disillusionment if the new technology creates more problems than it solves or if it is simply too immature to have productive applications. Neither customers nor vendors want to find themselves in what Gartner calls the "trough of disillusionment." It's a sad place to be. Customers and vendors alike have usually invested extensive resources and personnel into new-technology deployment, only to find it severely lacking.

Gradually, however, vendors and customers may discover viable uses for new products. Although not living up to the great expectations that were initially set, specific applications and solutions begin to be successfully deployed. During this period of slower penetration of the new technology, a critical juncture is reached. The technology either proves its viability and gradually ramps toward productive deployment, or it fails to establish compelling end-user value and goes into decline. This transition may be fairly brief, or may drag on for years until a more successful technology solution emerges.

There are numerous examples that conform to this model. ATM, for example, was launched as a new networking infrastructure that would merge every form of data into a uniform, high-performance network. Initial expectations, however, were quickly deflated as ATM vendors struggled to demonstrate working solutions for everything from switching in the WAN to ATM desktop applications. The "slope of enlightenment" for ATM occurred as customers realized that, although suitable for a WAN infrastructure, ATM was far too difficult to implement as a replacement for Ethernet LANs. ATM thus found a home in the core of wide area internetworking, but failed in establishing end-user value for the desktop.

Storage networking has similar stories to tell. The first high-performance serial storage implementation was IBM's Serial Storage Architecture (SSA).

After a brief spurt of unfulfilled expectations, SSA declined as Fibre Channel ascended its own slope. Fibre Channel promised to overturn all previous notions of storage access and largely succeeded in establishing the concept of SANs as the most viable solution for storage. Inflated expectious were initially punctured by the slow progress made toward interoperability, first by the arbitrated loop vendors, and by the fabric switch vendors. Management, security, and QoS shortcomings of Fibre Channel transport have also leveled the ramp from the trough of disillusionment to the slope of enlightenment. Productive applications for Fibre Channel SANs in the form of certified and supported solutions from the major server and storage providers have prevented Fibre Channel from following SSA into the oblivion of unmet user expectations.

The tempering effect on sustaining a productive plateau, and an additional data point not depicted in the Gartner Group chart, is the effect of the next new-technology wave. Fibre Channel end systems may represent the state-of-the-art in high-performance storage, but already the Fibre Channel fabric can easily be replaced with an IP storage fabric. As with ATM, a portion of the technology may endure for some time, while other building blocks fall from favor. Until native IP storage arrays become the default configuration shipped with certified solutions, Fibre Channel disk arrays and end systems will continue to extend the life of Fibre Channel as the fabric component may be superseded by IP SANs.

New-technology hype around IP storage has quickly placed it in the limelight of storage networking, with inflated expectations focused on ease of storage management and seamless integration. Storage management, because it combines elements of storage administration with network management, has inherent complexities that are protocol and topology agnostic. What IP storage simplifies is transport management, not storage administration. This still has a compelling value for end users, though, because IP network management tools are powerful and well established, and IP network administrators are more easily come by than experts in Fibre Channel fabric management. As for seamless integration of SANs with mainstream networking, IP storage vendors must offer migration strategies to integrate SCSI, Fibre Channel, and IP storage into a coherent solution. Convergence strategies should be able to integrate IP and conventional storage without stepping the customer through endless configuration menus or requiring a consultant to decode product offerings.

Life in high technology would be bearable if a customer only had to deal with a single new-technology introduction, or could face them sequentially rather than in parallel. The reality is that new technology waves pound against each other and against the market in such rapid succession that customers are just coming off the high of one set of inflated expectations when another new technology is launched. Troughs of disillusionment and slopes of enlightenment are overlapping so frequently that customers must consult a pile of product road maps to find their bearings.

This is not simply a case of vendors run amuck, but of new solutions concurrently attempting to address a wide variety of issues. Fibre Channel's solution for block storage networking was being established in the market when NAS introduced appliance-based file-oriented storage networking. Depending on vendor literature, NAS and SANs were either bitter enemies or the best of friends. Concurrently, InfiniBand's solution for server architecture arose. InfiniBand, however, did not restrict itself to reengineering the server, but promised to provide a completely new solution for storage I/O, as well presenting a third architecture for storage interconnect. IP storage has been introduced as yet another new-technology solution. Unlike its peers, however, IP storage is not a completely new contender for customer mindshare, but is founded on incumbent, mainstream IP technology. This has given it a marked advantage over Fibre Channel and InfiniBand in making the path from customer enlightenment to productive employment shorter.

As shown in Figure 14–2, the new-technology hype cycle for the storage market in general is a series of overlapping waves.

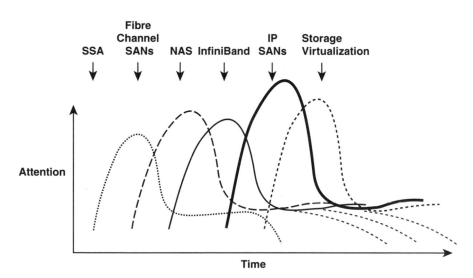

Figure 14–2 New-technology hype cycles for storage networking.

To avoid going the way of SSA, current storage networking technologies must converge on comprehensive solutions. Customers will not close their eyes and point toward a particular technology, but will gravitate to solutions that solve their problems. Selecting an infrastructure that will support legacy SCSI, Fibre Channel, NAS, InfiniBand, IP, and new solutions such as storage virtualization is a more obvious choice than locking in to a single architecture. Historically, only IP and Ethernet have demonstrated the flexibility to adapt to changing customer requirements while still maintaining a consistent open systems philosophy. Widespread adoption of shared storage solutions will therefore be more easily accomplished on the basis of IP SANs, as opposed to reshaping the world in the image of less flexible and unfamiliar architectures. If this is implemented in real IP storage products, then the great expectations and hype may be mostly realized after all.

14.2 Prerequisites for Successful IP Storage Deployment

For block storage data over IP to be successful, a series of technical thresholds must be crossed. These include standards compliance, interoperability, performance, management, and the ability to integrate the installed base of storage products. Given the momentum behind IP networking and the engineering resources available to solve IP-related issues, it is largely a matter of when, not if, these issues will be resolved.

14.2.1 Standards Compliance

The task of the standards initiatives within the IETF is to create the guidelines from which real products can be created. With all vendors designing to common standards, the likelihood of interoperability is greatly enhanced, and hopefully with no disruption to the Internet. Standards track status within the IETF does not guarantee that standardization will automatically occur. Issues must be resolved to the collective satisfaction of the working group, and value to the industry must be demonstrated. Concurrent with standards development, however, it is essential for vendors to verify constantly that their implementations are valid and interoperable.

For IP storage compliance testing, there are currently two venues for vendor interoperability validation. Cooperative marketing and plugfest events are organized through the IP Storage Forum of the SNIA. The SNIA has also created venues for interoperability demonstrations through the activity of the SNIA Interoperability Committee and Storage Networking World (SNW) conferences. Because the SNIA focuses more on upper layer applications, it is a venue for verifying compliance with other storage networking standards such as management MIBs and extended copy. In addition, lower layer protocol compliance testing is led by the University of New Hampshire (UNH) iSCSI Consortium. UNH has proven expertise in the development of rigorous standards compliance test suites that enable vendors to identify quickly areas in which standards specifications have been incorrectly interpreted or improperly defined. This testing is critical for accelerated development of products and features for IP storage end systems and switch interconnects.

Because the IP storage standards initiatives also include the iSNS discovery and management protocol, vendors must demonstrate compliance and interoperability of iSNS implementations so multivendor IP SANs can be deployed. Compared with the artificially prolonged development of Fibre Channel standardization and interoperability for distributed discovery and zoning mechanisms, the iSNS framework can give IP storage an early start in rationalizing the discovery process for multivendor IP SANs.

The other standards dependencies affecting IP storage relate to QoS initiatives such as DiffServ and MPLS. As these become standardized for the IP community at large, IP storage can leverage advanced QoS services for block storage traffic.

14.2.2 Interoperability

Theoretically, if IP storage vendors are engineering to the same standards specifications, their products should be compatible in real-world installations. Standardization of protocols and standards compliance testing alone, however, do not guarantee that products will be interoperable. Plugfest events that enable vendors to test interoperability, identify issues, and debug problems are essential for accelerating product development. Proactive interoperability testing also avoids having to discover compatibility problems at the customer site, a situation that neither customers nor vendors particularly enjoy.

IP storage also requires interoperability testing with a myriad of other storage technologies, including SCSI and Fibre Channel end devices as well as upper layer applications such as tape backup software. The industry venue for this level of interoperability testing is the SNIA Technology Center in Colorado Springs, CO. Although individual vendors may be competing for market share, it is in their collective interest to solve compatibility problems in concert and thus remove obstacles for technology adoption.

14.2.3 Performance

Although some early-market IP storage products have been able to demonstrate wire-speed gigabit performance, others have only demonstrated throughput at one third the speed of Fibre Channel. IP storage cannot displace Fibre Channel unless it has at least comparable gigabit performance.

Performance in IP SANs has two dependencies: bandwidth utilization on the link and host processing overhead. Although different gigabit transports provide comparable bandwidth, latency incurred by the respective switch or routing infrastructures may affect performance. Bandwidth utilization is also partly a function of protocol overhead. Framing overhead for TCP/IP, for example, is slightly more than Fibre Channel. In practice, however, the faster line rate of Gigabit Ethernet compensates for the delta in framing efficiency, giving both IP storage and Fibre Channel comparable data payload delivery rates. TCP ramping may also affect link utilization for storage applications that use small block sizes. Large block transfers typical of most storage applications, however, are not significantly affected by TCP ramping. For data center applications, use of UDP at the transport layer eliminates TCP ramping issues by mimicking Fibre Channel's burst mode mechanism.

Link utilization for wide area applications favors IP storage over Fibre Channel, simply due to the fact that Fibre Channel fabric switches typically do not have the buffering support for long-haul transactions. Optimized IP storage gateways can drive full link utilization much longer distances without auxillary equipment.

Host processing overhead can be addressed with TOEs embedded on IP storage NICs. Although it is unreasonable to expect that IP storage can be run on an ordinary Gigabit Etherent card, IP storage NICs can offer comparable CPU utilization with Fibre Channel HBAs. TCP off-load technology is being promoted for a wide variety of TCP/IP applications, which will drive down costs as volumes increase. IP storage is an opportunistic beneficiary of off-load technology in having a key problem resolved by other IP vendors.

Performance for IP SANs takes a quantum leap with 10-Gbps and higher speed Ethernet. Not only is Ethernet first to market with 10-Gbps performance, it also has the installed base of IP networking to support higher volumes and lower cost over time. Deployment of 10-Gbps Ethernet switches enables large enterprise-class SANs to be built that support hundreds or thousands of servers and storage devices, and facilitates applications such as centralized backup for reduced administrative overhead.

14.2.4 Management

One of the perhaps too aggressively marketed benefits of IP storage is simplified management. Management of any storage networking architecture requires management of data placement and management of data transport. Data placement, in the form of volume management, hierarchal storage management, and storage resource management sits above the SAN infra-structure. Integration of data placement and data transport management facilitates SAN design and problem resolution. Providing hooks into the upper layer storage management applications is therefore obligatory for IP storage plumbing providers.

Enhanced management of data transport for IP SANs is a substantial benefit of the technology. Unlike Fibre Channel, IP storage does not need to create its own set of management tools, but can leverage well-established and well-understood IP networking management applications. Identifying IP storage conversations across the network is easily accomplished using existing management platforms. This enables validation of connectivity and helps to identify and isolate problems more quickly without the need for specialized tools.

SAN management also includes QoS and security policies. The direct benefits IP storage offers for QoS is the ability to use a wide variety of IP-based mechanisms, including 802.1Q traffic prioritization, DiffServ, RSVP, and MPLS. These services are either already standardized or on standards track and are available in IP products today. For security, in addition to basic ACLs and public key mechanisms, advanced encryption capabilities are readily available from a variety of vendors. As with QoS, IP storage does not have to invent security solutions from scratch but can leverage existing technologies. Advanced QoS and security services for Fibre Channel only exist in vendor product road map slides.

As some IP storage vendors have already demonstrated via proof-of-concept configurations, combining IP storage products with other IP management, QoS, and security components enables the customer to scale a variety of solutions to meet application requirements.

14.2.5 Integration with Other Storage Technologies

Most enterprise networks must support several generations of equipment as new products are introduced and others are redeployed throughout the network. The ability to accommodate the installed base of still quite serviceable equipment enables a new technology to integrate into the network with minimal disruption and without forcing customers to bring out the forklifts simply to benefit from a new solution.

Depending on product selection, IP storage offerings may either replace or complement existing storage investments. As a replacement strategy, IP storage solutions may make sense for customers who have few legacy products. Most enterprises, however, have at least SCSI hosts and storage arrays, and possibly investments in Fibre Channel configurations as well. Accommodating both SCSI and Fibre Channel end devices for IP-based SANs offers more flexibility and essentially upgrades older products into state-of-the-art solutions. Gigabit Ethernet-to-SCSI bridges can bring both SCSI hosts and SCSI targets into a peer storage network. Bridge products may also be required to allow SCSI-attached tape libraries to be used in a shared or centralized backup configuration.

The ability to support either Fibre Channel or Gigabit Ethernet devices on any port of an IP storage switch provides flexibiliy in configuring IP SANs for various applications. A customer, after all, should not have to consult a configuration guide every time a new device is added to the network. In addition to Fibre Channel end devices, IP storage deployment is less problematic if IP storage switches can also support Fibre Channel loop hubs and fabric switches. This makes it possible to connect existing SAN islands to an integrated IP SAN without the usual concerns about Fibre Channel switch interoperabililty.

Although vendor data sheets may be useful guides for assessing product capabilities, customers should verify the SCSI and Fibre Channel support functionality of IP storage switches via demonstrated interoperability testing. Some offerings, for example, may provide SCSI or Fibre Channel device support, but have only limited support for Fibre Channel fabrics.

14.3 IP Storage Futures

IP-based storage networking has the potential to extend the shared storage model far beyond the top-tier enterprise networks. As native IP storage and tape devices and affordable IP storage NICs permeate the market, larger and more powerful storage networks can offer shared storage services that are not limited by distance. The ideal goal of shared storage technology is ubiquitous and high-speed data access. Within an enterprise, this may mean that users can securely log in and access block data regardless of their physical location, whether within an enteprise facility or across the Internet. The storage off-load model pioneered by storage service providers may become the de facto storage solution within the enterprise itself, simply because IP storage and intelligent virtualization engines make storage deployment and access relatively painless.

The challenge for vendors is to integrate advanced storage solutions with mainsteam IP networking, whether in the form of enhanced IP storage switches or storage-aware capabilities in Gigabit Ethernet switches, IP routers, and internetworking backbones. As storage and networking technologies become more tightly integrated, storage networking ceases to be a distinct entity and simply enters mainstream data communications. From a user perspective, this is ideal.

14.4 Chapter Summary

Great Expectations
- New-technology introductions are invariably accompanied by inflated expectations before real capabilities are proved.

- New technologies must, in the end, demonstrate compelling end-user value.

- The actual application a new technology finds may be quite different from its announced intentions.

- IP storage is driven by an incumbent and well-known technology.

- Storage networking is generating multiple, overlapping new-technology waves.

- IP storage may more readily accommodate peer technologies to provide comprehensive shared storage solutions.

Prerequisites for Successful IP Storage Deployment
- Standardization of IP storage protocols is required for successful product development and customer adoption.

- IP storage standards compliance venues include the SNIA and UNH.

- Standards dependencies for IP storage include development of DiffServ and MPLS.

- Standards compliance verification must be accompanied by interoperability testing.

- Interoperability for IP storage also includes interoperability with SCSI and Fibre Channel devices as well as upper layer applications.

- IP storage must demonstrate comparable performance with Fibre Channel.

- TOEs enhance IP storage performance by removing processing overhead from servers.

- 10-Gbps Ethernet provides a fundamental performance enhancement for IP storage.

- IP storage infrastructure management should integrate into storage management and IP network management frameworks.

- Management of IP SANs is enhanced by IP QoS and security features.

- IP SANs require bridge and gateway products to accommodate the installed base of SCSI and Fibre Channel end devices and interconnects.

IP Storage Futures
- IP storage technology enables widespread adoption of shared storage applications.

- Integration of IP storage capabilities with mainstream data communications facilitates and simplifies block data access.

Appendix A
IP Storage and Related Vendors

Product	Web Site URL
IP SAN Products	
3Ware	www.3ware.com
Adaptec	www.adaptec.com
ADVA	www.san.com
Agilent	www.agilent.com
Andiamo	www.andiamo.com
Cereva	www.cereva.com
Cisco	www.cisco.com
Confluence Networks	www.confluencenetworks.com
Emulex	www.emulex.com
Entrada	www.entradanetworks.com
Falconstor	www.falconstor.com
Hewlett-Packard	www.hp.com
IBM	www.ibm.com
Intel	www.intel.com
JNI	www.jni.com
Lucent	www.lucent.com
NetConvergence	www.netconvergence.com
Nishan Systems	www.nishansystems.com
Pirus Networks	www.pirus.com
Platys	www.platys.com

Product	Web Site URL
IP SAN Products *(continued)*	
Qlogic	www.qlogic.com
Rhapsody Networks	www.rhapsodynetworks.com
SANcastle	www.sancastle.com
SANRAD	www.sanrad.com
SAN Valley Systems	www.sanvalley.com
StoneFly Networks	www.stoneflynetworks.com
Troika Networks	www.troikanetworks.com
TrueSAN	www.truesan.com
Fibre Channel Extension	
Atto	www.attotech.com
Brocade	www.brocade.com
Chaparral	www.chaparralnet.com
CNT	www.cnt.com
Crossroads	www.crossroads.com
Gadzoox	www.gadzoox.com
InRange	www.inrange.com
Lucent	www.lucent.com
McData	www.mcdata.com
Vixel	www.vixel.com
Storage and Tape Vendors	
ADIC	www.adic.com
Compaq	www.compaq.com
Dell Computers	www.dell.com
EMC	www.emc.com
Eurologic	www.eurologic.com
Exabytes	www.exabyte.com
Hitachi Data Systems	www.hds.com
IBM	www.ibm.com

Product	Web Site URL
Storage and Tape Vendors *(continued)*	
LSI	www.lsilogic.com
MTI	www.mti.com
Overland Data	www.overlanddata.com
Quantum/ATL	www.atlp.com
Raidtec	www.raidtec.com
Siemens	www.sni.com
SpectraLogic	www.spectralogic.com
StorageTek	www.network.com
Sun Microsystems	www.sun.com
Unisys	www.unisys.com
SAN Management and Virtualization	
BMC	www.bmc.com
Compaq	www.compaq.com
Crossroads	www.crossroads.com
DataCore	www.datacore.com
Data Direct	www.datadirect.com
EMC	www.emc.com
FalconStor	www.falconstor.com
KOM Networks	www.komnetworks.com
Legato Systems	www.legato.com
SANavigator	www.sanavigator.com
StorageApps	www.storageapps.com
StoreAge	www.store-age.com
Sun Microsystems	www.sun.com
Tivoli	www.tivoli.com
Veritas Software	www.veritas.com
Vicom	www.vicom.com
XIOTech	www.xiotech.com

Product	Web Site URL
Gigabit Ethernet Vendors	
3Com	www.3com.com
Anritsu	www.anritsu.com
Avaya	www.avaya.com
Avici Systems	www.avici.com
Cisco	www.cisco.com
Extreme	www.extremenetworks.com
Foundry	www.foundrynetworks.com
Juniper	www.juniper.net
Nortel	www.nortelnetworks.com
RiverStone	www.riverstonenetworks.com
Test Equipment and Verification Labs	
Ancot	www.ancot.com
Finisar	www.finisar.com
Imation Labs	www.imation.com
I-Tech	www.i-tech.com
Medusa Labs	www.medusalabs.com
Mier Communications	www.mier.com
Network Associates	www.sniffer.com
SNIA Technology Center	www.snia.org
Solution Technology	www.soltechnology.com
Xyratex	www.xyratex.com

Appendix B
The Storage Networking
Industry Association

Industry associations embody the contradiction between competitive interests of vendors and their recognition that the success of individual vendors is tied to the success of the industry as a whole. The appropriate homily for industry associations is "rising waters raise all ships," although occasionally a gunboat will appear as a vendor's competitive drive goes unchecked. An industry association may focus primarily on marketing campaigns to raise end-user awareness of the industry's technology, or to combine marketing and technical initiatives to promote awareness and to formulate standards requirements. The Fibre Channel Industry Association (FCIA), for example, has organized promotional activity for out-bound messaging through Net-world+Interop, Comdex, and other venues as well as technical work on the SANmark program for standards compliance. For standardization, the FCIA has worked primarily through the NCITS T11 Committee, to the extent of holding FCIA meetings and NCITS T11 sessions concurrently.

The umbrella organization for all storage networking technologies is the SNIA. The SNIA has more than 250 members, representing vendors and customers from a wide variety of storage disciplines including management software, storage virtualization, NAS, Fibre Channel, IP storage, disk and tape, and solution providers who offer certified configurations and support. As with other industry associations, the SNIA is a volunteer organization with only a few paid staff positions. Its activity is funded by the monetary and personnel contributions of the membership. The general mission of the SNIA is to promote the adoption of storage networking technology as a whole, with the membership itself providing the momentum to accomplish this goal. The more the membership invests in terms of finances and volunteer resources, the more the organization can accomplish.

B.1 Board of Directors

As shown in the organizational chart in Figure B–1, the governing body of the SNIA is the board of directors. Board members are elected by the membership for two-year terms, and an individual board member may serve two consecutive terms. The ten elected board members are supplemented by three at-large board members appointed by the board itself. The board is responsible for establishing policies and managing resources of the organization to fulfill SNIA's mission and provides oversight to the SNIA committees, industry forums, Technical Council, Consumer Council, the Technical Director, and the SNIA Technology Center.

To ensure involvement in wider SNIA activity, board members are required to chair or provide leadership in SNIA committees and subgroups. Board members are also required to participate in six face-to-face meetings each year and are expected to represent the organization at public venues such as the SNW conferences. This volunteer activity represents a substantial contribution of time and resources for member companies who participate at the board level, and reveals their commitment to the industry as a whole. Of course, board representation also provides an opportunity to promote specific vendor agendas, although board representation is sufficiently diverse to discourage overt vendor-driven initiatives.

B.2 Executive Director and Staff

Board activity is supported by the executive director and staff. Robin Glasgow, the current executive director, and project managers Jennifer Cady and Yansu Ouyang conduct the day-to-day operations of the organization and provide logistical support for SNIA meetings and conference participation.

B.3 Board Advisors

The board may receive counsel on industry-related issues from the board advisors, typically former board members and interested parties who may attend board meetings and provide input to board discussions. Board advisors play a critical role in providing viewpoints on storage networking issues and in helping to promote the SNIA within the industry.

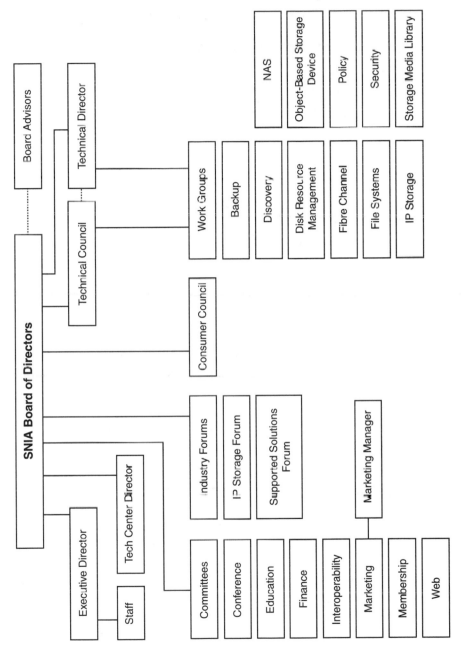

Figure B–1 SNIA organizational structure.

B.4 Technical Council

The technical activity and strategic technical vision of the SNIA is managed by the SNIA Technical Council. The Technical Council is composed of nine of the top experts within the storage networking community who volunteer their time and expertise to maintain the integrity of SNIA's technical initiatives. In 2001, the Technical Council produced the SNIA Shared Storage Model as a guide to understanding storage networking technologies. The Technical Council also oversees the activity of the technical work groups in cooperation with the Technical Director.

B.5 Technical Director

The SNIA Technical Director is a full-time staffed position funded by the SNIA budget. Responsibilities of the technical director include technical direction and project management of the SNIA work groups, SNIA liaison to standards bodies such as ANSI and IETF, technical input into the SNIA Technology Center, and support of SNIA committees.

B.6 Technical Center Director

The technical center director is also a full-time staffed position and is responsible for management of the SNIA Technology Center in Colorado Springs, CO. Over time, the technical center director will staff the SNIA Technology Center for a variety of SNIA-sponsored initiatives.

B.7 SNIA Technology Center

The SNIA Technology Center in Colorado Springs was launched in the spring of 2001 as a multipurpose facility. The SNIA Technology Center was made possible by a $3.5-million grant from Compaq Computer Corporation to the SNIA. It supports 14,000 square feet of lab and classroom space and is operated as a vendor-neutral facility by the SNIA. Uses of the SNIA Technology Center include interoperability demonstrations, standards compliance testing, proof-of-concept and evaluation configurations, technology development in support of SNIA technical work group activity, and training in storage networking technology.

As with other SNIA activities, the SNIA Technology Center is dependent on contributions of money and equipment by member companies. Network

Appliance was one of the first vendors to contribute more half a million dollars worth of equipment in the form of fully configured NetApp filers, and other vendors have been contributing sponsorships and equipment to get the center operational. The SNIA Technology Center is a significant and practical step for the SNIA in providing its members and the customer community a venue for accelerating storage networking adoption.

B.8 Consumer Council

Because vendors alone do not determine the useful purposes to which technology will be put, the SNIA has organized a consumer council to solicit customer representation within the SNIA and to solicit customer input into storage networking strategies. The consumer council will hold events in the United States, Europe, and Asia to generate end-user input that can be fed back to the vendor community.

B.9 Committees

Much of the nontechnical activity of the SNIA is conducted through committees. Committees may be chaired by SNIA board members or other volunteers, with volunteer participation by member companies. Committees are chartered with various tasks that must be performed within the vendor-neutral culture of the mother organization. Committees and work groups have face-to-face meetings at least four times a year, plus periodic conference calls to track their progress and to assign tasks.

The Conference Committee is responsible for organizing SNIA participation in SNW and other major events. SNW is the product of a cooperative agreement between the SNIA and Computerworld. SNW conferences are held twice a year, typically in Palm Desert, CA, in the spring and Orlando, FL, in the fall. Attendance at SNW events has grown from a few hundred to several thousand, and SNW has become the premier event for storage networking.

The Education Committee is responsible for creating training and certification programs for the SNIA. This activity ranges from training classes held at the SNIA Technology Center to technology certification through various partnerships. The Education Committee has also produced the *SNIA Dictionary of Storage Networking Terminology*.

The Finance Committee is responsible for developing the SNIA annual operating buget and for ensuring that fiscal responsibilities of the organization are met.

The Interoperability Committee has had multiple responsibilties, including initial organization of the SNIA Technology Center, development of standards compliance test suites, and staging of interoperability demonstrations at SNW and other events. Of these activities, the visibility provided by the SNW Interoperability Lab has encouraged participation in the Interoperability Committee, with more than 65 vendors represented in recent SNWs. For test suite development, the Interoperability Committee has solicited contributions of code and programming expertise from member companies to accelerate standards compliance test development.

The Marketing Committee is responsible for press releases, press and analyst reviews, marketing collateral, and marketing event coordination in support of SNIA committees and work groups.

The Membership Committee is responsible for recruitment and maintenance of the SNIA membership, and for formulating the benefits of SNIA participation to vendors and customers.

The Web Committee has assumed the task of maintenance and revision of the SNIA Web site. The SNIA URL (www.snia.org) is a resource for customers and members, and includes information on SNIA activity as well as technical resources such as the SNIA dictionary and source code.

Depending on time and resources, SNIA member companies may participate in any or all of the SNIA committees. Although committee activity is vendor neutral and is focused on the industry as a whole, participation is a means of ensuring that a company is adequately represented in the creation of policies, processes, and events that provide visibility in the marketplace. Committee participation is also a means of monitoring the state of the industry and thus shaping vendor strategies to the consensus of industry peers.

B.10 Technical Work Groups

The SNIA technical work groups have been instrumental in formulating requirements for technology standards that may then be forwarded to the appropriate standards body for further work. Additional detail on the activity of each technical work group may be found on the SNIA Web site. SNIA work groups have produced open source code for the Common Information Model Object Model and the HBA application programming interface, both of which are available via the SNIA site. Technical work groups support a diversity of interests, from management and backup to security issues.

For IP storage, the SNIA IP Storage Work Group was formed to create requirements for standards for IP-based SANs. These requirements documents will then be forwarded to ANSI, IETF, or the appropriate standards organization.

B.11 Industry Forums

To accommodate new storage networking trends within the SNIA umbrella, the SNIA has created a category of SNIA industry forums as a vehicle for organization and marketing. SNIA industry forums enjoy some autonomy within SNIA, but are chartered within the general guidelines of SNIA policy. The forum concept enables emergent technologies and services to leverage the SNIA infrastructure and thus accelerate development without the need to create separate industry associations.

B.11.1 SNIA IP Storage Industry Forum

The first forum created under the industry forum defnition was the IP Storage Forum. After some initial discussion on its scope, the IP Storage Forum now represents all vendors who are developing block storage data over IP solutions. Currently, subgroups have been created for FCIP, iFCP, and iSCSI protocols. More than 40 SNIA member companies are enrolled in the forum, including new IP storage vendors as well as established storage networking vendors who are developing IP-based interfaces for their products. The focus of the IP Storage Forum is marketing and promotion of IP SAN technology. It thus complements the technical work of the IPS Work Group.

B.11.2 SNIA Supported Solutions Forum

The SNIA Supported Solutions Forum was created to promote storage networking solutions that are interoperable and have vendor backing for customer service. As with other SNIA subgroups, the Supported Solutions Forum is open to any SNIA member company. The focus on this forum is to configure and test multivendor solutions for specific applications and to create a support infrastructure that will streamline problem resolution for the customer. Ideally, a customer will only have to make a single problem call and the vendors themselves will troubleshoot, isolate, and repair without further customer intervention.

B.12 Relationship of SNIA to Other Industry Associations

The SNIA has cooperative relations with other industry associations, including the FCIA, the IBTA, and the UNH iSCSI Consortium. The SNIA Interoperability Committee and the FCIA have been jointly addressing the issue of mid- and upper layer interoperability testing for the FCIA SANmark program. The FCIA's work has centered on physical and transport layer issues, whereas the SNIA has focused on application and management issues. The SNIA Technology Center and Interoperability Committees have met with the IBTA to discuss InfiniBand testing, and the IBTA has participated in the SNIA Interoperability Committee's Interoperability Lab at SNW conferences. In addition, the SNIA Interoperability Committee, SNIA IP Storage Forum members, and UNH representatives have discussed using the SNIA Technology Center to hold IP storage plugfest events for interoperability testing.

B.13 Summary

The SNIA represents a diversity of technologies that meet on the common ground of storage networking. Software vendors, hardware vendors, solutions providers, integrators, consultants, and customers committed to shared storage can work within the SNIA to advance their individual and collective interests. As a volunteer organization, the SNIA solicits involvement by its members and interested individuals for committee and work group activity. Additional information on membership and services of the SNIA is available at www.snia.org.

Bibliography

Bibliographic Entries

Benner, Alan F. *Fibre Channel*. New York, NY: McGraw-Hill, 1996.

Breyer, Robert, and Sean Riley. *Switched, Fast, and Gigabit Ethernet*. Indianapolis, IN: Macmillan, 1999.

Clark, Tom. *Designing Storage Area Networks: A Practical Reference for Implementing Fibre Channel SANs*. Reading, MA: Addison-Wesley, 1998. Also in Japanese translation, Nanosoft, 2000, ISBN 89471-272-5.

Cunningham, David, and William Lane. *Gigabit Ethernet Networking*. Indianapolis, IN: Macmillan, 1999.

Davie, Bruce, et al. *Switching in IP Networks*. San Francisco, CA: Morgan Kaufmann, 1998.

Farley, Marc. *Building Storage Networks*. Berkeley, CA: Osborne, 2000.

Field, Gary, et al. *The Book of SCSI*. San Francisco, CA: No Starch Press, 1999.

Kembel, Robert W. *The Fibre Channel Consultant: Arbitrated Loop*. Tucson, AZ: Northwest Learning Associates, 1997.

Kembel, Robert W. *The Fibre Channel Consultant: A Comprehensive Introduction*. Tucson, AZ: Northwest Learning Associates, 1998.

Kembel, Robert W. *The Fibre Channel Consultant: Fibre Channel Switched Fabric*. Tucson, AZ: Northwest Learning Associates, 2001.

Perlman, Radia. *Interconnections*. 2nd ed. Boston, MA: Addison-Wesley, 2000.

Seifert, Rich. *Gigabit Ethernet*. Reading, MA: Addison-Wesley, 1999.

Stai, Jeffrey D. *The Fibre Channel Bench Reference*. Saratoga, CA: ENDL Publications, 1996.

Stevens, W. Richard. *TCP/IP Illustrated.* 3 vol. Boston, MA: Addison-Wesley, 2000.

Toigo, Jon William. *The Holy Grail of Data Storage Management.* Upper Saddle River, NJ: Prentice Hall, 1999.

Standards and Proposals

ANSI/NCITS T10 FCP-2 *Fibre Channel Protocol for SCSI (Second Version)* March, 2001

ANSI/NCITS T11 FC-GS-3 *Fibre Channel—Generic Services 3* November, 2000

ANSI/NCITS T11 FC-SW2 *Fibre Channel—Fabric Switch—2* July 19, 2001

IEEE 802.1p/Q *Virtual Bridged Local Area Networks* December, 1998

IEEE 802.3x *IEEE 802.3 Part 3: Carrier sense multiple access with collision detection (CSMA/CD) access method and physical layer specifications* 2000 Edition

IEEE 802.3z *IEEE 802.3 Part 3: Carrier sense multiple access with collision detection (CSMA/CD) access method and physical layer specifications* 2000 Edition

ITU X.509 *Information technology—Open Systems Interconnection—The Directory: Public-key and Attribute Certificate Frameworks* March, 2000

RFC 768 Postel, J. 1980, *User Datagram Protocol* IETF

RFC 793 Information Sciences Institute, 1981, *Transmission Control Protocol* IETF

RFC 1349 Almquist, P. 1992, *Type of Service in the Internet Protocol Suite* IETF

RFC 16333 Branden, R. et al. 1994, *Integrated Services in the Internet Architecture: an Overview* IETF

RFC 1737 Sollins, K., et al. 1994, *Functional Requirements for Uniform Resource Names* IETF

RFC 2205 Branden, R. et al. 1997, *Resource ReSerVation Protocol (RSVP)* IETF

RFC 2401 Kent, S. and Atkinson, R. 1998, *Security Architecture for the Internet Protocol* IETF

RFC 2402 Kent, S. and Atkinson, R. 1998, *IP Authentication Header* IETF

RFC 2406 Kent, S. and Atkinson, R. 1998, *IP Encapsulating Security Payload (ESP)* IETF

RFC 2474 Nichols, K. et al. 1998, *Definition of the Differentiated Services Field (DS Field) in the IPv4 and IPv6 Headers* IETF

RFC 2475 Blake, S. et al. 1998, *An Architecture for Differentiated Services* IETF

RFC 2597 Heinanen, J. et al. 1999, *Assured Forwarding PHB Group* IETF

RFC 2598 Jacobson, V. et al. 1999, *An Expedited Forwarding PHB* IETF

RFC 2748 Durham, D. ed. 2000, *The COPS (Common Open Policy Service) Protocol* IETF

RFC 3031 Rosen, E. et al. 2001, *Multiprotocol Label Switching Architecture* IETF

Standards and Proposals Web Links

IETF Requests for Comments

www.ietf.org
(Internet Engineering Task Force)

ftp://ftp.isi.edu/in-notes
(Univesity of Southern California School of Engineering Information Sciences Institute—RFC download)

IETF IP Storage Internet Drafts

www.ietf.org/internet-drafts
(IETF Internet drafts)

www.haifa.il.ibm.com/satran/ips
(Julian Satran's IP storage archive)

Gigabit Ethernet

http://standards.ieee.org/
(IEEE standards site)

www.manta.ieee.org/groups/802/3/
(IEEE Ethernet Working Group)

Fibre Channel Standards

www.T10.org
(NCITS T10 Technical Committee)

www.T11.org
(NCITS T11 Technical Committee)

www.cern.ch/HSI/fcs
(European Laboratory for Particle Physics)

InfiniBand

www.infinibandta.org
(InfiniBand Trade Association)

www.fabric-io.com
(InfiniBand)

IP Storage Technical and Marketing

http://www.ietf.org/html.charters/ips-charter.html
(IETF IPS Work Group)

http://www.snia.org/English/Products/Products_FS.html
(SNIA IP Storage Forum)

www.iol.unh.edu/consortiums/iscsi
(UNH iSCSI Consortium)

Other Related Web Resources

www.snia.org
(Storage Networking Industry Association)

www.10gea.org
(10 Gigabit Ethernet Alliance)

www.scsi.org
(SCSI homepage)

http://www.aberdeen.com
(Aberdeen Group)

www.searchstorage.techtarget.com
(TechTarget storage site)

http://www.bswd.com/cornucop.htm
(Berg Software Design—Storage Cornucopia)

http://www3.gartner.com/Init
(Gartner)

http://is.pennnet.com/home.cfm
(InfoStor)

http://www.computerworld.com/
(ComputerWorld)

http://www.illuminata.com/
(Illuminata)

http://www.lightreading.com
(LightReading)

http://www.byteandswitch.com
(Byte and Switch)

http://www.periconcepts.com
(Peripheral Concepts)

http://www.sresearch.com
(Strategic Research)

Glossary

802.1p/Q   IEEE standard for frame prioritization

802.1Q   IEEE standard for VLAN tagging

802.3a   IEEE standard for 10-Gbps Ethernet

802.3ad   IEEE standard for link aggregation

802.3x   IEEE standard for link-layer flow control using PAUSE frames

802.3z   IEEE standard for Gigabit Ethernet

8b/10b encoding   an encoding scheme that converts an 8-bit byte into two possible 10-bit characters; used for balancing ones and zeros in high-speed transports

access method   the means used to access a physical medium to transmit data

ACK   acknowledgment; a packet sent by a destination to verify receipt of data

ACL   access control lists; a list of authorized IP addresses maintained by an IP router or switch to provide security for network access

active copper   a gigabit physical cabling connection that allows as much as 30 m of copper cabling between devices

address identifier   in Fibre Channel, a 24-bit value used to indicate the link-level address of communicating devices; in a frame header, the address identifier indicates the source ID and destination ID of the frame

AH   Authentication Header, an IPSec header used to establish authorized communication between two network devices

AIT   Advanced Intelligent Tape

AL_PA   Arbitrated Loop Physical Address; an 8-bit value used to identify a participating device in an Arbitrated Loop

ANSI   American National Standards Institute; a governing body for technology standards in the United States

appliance   a network product designed to perform a specialized task with minimal user administration

application programming interface   an interface used by an application to request services from other applications or software components

arbitrated loop   a shared 100-MBps Fibre Channel transport supporting as many as 126 devices and 1 fabric attachment

arbitration   a means for gaining orderly access to a shared loop topology

ARP   Address Resolution Protocol; an IP function that correlates an IP network address to a link-level MAC address

ASIC   application-specific integrated circuit; an integrated circuit engineered for a specialized application

Assured forwarding   a DiffServ class-of-service for packet aggregation on the basis of data type or source

ATM   asynchronous transfer mode; a high-speed cell switching transport used primarily in WANs

Authentication   a means of verifying the identity of a network device before data transmission is initiated

authentication header   an IPSec header used to establish authorized communication between two network devices

back up   securing disk data to tape or optical media

backup window   the time required to perform nondisruptive tape backup of disk data

bandwidth   data transmission capacity of a link or system

BGP   Border Gateway Protocol; a routing protocol used for determining optimal paths between autonomous systems within an extended IP network

binary   a base-two numbering system using ones and zeros to indicate numerical value

bit   the smallest unit of binary information used in computer systems

block   a unit of contiguous data stored on disk or tape devices

BOOTP Bootstrap Protocol; a mechanism for automating IP address assignment and download of operating system or configuration data to a network device.

B_Port In Fibre Channel, a switch port supporting attachment to an interswitch backbone

broadcast the simultaneous transmission of a message to all possible destinations on a network or network segment

broadcast storm unintended flooding of a network with broadcast messages

bus a parallel data and control signal path typically implemented on a motherboard and used to support adapter cards and interfaces

bypass circuitry circuits that automatically remove a device from the data path when valid signaling is lost

byte a contiguous string of eight binary digits, typically representing a unit of information such as an alphanumerical character

CA channel adapter; defined by InfiniBand to decouple memory queueing, memory protection, and I/O from the CPU

cascade connecting two or more Fibre Channel hubs or fabric switches to increase the number of ports or to extend distances

CDB command descriptor block

CDR clock and data recovery circuitry; used to recover intelligible data from a continuous bit stream

certificate a formatted file used as a digital signature for device authentication

checksum a count of the number of bits in a protocol unit that is transmitted with a packet to verify proper receipt of data

CIDR classless interdomain routing; currently used in place of traditional IP addressing based on classes to create more usable IP addresses

CIFS Common Internet File System; a cross-platform file access protocol similar to the Network File System

class 1 in Fibre Channel, a connection-oriented class of service that requires acknowledgment of frame delivery

class 2 in Fibre Channel, a connectionless class of service that requires acknowledgment of frame delivery

class 3   in Fibre Channel, a connectionless class of service that requires no notification of frame delivery

class 4   in Fibre Channel, a class of service that defines virtual circuits via fractional bandwidth and QoS parameters

class 6   in Fibre Channel, a class of service that provides multicast frame delivery with acknowledgment

class A   in IP networking, an address class providing 126 networks with 16.5 million hosts per network

class B   in IP networking, an address class providing 16,000 networks with more than 65,000 hosts per network

class C   in IP networking, an address class providing more than two million networks with 254 hosts per network

class of service   prioritization and delivery guarantees of different types of data during transport

command line interface   typically a serial or TELNET text-driven management interface

common information model   a management structure enabling disparate resources to be managed by a common application

connection allegiance   Use of a single TCP connection for individual iSCSI command/response pairs

connection identifier   used on SCSI to identify one of many potential TCP connections between two communicating devices

connectionless service   communication between two network devices that does not require session setup in advance of data exchange

connection-oriented service   communication between two network devices that requires session establishment before data exchanges begin

consumer   in InfiniBand, an upper layer application

context switching   concurrent processing of multiple SCSI transactions by an initiator

convergence   the time required for a network to regain stability and updated routing information after a disruption

COPS   Common Open Policy Service; a centralized method of authenticating permissions for QoS requests

CPU   central processing unit; typically a microprocessor in a workstation or server

CRC   cyclic redundancy check; an error detection method

cut-through   a switching technique that allows a routing decision to be made as soon as the destination address of a frame is received

DA   destination address

DAFS   Direct Access File System; a protocol used for file transfer directly to system memory over VI

datagram   a message transmitted over a network with no link-level acknowledgment of delivery

DDS   discovery domain set

DES   Data Encryption Standard; a method of key encryption of data allowing for as many as 72 quadrillion possible encryption keys

destination   the intended recipient of a network transmission

device discovery   in storage networking, any mechanism used by initiators to discover targets

DiffServ   differentiated services; policy-based class of service for IP networks based on PHB rules

disaster recovery   ensuring business continuance by safeguarding data at a geographical distance from a primary data center

discovery domain   in the iSNS protocol, a grouping of initiators and targets that are authorized to communicate

discovery domain sets   groupings of initiators and targets that have been previously defined within the same zone or domain

disparity   the relationship of ones and zeros in an encoded character; positive disparity contains more ones; negative disparity contains more zeros; neutral disparity contains an even number of ones and zeros

distance vector protocol   a routing protocol that calculates optimal paths through the network on the basis of the number of hops (routers) through which a packet must traverse

DNS   domain name server; used to resolve human-readable network domain names to IP addresses

DSCP   DiffServ code point; use of the IP header TOS field to specify additional class of service parameters

DWDM   dense wave division multiplexing; use of multiple optical wavelengths within a single fiber to transmit different data streams concurrently

Dynamic Host Configuration Protocol   a means of automating the task of IP address assignment by providing temporary address leases

E_D_TOV   error detect timeout value; a timing parameter used in Fibre Channel to monitor frame transmission

EIGRP   Enhanced Interior Gateway Routing Protocol; a Cisco proprietary routing protocol

ELS   extended link services; status and command frames exchanged between switches or gateways

EMI   electromagnetic interference

enterprise   a large corporation, institution, or government entity

EOF   end of frame; a field used to delineate the end of a frame

E_Port   an expansion port connecting two Fibre Channel fabric switches

ESI   entity status inquiry; used by iSNS to monitor the status of end devices via periodic polling

ESP   encapsulating security payload; an IPSec mechanism for data encryption

expedited forwarding   a premium class of service provided by DiffServs for timely delivery of frames

extended copy   a SCSI command extension that enables an application to read from one storage device and write to another without server intervention

fabric   one or more switches in a homogeneous switched networked topology

fabric login   a process by which a node establishes a logical connection to a fabric switch

FC_BB   Fibre Channel backbone

FCIA   Fibre Channel Industry Association

FCIP   Fibre Channel over IP

FCP   Fibre Channel Protocol; the upper layer protocol for Fibre Channel serial SCSI-3 defined by ANSI T10

FC SAN   a storage network based on Fibre Channel hubs or switches

FEC   forwarding equivalence classes; a mechanism used by MPLS to aggregate packets for label assignment

Fibre Channel an ANSI standard for serial gigabit transport, typically used for serial SCSI-3 upper layer protocol support

file a data object composed of an ordered set of data bytes stored on disk or tape and identified by a symbolic name and read/write permissions

FIN finish bit

flag bits within a parameter field of a frame header that specify status or actions appropriate to packet transport

flow control a mechanism for pacing traffic between source and destination over the network

flow specification QoS requirements for an RSVP connection

F_Port a port on a Fibre Channel switch that supports an N_Port

FL_Port a port on a Fibre Channel switch that supports arbitrated loop devices

frame a data unit composed of an SOF delimiter, header, data payload, CRC, and EOF delimiter

FSPF Fabric Shortest Path First; a routing protocol for Fibre Channel fabrics; a subset of the IP OSPF protocol

full duplex concurrent transmission and reception of data on a link

GBIC gigabit interface converter; a removable transceiver module for Fibre Channel and Gigabit Ethernet physical layer transport

Gbps gigabits per second

gigabit for Fibre Channel, 1,062,500,000 bits per second; for Gigabit Ethernet, 1,250,000,000 bits per second

Gigabit Ethernet the IEEE 802.3z standard for Ethernet over a switched serial gigabit transport

Gigabit Ethernet-to-SCSI bridge a device that enables parallel SCSI devices to attach to an IP storage network

Gigabit media independent interface a physical layer interface for adapting Gigabit Ethernet to a variety of physical media types

globally unique identifier unique naming convention for InfiniBand

G_Port a port on a Fibre Channel switch that supports either F_Port or E_Port functionality

GUI graphical user interface; typically a graphical menu system for device management and configuration

hard zoning   segregation of SAN devices based on port attachment

HBA   host bus adapter; an interface between a server or workstation bus and the Fibre Channel network

HCA   host channel adapter; defined by InfiniBand to service memory and I/O processes for a CPU

header   leading bytes of addressing and parameter information attached to a packet payload

high-voltage differential   a SCSI parallel cable interface

HTTP   Hypertext Transfer Protocol

hub   in Fibre Channel, a wiring concentrator that collapses a loop topology into a physical star topology

IBTA   InfiniBand Trade Association

ICANN   Internet Corporation for Assigned Names and Numbers

ID   identification

IEEE   Institute of Electrical and Electronics Engineers

IETF   Internet Engineering Task Force; the standards body responsible for IP-related standards

iFCP   Internet Fibre Channel Protocol; Fibre Channel layer 4 FCP over TCP/IP

in-band   transmission of management protocol over the network transport

InfiniBand   an architecture that defines a server switch matrix as a replacement for the conventional server bus, as well as direct memory access data transfer

initiator   typically a server or workstation on a storage network that initiates transactions to disk or tape targets

intercabinet   a specification for copper cabling that allows as much as 30 m between enclosures

intermix   in Fibre Channel, allows any unused bandwidth in a class 1 connection to be used by class 2 or class 3 transactions

intracabinet   a specification for copper cabling that allows as much as 13 m within a single enclosure

I/O   input/output; an operation that transfers data to or from a computer

IP   Internet Procotol; the most widely used layer 3 network protocol

IPC interprocess communications; high-performance multiprocessor and server cluster communication

IPS IP storage

IP SAN a storage network based on IP switches and routers with native IP, Fibre Channel, or SCSI end devices

IPSec IP Security; an architecture for device authentication and data encryption over IP networks

IP storage block data transfer using serial SCSI-3 over an IP network

IPS Work Group the standards workgroup within the IETF currently developing IP storage protocol standards

IPv4 Internet Protocol version 4; uses a 32-bit address scheme

IPv6 Internet Protocol version 6; uses a 128-bit address scheme

iSCSI Internet SCSI; serial SCSI-3 over TCP/IP

iSCSI Consortium a multivendor organization established by UNH for standards compliance testing

iSCSI node an iSCSI initiator or target, identified by a 255-byte name

ISID in iSCSI, an initiator session ID used to monitor transactions

iSNS Internet Storage Name Server; a discovery and management protocol for IP storage networks

iSNSP the iSNS Protocol

ISP Internet service provider

IT information technology

ITU International Telecommunications Union

IU information units

JBOD just a bunch of disks; typically configured as a Fibre Channel arbitrated loop segment in a single chassis

jitter deviation in timing that a bit stream encounters as it traverses a physical medium

K28.5 a special 10-bit character used to indicate the beginning of a Fibre Channel command

Kerberos a security protocol for requesting services from a computer system

LAN   local area network; a network linking multiple devices in a single geographical location

LDP   Label Distribution Protocol; a protocol used by LSRs to bind groups of packets to labels for forwarding through the network

Lightweight Directory Access Protocol   a protocol used for locating resources or devices on the network

link-state protocol   a routing protocol that calculates optimal paths through the network based on the number of hops (routers), link bandwidth, and current traffic loads between routers

LLC   logical link control; a data link sublayer that interfaces between MAC and upper layer network protocols

local identifier   in InfiniBand, an address used for subnet switching

logical unit   the entity within a storage target that executes SCSI I/O commands

loop   arbitrated loop; a shared Fibre Channel gigabit topology

loop initialization primitive   used to initiate a procedure that results in unique addressing for all nodes; used to indicate a loop failure or to reset a specific node

loop port state machine   logic that monitors and performs the tasks required for initialization and access to the loop

LSR   label switch router; an IP router or switch supporting MPLS

LUN   logical unit number; a SCSI identifier for a logical unit within a storage target

LUN masking   a mechanism for making only designated LUNs visible to an initiator

LVD   Low-voltage differential; a SCSI parallel cable interface

MAC   media access control; a sublayer interface at the data link level that controls access to the physical media

MAN   metropolitan area network; typically with a circumference of less than 100 km

MBps   megabytes per second

Mbps   megabits per second

MBZ   must be zero; a zeroed bit in the TOS field in an IP header

mFCP Metro Fibre Channel Protocol; Fibre Channel layer 4 FCP over UDP/IP

MIB management information base; an SNMP structure for device management

mirror an exact copy of disk data written to a secondary disk or array

MPLS Multiprotocol Label Switching; a QoS mechanism for accelerating frame transmission based on data type

multicast a network transmission from a single source to multiple destinations concurrently

multimode a fiber-optic cabling specification that allows as much as 500 m between devices

narrow SCSI a SCSI parallel interface with eight data lines

NAS network-attached storage; a disk array connected to a controller that provides file access over a LAN transport

NAT network address translator

native IP a networked device with an assigned IP address and TCP/IP or UDP/IP protocol stack processing

NCITS National Committee of Information Technology Standards

network entity an object for defining an IP storage client or server

network operations center an IP network monitoring and management facility

NFS Network File System; a cross-platform file access protocol

NIC network interface card

NL_Port node loop port; a port that supports the arbitrated loop protocol

node a Fibre Channel entity that supports one or more ports

Node_Name a unique 64-bit identifier assigned to a Fibre Channel node

N_Port a Fibre Channel port in a point-to-point or fabric connection

OC-3 a communications link supporting 155 Mbps

OC-12 a communications link supporting 622 Mbps

OC-48 a communications link supporting 2.5 Gbps

ordered set a group of low-level protocols used to manage frame transport, initialization, and media access

OSI   open systems interconnection

OSI Reference Model   a seven-layer abstraction of common data networking functions

OSPF   Open Shortest Path First; a link-state routing protocol used in IP networking

out-of-band   transmission of management protocol outside the Fibre Channel network, typically over Ethernet

packet   a unit of data transported over a network

parallel   the simultaneous transmission of multiple data bits over multiple lines in a single cable plant

passive copper   a low-cost Fibre Channel connection that allows as many as 13 m of copper cable lengths

PAUSE frame   a frame used by IEEE 802.3x for traffic pacing

PCI   peripheral component interconnect; an interface specification for a computer bus providing 66-MHz performance

PCI-X   peripheral component interconnect extended; an interface specification for a computer bus providing 133-MHz performance

PDP   policy decision point; typically a network policy server that authenticates requests for service via the COPS protocol

PDU   protocol data unit; in iSCSI, the frames used for SCSI commands, status, and data

PHB   per hop behavior; a policy-based mechanism used by DiffServs to establish class of service through an IP network

ping   an IP query used to verify the presence of a network device

PKI   public key infrastructure; a security mechanism for authentication and data encryption

PLOGI   in Fibre Channel, a port-to-port login process by which initiators establish sessions with targets

point-to-point   a dedicated network connection between two devices

policy enforcement points   typically switches or routers in the network that police QoS connection requests

port   a physical entity that connects a node to the network

portal   an iSNS object that uses an IP address and a TCP port number to identify an IP storage resource attached to the network

Port_Name in Fibre Channel, a unique 64-bit identifier assigned to a Fibre Channel port

port number in TCP and UDP, a 16-bit integer used by the transport layer to associate transactions with upper layer applications

primitive sequences ordered sets that indicate or initiate state changes on the transport and require at least three consecutive occurrences to trigger a response

primitive signals ordered sets that indicate actions or events and require only one occurrence to trigger a response

private loop a free-standing arbitrated loop with no fabric attachment

private loop device an arbitrated loop device that does not support fabric login

public loop an arbitrated loop attached to a fabric switch

public loop device an arbitrated loop device that supports fabric login and services

QoS Quality of service; frame delivery preference based on acknowledgment, prioritization, and bandwidth parameters

R2T ready to transmit; an iSCSI protocol data unit used for flow control during SCSI read/write operations

RAID redundant array of independent disks

RARP Reverse Address Resolution Protocol; an IP function that correlates a link-level MAC address with a corresponding IP address

R_A_TOV resource allocation timeout value; a timing parameter used in Fibre Channel to monitor availability of switch resources

RDMA Remote Direct Memory Access; in InfiniBand, a method for reading or writing data directly to memory

registered SCN a switch function that allows notification to registered nodes if a change occurs to other, specified nodes

repeater a circuit that uses recovered clock to regenerate the outbound signal

retimer a circuit that uses an independent clock to generate an outbound signal

RFC Request for Comment; standards document used by the IETF as a vehicle for consensus on standards and further standards development

RIF   routing information field; used in source route bridging to record a path traversed through the network

RIP   Routing Information Protocol; a legacy distance-vector protocol used in IP networks

route flapping   erratic changes in routing information resulting from unstable links or router ports

R_RDY   receiver ready

RSVP   Resource Reservation Protocol; a QoS method for dedicating specified bandwidth through an IP network

SA   source address

SAM-2   the SCSI Architectural Model

SAN   storage area network; a network linking servers or workstations to disk arrays, tape backup subsystems, and other devices, typically over gigabit transports such as Fibre Channel or Gigabit Ethernet

SAN island   a stand-alone storage network installation

SCN   state change notification; a mechanism for proactively alerting initiators to changes in the availability of storage targets

SCSI   small-computer systems interface; both a protocol for transmitting large blocks of data and a parallel bus architecture

SCSI-3   a SCSI standard that defines transmission of the SCSI protocol over serial links

SCSI enclosure services   a subset of the SCSI protocol used to monitor power, temperature, and fan status of enclosures

segmentation   the division of data blocks into sequential frames or packets for transmission over a network

sequence number   a 32-bit field in a TCP packet header used to monitor the number of bytes transmitted and received during a TCP connection

SerDes   serializing/deserializing circuitry; a circuit that converts a serial bit stream into parallel data characters, and parallel into serial

serial   the transmission of data bits in sequential order over a single line

server   a computer that processes end-user requests for data and/or applications

single mode   a fiber-optic cabling specification that provides as much as 10 km between devices

skew   the time frame within which all bits in a parallel transmission must be received

sliding window   a flow control mechanism that allows transmission of multiple packets before acknowledgments are received

slow start   a ramping algorithm used by TCP to monitor bandwidth availability in the network

SLP   Service Locator Protocol; a protocol for querying lists of network resources

SNACK   sequence number acknowledgment; used by iSCSI to solicit retransmission of specified packets within a sequence

SNIA   Storage Networking Industry Association

SNMP   Simple Network Management Protocol; a network management protocol designed to run over TCP/IP-routed networks

SNS   simple name server; a service provided by a fabric switch that simplifies discovery of devices

SNW   Storage Network World; storage networking conferences sponsored by SNIA and Computerworld

socket   a unique identifier based on a TCP port number and an IP address that facilitates communication to upper layer applications

SOF   start of frame; a field used to delineate the beginning of a frame

soft zoning   segregation of SAN devices based on WWN or network address

source   the origin of a network transmission

spanning tree   a protocol for preventing duplicate data paths through a bridged network

spoof   to assume the identify of a network device by manipulating the source address in a frame header

SRDF   Symmetrix Remote Data Facility; EMC's disk-to-disk mirroring for data replication or disaster recovery

SRP   Serial Remote Direct Memory Access Protocol; an ANSI standards initiative for mapping serial SCSI-3 to InfiniBand

SSA   serial storage architecture; a gigabit serial storage transport superseded by Fibre Channel

storage   any device used to store data; typically, magnetic disk media or tape

storage NIC   a network interface card with optimized logic for TCP and serial SCSI-3 processing

storage resource management   management of disk volumes and file resources

store-and-forward   a switching technique that requires buffering an entire frame before a routing decision is made

striping   a RAID technique for writing a single file to multiple disks on a block-by-block basis

subnet   organization of secondary groups of hosts within an IP network by manipulating network and host components of an IP address range

switch   a device providing full bandwidth per port and high-speed routing of data via link-level or network addressing

SYN   synchronization bit

T3   a serial communications link supporting 45 Mbps

tape subsystem   a tape backup device, typically a tape library with multiple tape drives in a single enclosure

target   typically a disk array or tape subsystem on a storage network

TCA   target channel adapter; defined by InfiniBand to provide peripheral, network, and storage access

TCP connection   a session established between two network devices to ensure reliable data exchange

TCP/IP   Transmission Control Protocol/Internet Protocol

TELNET   a virtual terminal emulation facility over TCP/IP

tenancy   possession of an arbitrated loop by a device to conduct a transaction

terabyte   a measure of storage capacity equivalent to a thousand billion bytes of data

TFTP   Trivial File Transfer Protocol

third-party copy   a SCSI command extension that enables an application to read from one storage device and write to another without server intervention

TOE   TCP off-load engine; typically embedded on an NIC for processing the TCP/IP protocol stack

topology the physical or logical arrangement of devices in a networked configuration

TOS type of service; a field in an IP header used to specify class of service for packet delivery

transceiver a device that converts one form of signaling to another for both transmission and reception; in fiber optics, conversion from optical to electrical

TSID in iSCSI, a target session identifier used to monitor transactions

tunneling encapsulation of entire frames of a protocol for transport through an IP network

UDP User Datagram Protocol; a connectionless, unacknowledged delivery service

UNH University of New Hampshire; organizer of the iSCSI Consortium for protocol standards compliance testing

URG urgent bit; a bit set in a TCP header signifying that the urgent pointer field in the header should be processed

URL uniform resource locator

URN uniform resource names; an IETF standard for formatting human-readable network resource names

vaulting archiving tape backups, typically via remote tape backup over a WAN

VI virtual interface; a protocol for direct memory reads and writes of data that does not require a protocol stack such as TCP/IP

virtual lanes defined by InfiniBand to enable concurrent transactions over a single link

virtualization in storage networking, a technology that makes multiple physical disks or tape resources appear as a single logical resource to an initiator

VL virtual lane

VLAN virtual LAN; an IEEE 802.1Q standard for creating logical subnets of network nodes regardless of physical attachment to the network

VLAN tagging setting a 12-bit identifier in an Ethernet frame to designate 1 of 4,096 possible VLANs

VLSM variable-length subnet masking; a technique for creating subsets of IP hosts within a single network address space

VPN virtual private network

WAN wide area network; a network linking geographically remote sites

Wide SCSI a SCSI parallel cable interface with 16 data lines

word Typically four contiguous bytes processed as a single instruction by a computer processor

world-wide name a registered, unique 64-bit identifier assigned to nodes and ports

WWN world-wide name

WWUI world-wide unique identifier; an identifier used by iSCSI, comparable with a Fibre Channel WWN

zoning a function provided by fabric switches or hubs that allows segregation of nodes by physical port, name, or address.

Index

Also by Tom Clark

Designing Storage Area Networks
A Practical Reference for Implementing Fibre Channel SANs

0-201-61584-3
Paperback
224 pages
Addison-Wesley
© 1999

Written for network developers, technical staff, IT consultants, administrators, and managers, *Designing Storage Area Networks* goes far beyond a straight description of Fibre Channel specifications and standards; it offers practical guidelines for implementing and utilizing SANs to meet the real-world needs of business networks.

**For more information on this book, and others in the
Addison-Wesley Networking Basics Series, visit
http://www.aw.com/cseng/networkingbasics.**

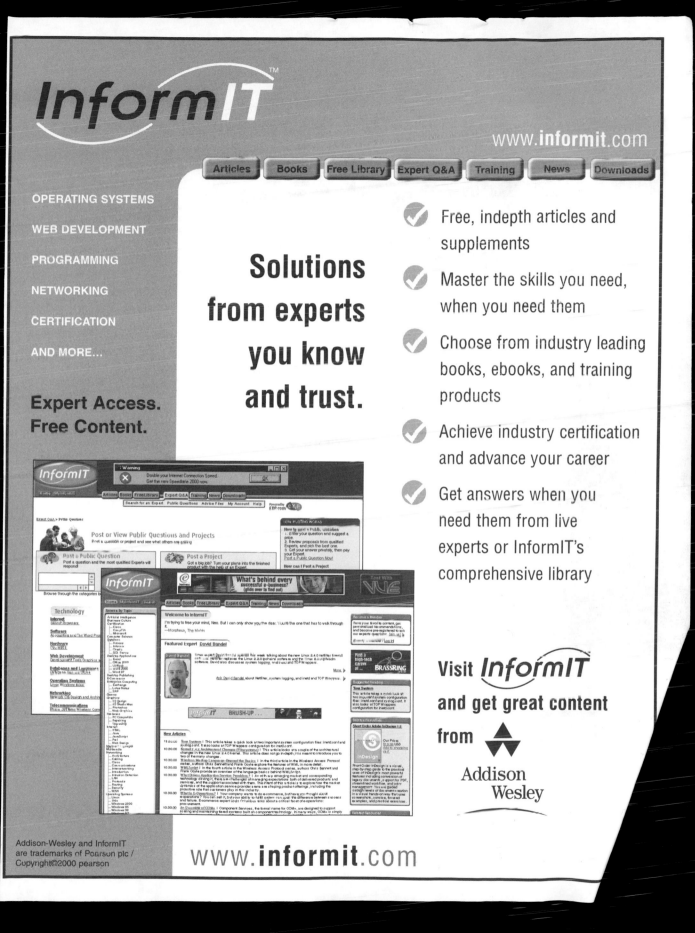